THE
TERRORIST
NEXT DOOR

THE TERRORIST NEXT DOOR

HOW THE GOVERNMENT IS DECEIVING YOU ABOUT THE ISLAMIST THREAT

ERICK STAKELBECK

Since 1947
REGNERY
PUBLISHING, INC.
An Eagle Publishing Company • Washington, DC

Cataloging-in-Publication data on file with the Library of Congress
ISBN 978-1-59698-152-2

Published in the United States by
Regnery Publishing, Inc.
One Massachusetts Avenue, NW
Washington, DC 20001
www.regnery.com

Manufactured in the United States of America

10 9 8 7 6 5 4 3 2 1

Books are available in quantity for promotional or premium use. Write to Director of Special Sales, Regnery Publishing, Inc., One Massachusetts Avenue NW, Washington, DC 20001, for information on discounts and terms or call (202) 216-0600.

Distributed to the trade by:
Perseus Distribution
387 Park Avenue South
New York, NY 10016

In loving memory of my father, Fred Stakelbeck, Sr.
Without your guidance and support, this book
would not have been possible.

CONTENTS

FOREWORD

BY MICHELLE MALKIN

Blind diversity is suicide; political correctness is the handmaiden of Islamic terrorism; and the so-called "tiny minority" of "fringe" radical Muslims who support violent jihad is actually a mainstreamed legion of hundreds of millions that hides behind the deceptive banner of the "Religion of Peace."

These are the inconvenient truths that should have jolted Americans into post-9/11 reality a decade ago.

Instead, we hit the snooze button.

More American civilians and soldiers died at the hands of Allah's soldiers. More of Mohammed Atta's spiritual brethren infiltrated our shores. More lethal hatred for infidels festered in caves and on college campuses, in refugee enclaves and in jails, and on military bases here at home and abroad.

Intrepid journalist Erick Stakelbeck shouldn't have had to write this book.

But Americans—lulled by the passage of time and the passivity of their government—need another blood-boiling wake-up call to pierce the fog of apathy that has set over the West.

You are holding in your hands the unvarnished, invaluable reporting that the rest of the "mainstream media" can't or won't do. My friend Erick has traveled the world to interview terrorists who are plotting the establishment of a global Islamic caliphate—and who have succeeded in Islamicizing large swaths of Europe. He has investigated fifth column organizations on our soil that pledge allegiance not to our Republic, but to sharia law. In *The Terrorist Next Door*, he also blows the whistle on how the same reckless, open-borders policies I exposed in *Invasion* nine years ago continue to aid and abet jihadi-sympathizers from Somalia and elsewhere.

Erick's on-the-ground investigative work in Muslim enclaves and mosques covers every corner of our country. Jihad doesn't just threaten Washington, D.C., New York, and other metropolitan areas. It's spreading across the South and the heartland. Radical Islam's virulently anti-American, anti-Western virus has infected a swelling army of homegrown jihadist wannabes—not just the sons and daughters of Muslim refugees, as Erick shows you, but also white suburban women, ethnic gang members, and alienated geeks.

On 9/11, I lived in the D.C. metro area. From a high-rise building in Montgomery County, Maryland, you could see the smoke plumes from the Pentagon, targeted by jihadi pilot Hani Hanjour and the suicide crew who hijacked American Airlines Flight 77. A year later, Muslim convert John Allen Muhammad and his young conspirator Lee Malvo murdered ten innocent men and women on a terrifying, three-week-long killing spree in the Beltway area. "We will kill them all, jihad," Malvo had scrawled in jailhouse notes.[1]

Several years later, my family and I moved to Colorado. The Rockies, I thought, would be a sanctuary from terrorism. The lesson for us—and for all Americans—is that there is no such thing as a safe haven from Islamic jihad. In February 2010, Afghan-born Muslim Najibullah Zazi of Denver pleaded guilty to terrorism charges related to his railway bombing plot hatched in Colorado and New York City. In April 2010, the feds charged Leadville, Colorado mom Jamie Paulin-Ramirez with conspiracy to provide material support to terrorists as part of a wider plot to murder Swedish cartoonist Lars Vilks, who tested the narrow limits of Muslim tolerance by depicting Mohammed as a pig. And in February 2011, 20-year-old Saudi student Khalid Ali-M Aldawsari was arrested in connection with a plot to bomb former President George W. Bush's Dallas home—along with twelve reservoir dams in California and in my adopted home state of Colorado.

Once again, the U.S. State Department's sloppy solicitousness of foreign students from jihad-coddling countries came back to bite us. Remember: it was thanks to Saudi-pandering Foggy Bottom programs that several of the 9/11 hijackers were able to circumvent regular visa screening procedures and obtain entry into our country despite incomplete applications and deadly intentions.[2] As the *Fort Worth Star Telegram* article on Aldawsari makes clear, the visa screeners fell down on the job again:

> Evidence seized from Aldawsari's apartment included bomb materials, a gas mask, a hazmat suit and lab equipment, the Justice Department said. Aldawsari also e-mailed himself instructions on how to convert a cellphone into a remote detonator and prepare a booby-trapped vehicle using items available in every home, the affidavit alleges.
>
> FBI agents also seized a journal with entries showing that Aldawsari, enrolled at South Plains College near Lubbock, had been planning the attack for years, according to the affidavit.
>
> Entries say Aldawsari worked to master English and sought and obtained a particular scholarship so he could come to the U.S. to target "infidel Americans."[3]

Young. Male. Saudi. Muslim. No independent means of income. These should have been automatic red flags. Yet, our anti-profiling national security agencies have shown a mind-boggling obliviousness to the sea of red flags flapping in the wind. Most alarming: the same bureaucratic incompetence that cripples our State Department and Homeland Security Department officials has emasculated our first line of defense—the U.S. military.

American soldiers on U.S. soil have paid a bloody price for these bipartisan failures of imagination and comprehension.

Political correctness is a gangrenous infection. For decades, American culture has submitted to a toxic diet of multiculturalism, identity politics, anti-Americanism, and entitlement. The problem metastasized under the Bush administration. Despite 9/11, government at all levels refused to screen out jihadi-apologizing influences in our military, at the FBI, in prisons, and even in city fire departments. Despite the bloody consequences of open borders, the Bush Pentagon allowed illegal aliens to enter the military. And the grievance lobby succeeded in plying the Muslim-jihadist-as-victim narrative to a sympathetic media. Homeland security has weakened further under the Obama administration—led by a chief executive who believes more empathy and education is the cure for Islamic imperialism.

The Fort Hood massacre is the starkest example since 9/11 of the continued perils of progressive political correctness. The violence at Fort Hood, President Obama told mourners, was "incomprehensible." The "twisted logic that led to the tragedy," he reiterated, may be "too hard to comprehend." But what exactly was so hard to comprehend? Accused Fort Hood jihadist Nidal Hasan made his means, motives, and Koranic inspiration all too clear for those willing to see and hear. His jihadi colors flashed like bright neon lights on the Las Vegas strip—and everyone in authority looked away:

- The belligerent Hasan carried a business card proclaiming himself a "Soldier of Allah."
- In his 2007 slide presentation to fellow Army doctors on "The Koranic World View As It Relates to Muslims in the Military," Hasan spelled it out: "We love death more then (sic) you love life!"
- Hasan exposed the deadly tension between his adherence to Islam and service in the U.S. military. Slide 11 stated: "It's getting harder and harder for Muslims in the service to morally justify being in a military that seems constantly

engaged against fellow Muslims." Slide 12 cited Koranic injunctions against killing fellow believers. And Hasan made clear he wasn't alone among Muslim soldiers who "should not serve in any capacity that renders them at risk to hurting/killing believers unjustly."

- Slide 13 ominously listed "adverse events" involving Muslim soldiers—including the fatal 2003 fragging attack on American soldiers in Kuwait by Sgt. Hasan Akbar (who was sentenced to death but remains alive while his case is on appeal); the desertion case of Lebanon-born Muslim Marine Wassef Ali Hassoun; and the espionage case of Muslim chaplain James Yee (the charges were dropped, but the case raised lingering security concerns about Muslim chaplains at Gitmo and elsewhere trained by terror-linked, Saudi-subsidized institutes).

Hasan missed a few "adverse events" that have faded from public memory in our reflexive age of "Islam is peace" emotionalism-over-comprehension:

- John Muhammad, the Beltway jihadist I mentioned above, was a member of the Army's 84th Engineering Company. Muhammad was suspected of throwing a thermite grenade into a tent housing sixteen of his fellow soldiers as they slept before the ground-attack phase of the Gulf War in 1991. Muhammad was admitted to the Army despite having been court-martialed for willfully disobeying orders, striking another noncommissioned officer, wrongfully taking property, and being absent without leave while serving in the Louisiana National Guard.
- Although Muhammad was led away in handcuffs and transferred to another company pending charges for the grenade attack, an indictment never materialized.

Muhammad was honorably discharged from the Army in 1994 before brainwashing young Lee Malvo in black nationalism and jihad—and then carrying out the three-week killing spree in the name of Allah.

- Muslim American soldier Hassan Abu-jihaad was convicted in 2008 on espionage and material terrorism support charges after serving aboard the USS *Benfold* and sharing classified info with al-Qaeda financiers, including movements of U.S. ships just six months after al-Qaeda operatives had killed seventeen Americans aboard the USS *Cole* in the port of Yemen.

- Jeffrey Leon Battle was a former U.S. Army reservist convicted of conspiring to levy war against the United States and "enlisting in the Reserves to receive military training to use against America." He had planned to wage war against American soldiers in Afghanistan.

- Egyptian Ali A. Mohamed joined the U.S. Army while a resident alien despite being on a State Department terrorist watch list before securing his visa. An avowed Islamist, he taught classes on Muslim culture to U.S. Special Forces at Fort Bragg and obtained classified military documents. He was granted U.S. citizenship over the objections of the CIA. Honorably discharged from the Army in 1989, Mohamed then hooked up with Osama bin Laden as an escort, trainer, bagman, and messenger. Mohamed used his U.S. passport to conduct surveillance at the U.S. Embassy in Nairobi; he later pled guilty to conspiring with bin Laden and admitted his role in the 1998 African embassy bombings that killed more than 200 people, including a dozen Americans.

As Erick details for you in *The Terrorist Next Door*, the list of jihadist plotters within our own borders is growing. Later this year, America will mark the tenth anniversary of the 9/11 attacks. Remembrance is worthless without resolve. And resolve is useless without recognition. You can't know our enemies, let alone defeat them, with your head buried in the sand and your government's collective hands grasping a whitewash brush. The first step every American must make to combat the radical tide of jihad in our midst is to get angry, get active, and get informed. Turn the page and turn the tide—now.

KNOW YOUR ENEMY

"You know the plane they found a bomb on today—the one that flew out of Yemen? I was on that plane."

The voice on the other end of the phone was a trusted intelligence source, one of the many Jack Bauer types I've formed relationships with in my ten years of covering the global jihad. He doesn't call often, so when he does I know he has something important to say. This call, on October 29, 2010, was no different.

"I flew out of Sana'a [the Yemeni capital] this morning, bound for Dubai," he continued. "I'm not surprised that they found a bomb on the plane. You wouldn't believe the scene at the airport in Yemen. Total chaos."

Authorities in Dubai had found an explosive device concealed inside a computer printer aboard my source's Qatar Airways flight. That same day, a similar bomb was found on a UPS cargo plane at the East Midlands Airport in Great Britain. The explosive had made its way to Britain from Yemen on a passenger aircraft before being transferred onto the UPS plane. Both packages were addressed to synagogues in Chicago—

a symbolic threat to Islam's eternal target, the Jews. But the terrorists who assembled the bombs likely planned for them to go off in mid-air aboard the passenger flights, hoping to kill hundreds of civilians in a Lockerbie-style massacre.[1]

My source told me he had a pretty good inkling as to how the bombs made it onto the planes. He described for me how pre-teen boys were pulling bags out of X-ray machines at the Yemen airport and essentially acting as porters, complete with uniforms. No word yet on whether they've been hired by the TSA, but give it time. My source also noticed a good deal of large bags, "thirty or forty of them," being brought by porters—grown men, this time—to the personal baggage terminal, rather than to the cargo terminal.

"This was odd," he told me. "Some of these packages looked like they could fit a piano inside. But no one said a thing."

He added that virtually all the women on his Yemen-to-Dubai flight wore full-body Islamic garb, yet security did not ask them to remove their face coverings. Considering that male terrorists have repeatedly disguised themselves under burqas, who knows who could have been under there? When jihadists stage mini-reenactments of *Some Like It Hot*, a lot of innocent people can get burnt.

Yet according to my source, none of the Yemeni airport employees seemed to have a care in the world about the circus atmosphere unfolding around them, acting as if it was all just business-as-usual.

"People need to know what's going on at that airport in Yemen," he told me firmly before hanging up. "It's a threat to our national security."

Given the insane conditions my source had seen firsthand, it isn't hard to imagine how two suspicious packages made their way onto the planes. It also isn't difficult to imagine that al-Qaeda has sympathizers or opera-tives actually working at the Yemen airport who would help get explosives onto flights. After all, something similar happened in Britain, where in March 2011 an Islamist working as a computer expert for British Airways was convicted of plotting with al-Qaeda cleric Anwar al-Awlaki to blow up in mid-flight a U.S.-bound passenger airplane. A jury found Rajib Karim had secured a job with British Airways specifically to advance his terrorist plan. As a prosecutor on the case said, "The most chilling element...is probably the fact that Karim tried to enroll as cabin crew and anyone can imagine how horrific the consequences of this could have been, had he succeeded."[2]

As for the so-called Yemen Cargo Plane Plot, we indeed soon learned that it was an al-Qaeda creation hatched by the group's Yemen branch, known as al-Qaeda in the Arabian Peninsula (AQAP)—the same al-Awlaki-connected outfit that was behind the British Airways plot as well as the failed Underwear Bomber scheme to blow up a Detroit-bound plane on Christmas Day 2009.

My source in Yemen told me that AQAP was growing in size and influence—with thousands of indigenous new fighters, particularly from south Yemen, lining up to join the cause. While troubling, this news was hardly shocking. With al-Qaeda's leadership in the tribal regions of Pakistan feeling increased pressure in recent years due to a steady barrage of CIA predator drone strikes, the organization's operational focus has gradually been shifting to other AQ hotspots like North Africa, Somalia, and yes, Yemen.[3]

If Yemen's airport was unsecure then, imagine the situation now as Yemen—like Egypt, Tunisia, Libya, Oman, Bahrain, and other Middle Eastern countries—is roiled by civil unrest. The revolutions sweeping the Middle East have given rise to a host of national security problems that the Obama administration has utterly failed to address or even comprehend. In most of the Arab countries now gripped by revolutionary fervor, there is a well-organized Islamist movement waiting in the wings. In Egypt, the Muslim Brotherhood comprised the most popular opposition movement to now-deposed strongman Hosni Mubarak. In Yemen and Libya, the tottering regimes, though brutal, have found it in their own interests to suppress al-Qaeda-linked terrorist organizations. Those same terrorists would likely find a friendly safe-haven in both countries if central authority collapsed or fell into the hands of Islamic radicals.

No one knows the shape of the new Middle East that will emerge from the current chaos. But considering the rising popularity of Islamism throughout the region and the poisonous hostility to America—notwithstanding President Obama's seemingly endless tributes to the "peace and justice and fairness and tolerance" of Islam, as he puts it[4]—there is a good chance the outcome will not be favorable to America's national security. The Mubarak government and various now-unstable Arab regimes formed a bulwark against the malign influence of Iran, which stands to emerge from the wreckage greatly empowered. As argued in chapter seven of this book, Iran is the epicenter of the global jihad, a nation whose threatening activities—from developing its own arsenal of nuclear weapons to helping turn Venezuela into a jihadist safe haven in our own backyard—the Obama administration has entirely failed to restrain. But the fact that Obama officials seem indifferent to the rising global tide of Islamic fanaticism is, sadly, unsurprising, considering their duplicity in coping with the same threat we are facing right here at home.

For example, the administration is recklessly downplaying a crucial new strategy adopted by al-Qaeda. Even while pursuing spectacular, 9/11-style attacks, the terror group is increasingly interested in smaller-scale assaults on softer targets—such as the foiled 2009 attempt to bomb the New York City subway system; the failed Times Square bombing plot of 2010; the 2009 attack on an Army recruiting office in Little Rock that left one soldier dead and another seriously wounded; and the gruesomely successful jihadist massacre at Fort Hood. Even as I write these words, we are receiving news that two U.S. servicemen were shot and killed in a jihadist attack at Germany's Frankfurt airport by a gunman yelling "Allahu Akbar."

As described in chapter two, al-Qaeda has endorsed this modus operandi, which I call the Chip Away strategy, in its own publications and in video statements by its spokesmen. Yet the Obama administration insists that every new terrorist attack is the work of a lone "isolated extremist." Prevented by their "Islam-is-peace" dogma from analyzing these attacks as part of a wider strategy, Obama officials are allowing key vulnerabilities in our national security to remain in place.

In recent decades, we've seen a growing number of homegrown terrorists in America, both converts to Islam and those raised Muslim. You'll meet these American jihadists throughout the pages of this book; people like Daniel Patrick Boyd, an all-American kid, former high school football player, and son of a Marine who converted to Islam and pled guilty in 2010 to charges stemming from a plot to massacre U.S. soldiers at Quantico, Virginia; Adam Pearlman Gadahn, a former heavy metal fan who was raised Christian by hippie parents before adopting Islam and becoming al-Qaeda's chief English-language propagandist; and Anwar al-Awlaki, the aforementioned AQAP honcho who is, in fact, a New Mexico-born U.S. citizen and alum of Colorado State University.

Far from being the proverbial "isolated extremists," these individuals moved within a rapidly growing American Islamic community. And if that community is dedicated to peace and tolerance and co-existence, as its spokesmen and government officials both emphatically claim, a lot of its own members have yet to get the message. In chapter five I describe my investigation of Halalco, the largest Islamic supermarket in the Washington, D.C. area, where I found for sale scores of jihadist tracts including dozens of propaganda videos by none other than Anwar al-Awlaki. Likewise, in chapter three you will read about my visit to one of many secretive Islamic compounds springing up across America, this one located in the rural town of Red House, Virginia, where neighbors listen to the enclave's residents conduct firearms training and where a back country road is named after a notorious jihadist leader from Pakistan.

Another unspeakable truth for the Obama administration is that the threat of domestic Islamic terrorism increases along with the rising number of Muslims in America. According to a Pew Research Center report, America's Muslim population is projected to nearly triple, from 2.6 million to 6.2 million, by 2030.[5] As Islam spreads, so does the main location for preaching Islam: mosques. As recounted in chapter one, American

Muslims are already engaged in a nationwide campaign of mosque-building—including in the very heart of the Bible Belt. Consequently, there are currently over 2,000 mosques operating in the United States and an untold number of Islamic schools. To put it in perspective, in the year 2000, there were only 1,200 mosques in the United States[6]—so in just over ten years, their number has nearly doubled, despite the 9/11 attacks and an unceasing onslaught against the West by Islamic jihadists during that same timeframe.

There is plenty of evidence that the creed being preached at American mosques is often not the "tolerant" doctrine that Obama officials tell us constitutes "mainstream" Islam. Take, for example, my visit to one of the largest mosques in America, the Islamic House of Wisdom in Dearborn, Michigan. As described in chapter eight, the imam there is an unabashed supporter of the Ayatollah Khomeini and of the Hezbollah terrorist group. While that mosque is Shia, Sunni mosques don't seem particularly interested in co-existence either; many of them are funded by Saudi Arabia and are highly influenced by Saudi-style Wahhabism, replete with all the hatred for Christians and Jews for which that ideology is rightly infamous.

As explained in chapter three, these rapidly growing Islamic communities have taken root not just in the traditional coastal gateway cities, but in rural areas and heartland states like Tennessee, where the local culture is being fundamentally altered by the erection of mosques, the appearance of burqa-clad women, and the insistence on "accommodations" for Islamic traditions and religious practices. One of the fastest growing segments of Islamic America today consists of Somali immigrants. As described in chapter four, the continued arrival of thousands of Somali immigrants every year is part of a fraud-ridden State Department program whose overseers, believing in diversity-uber-alles, seem unconcerned by the growing number of terrorism cases related to the Somali newcomers. The most recent such example is the November 2010 alleged attempt by Somali-American Mohamed Osman Mohamud to massacre thousands of gatherers at a Christmas tree lighting ceremony in Portland, Oregon.

All of these threats to American security are being allowed to fester due to the Obama administration's steadfast refusal to acknowledge the violent jihadist impulse within Islam. Insisting, in the face of all evidence, that Islam is inherently peaceful, government officials recoil from listening to our enemies' explanation of why they are attacking us—that is, because Islamic scripture commands them to do so.

This was the constant refrain I heard when I travelled to England to interview some of the world's most notorious jihadists, all of whom walk the streets of London as free men. As described in chapter six, I spoke to Saad al-Faqih, a reputed associate of Osama bin Laden himself, who explained to me the inner workings of al-Qaeda and warned of coming attacks against the West that will be bigger than 9/11; Yasser al-Sirri, a longtime al-Qaeda associate who earned a death sentence in Egypt for his part in a jihadist assassination attempt against a former Egyptian prime minister; and Anjem Choudary, the leader of Britain's most notorious Islamist organization, who uttered to me, on the record, a thinly veiled terrorist threat against the British state.

The overall ideological threat we face is known by various names, including *Islamic supremacism, Islamism,* and *jihadism.* With those terms, I'm referring to everyone from Armani-wearing stealth jihadists like the Muslim Brotherhood to violent ones like al-Qaeda and Hezbollah. Some Islamists are Sunni Muslims and some are Shia. As you will see throughout this book, some conduct their jihad through legal, subversive means, while others use terrorism as the means to their end. But while they may employ different tactics, all of them—from the Saudi Wahhabis to the Iranian regime to the Taliban to Hamas and beyond— share a similar desire: to see the world subjugated to Islamic law, or *sharia,* and to see all non-Muslims bow to the will of Allah.

I realize that not all of the world's 1.6 billion Muslims subscribe to this line of thinking, and I'm sure that most just want to raise their families and be left alone. But credible polls show that roughly 10 percent of the world's Muslims do hold Islamist views and, in the very least, support terrorism against non-Muslims.[7] Ten percent of 1.6 billion means that roughly 157 million of the world's Muslims are Islamic supremacists who loathe the United States and Israel and are partial to Osama bin Laden. That's problematic, to say the least. So are polls showing that 13 percent of American Muslims support at least some instances of suicide bombings, with that number rising to 26 percent among young American Muslims.[8] Furthermore, because violent jihad and Islamic supremacism is advocated throughout Islam's fundamental texts, those who believe in those concepts dominate the discussion within Islam. They control most of the world's mosques, the main Islamic seminaries, and the Islamic political parties, as well as the U.S.-based Islamic interest groups.

Like other totalitarian movements, Islamism—in its various reincarnations over the past 1,400 years—has always sought world domination. At times, it has come awfully close to achieving that goal, mainly through *jihad*: holy war, as mandated by Allah through his prophet, Mohammed, in the Koran:

> Fight those who believe not in Allah nor the Last Day, nor hold that forbidden which hath been forbidden by Allah and His Messenger, nor acknowledge the religion of Truth, (even if they are) of the People of the Book, until they pay the Jizya with willing submission, and feel themselves subdued. (9:29)

This is the infamous "Verse of the Sword." It is one of Mohammed's final "revelations" in the Koran, and throughout the ages, it has been interpreted by a sizable chunk of Muslims as an open-ended call to violent jihad, for all times. The "People of the Book" that the verse refers to are Jews and Christians. The "jizya" is a crushing tax that non-Muslims living in Muslim lands are forced to pay to remind them that they are vassals of Islam—and that is the precise status to which millions of Muslims are fighting to reduce "infidels" like you and me, including here in America.

★ ★ ★

Baby boomers still remember exactly where they were on the day JFK was assassinated. Likewise, a defining question for my generation has become, "Where were you on 9/11?" As for myself, when the first plane rammed into the World Trade Center, I was a 25-year-old kid working on a freelance article in my Philadelphia home. As I turned on the TV to see the World Trade Center engulfed in flames, it was clear to me that America was facing the kind of sink-or-swim moment it hadn't seen since Pearl Harbor: would we fight or would we fold?

My thoughts immediately turned to the friends I had made during a recent stint working in New York City, including some who lived near the Twin Towers. As footage of the Towers' collapse exploded across my television screen, I feared for their safety. That concern quickly turned to anger. Then alarm. Since Philly is a major city rich in national landmarks that lies in between Manhattan and Washington—where the Pentagon had also been struck—I thought it might very well be next on the terrorists' target list.

I called my brother right away because he, at the time, worked in a federal government building in downtown Philly. He was already preparing to board the train and head home to his family, as were tens of thousands of confused, frightened people who had been deeply shaken by the apocalyptic images they had just witnessed on television. I next called my parents' house, reaching my father. Little did I know that I was about to have a conversation that would help change the direction of my life.

My dad was a former paratrooper in the 101st Airborne: the legendary Screaming Eagles. A self-made man through and through, he possessed a razor-sharp mind and was one of the most well-read people I have ever known. Before passing away in 2003 at the age of sixty, he was a student of military history, a Christian Zionist before I even knew what the term meant, and an all around bad dude—respected at home and on the street. He had grown up in one of the toughest neighborhoods in Philly, a decaying cauldron named Kensington that had a reputation for turning out fierce brawlers. My dad—who in his heyday was 6' 2", 260 pounds of solid muscle—certainly fit that bill. Up to that point I had only seen him cry once in my entire life. But that morning when he answered the phone, he was sobbing.

"Those bastards," he rasped. "If I was younger, I'd sign back up and go over there tomorrow."

His emotional, patriotic call to action was jarring. Once he calmed down, he hit me with what would prove to be an even bigger bombshell.

"It was bin Laden," he said, lowering his voice to a hoarse whisper. "He hit us in Africa, now he's hitting us here."

You couldn't live under my father's roof and not have a solid knowledge of current events and foreign affairs, particularly concerning the Middle East. Growing up, my brother, sister, and I were treated to nightly lessons from my encyclopedic father on everything from Alexander the Great to King David to Stalingrad.

On the night of September 11, after devouring hours of news coverage and watching President Bush address the nation, my father's words echoed in my ears: "Know your enemy," he had always told me, quoting *The Art of War*, Sun Tzu's ancient masterpiece of military tactics. It dawned on me that I needed to read everything I could get my hands on about Islam, terrorism, al-Qaeda, and the Middle East. And I had to do it immediately. Though I already had a solid background knowledge courtesy of my dad, I soon learned that I had a long way to go to fully understand this latest installment of a 1,400-year war waged by Islamic supremacists against the West.

The next day, I began studying the Koran and poring over Islam's other core texts. I wanted to know more about the people who had attacked us: their culture, their motivations, their strengths and weaknesses, and their history and ideology. In essence, I did what our elected officials in every branch of government should have done, but didn't: I set about getting to know the enemy, with zero consideration given to political correctness or my own preconceived notions.

I already knew of Islam's bloody legacy of conquest; how it spread by the sword out of the Arabian Peninsula in the seventh century, covering the entire Middle East, North Africa, and South Asia. Parts of Europe were also subjugated—Spain and Sicily in the first great jihad, and later, Greece and the Balkans at the hands of the Turkish-led Ottoman Empire. But I didn't yet know the full extent of the oppressive tyranny that the conquered peoples suffered—those who were not butchered or bullied into converting to Islam were deprived of basic rights, frequently physically and psychologically abused, restricted from building new houses of worship, and sometimes forced to wear distinctive yellow garments identifying them as non-Muslims.[9]

All of this was in accordance with Islamic law, or *sharia*, a system that dictates every aspect of a Muslim's life, from how and when they should wage jihad, to how they wear their pants, to how they treat their wives, to how they are to deal with non-believers. A handy summary of what the West could expect under sharia law—if Islamists were to some day get their way—is provided in an indispensible little pamphlet called *Sharia Law for the Non-Muslim*, published by the Center for the Study of Political Islam:

> Sharia: Sharia is based on the principles found in the Koran and other Islamic religious/political texts. There are no common principles between American law and Sharia.
>
> Under Sharia law:
>
> • There is no freedom of religion.
> • There is no freedom of speech.

- There is no freedom of thought.
- There is no freedom of artistic expression.
- There is no freedom of the press.
- There is no equality of peoples—a non-Muslim, a Kafir, is never equal to a Muslim.
- There is no equal protection under Sharia for different classes of people.
- Justice is dualistic, with one set of laws for Muslim males and different laws for women and non-Muslims.
- There are no equal rights for women.
- Women can be beaten.
- A non-Muslim cannot bear arms.
- There is no democracy, since democracy means that a non-Muslim is equal to a Muslim.
- Our Constitution is a man-made document of ignorance, "ahiliyah," that must submit to Sharia.
- Non-Muslims are dhimmis, third-class citizens.
- All governments must be ruled by Sharia law.
- Unlike common law, Sharia is not interpretive, nor can it be changed.
- There is no Golden Rule.[10]

Not exactly what the Founders had in mind.

By the fall of 2002, I had begun focusing all my work on national security and the jihadist threat to the West. I contributed articles to websites and major newspapers, became a senior writer and analyst for Steven Emerson's Investigative Project on Terrorism (IPT), and appeared as an IPT terrorism analyst on nationally syndicated radio programs and TV networks. I eventually moved on to the Christian Broadcasting Network, where I'm host of my own show, *Stakelbeck on Terror*.

To my great distress, my work has brought me to realize that today, ten years after 9/11, America is losing the war against Islamic fascism. Yes, we have had military successes against the jihadists and have killed or captured several top al-Qaeda leaders, hearing the usual self-congratulatory rhetoric out of Washington whenever an attack is thwarted. However, in the war of ideas—the ideological war, which is even more important than the military sphere against this particular enemy—America is getting its tail kicked. Why are we letting the Islamic supremacist government of Saudi Arabia fund mosque-building across our nation and help place textbooks in American public schools that give the Saudi version of Islamic history? Why is the Obama administration openly embracing groups that have intimate ties to the Muslim Brotherhood, a jihadist organization whose Palestinian branch is none other than the genocidal terror group Hamas? Why was a Brotherhood-linked Islamist invited to speak to U.S. troops at Fort Hood in 2009—one month after the terrorist massacre there? Why are our schools devaluing Judeo-Christian civilization but teaching our children that, in the unenlightened words of Presidents Bush and Obama, Islam is a "religion of peace?"

We are facing an existential threat, yet Islamic terrorism remains the enemy we dare not name. "Violent extremism," anyone?

Yes, there are moderate Muslims who want no parts of jihad, sharia, or the caliphate. I know such Muslims, and I fully support and appreciate them. I pray that they can spearhead an Islamic Reformation that brings their faith into the twenty-first century and somehow mitigates sharia and the many calls to violence against non-Muslims that are found in the Koran and the hadiths. But I am not optimistic. The pushback against such a movement in the Muslim world is just too strong.

The surging tide of Islamic supremacism, and the vulnerable position occupied by the few brave souls in the Islamic world who oppose it, was starkly illustrated by the January 2011 assassination of Pakistani governor Salman Taseer and, two months later, the killing of Pakistan's sole Christian government minister, Shabaz Bhatti—both men gunned down for their efforts to reform Pakistan's blasphemy laws, which can impose the death penalty for the crime of insulting Islam. A correspondent for

The Economist issued the following report a month after Taseer was murdered by his own bodyguard:

> Lawyers showered [Taseer's] traitorous bodyguard with rose petals. The killer has become a hero. It has been almost impossible to find a judge who will dare take on the case. In parliament no senator would lead a prayer to commemorate the slain politician. Almost none of Pakistan's articulate and educated liberal voices have dared speak out in his defence. Even Mr Taseer's allies mostly stayed away from his funeral. By contrast, in Lahore on Sunday, I was caught up in a huge crowd of Islamists celebrating noisily the death of the hated liberal.[11]

This is no time to mince words, and we need to face the harsh reality that, while there are moderate Muslims, Islam itself is not moderate.

In fact, if followed to the letter, Islam is inherently incompatible with Western democracy and values. I sincerely wish it weren't so. But based on Islam's core texts, the example of its warrior prophet, Mohammed, and a review of Islamic history—both recent and older—no intellectually honest individual could say with a straight face that Islam is a religion of peace. The evidence against this is just too overwhelming to ignore.

I've interviewed Islamic jihadists who have told me to my face that Islam is much more than a religion: that it is an all-encompassing ideological system that is destined to achieve global domination. Leading Islamic scholars throughout the ages, up to the modern day, have seconded this notion. Before more Americans needlessly get killed, the U.S. government needs to accept this unpleasant fact and adjust its policies for what the Obama administration has laughably dubbed the "War Against Violent Extremism." At stake is not only our country but also Western, Judeo-Christian civilization—which, despite its human flaws, has been a gift from God and a gift to the world overall.

That's why I'm writing this book. It's both an educational tool and a call to action to our government and our people.

Too many have forgotten. I never will.

Because I don't want to see my daughters or my wife forced to cover up, confined to the house and deprived of any form of joy or opportunities. I refuse to wear a special badge or pay a special tax that marks me as a non-Muslim "dhimmi." I want to be able to laugh, dine, and converse with my Jewish friends around the world just as I always have, without fear of them being snatched up by Islamic stormtroopers. I want to be able to read the Bible in public and attend church freely. I want to live in a society where art, education, science, and culture are encouraged and valued. I want to be able to worship, speak, read, and socialize wherever and with whomever I see fit. And I refuse to even entertain the possibility of a day when the state of Israel does not exist. Under an Islamic sharia system—the kind that is slowly gaining traction in Western societies—none of these things would be possible.

To quote my friend, the courageous Dutch politician Geert Wilders, I want my children to be raised with the values of Athens, Rome, and Jerusalem, and not the values of Gaza, Mecca, and Tehran.

If 9/11 seems to you like a faraway event that happened to somebody else in another lifetime, it's about time you stopped forgetting and started fighting to preserve your way of life.

Believe me when I say the barbarians are not just at the gates: they're inside them. And as you are about to find out, time is shorter—much shorter—than you think.

CHAPTER ONE

MEGA-MOSQUE NATION

We were staring down at a shallow, freshly dug grave. And we weren't in a cemetery.

It was August 2010, around the time a nationwide controversy was raging over a proposed $100 million mega-mosque to be built just two blocks from Ground Zero in New York City. Yet as the nation focused on the Islamist project in lower Manhattan, I was hundreds of miles away, in rural Murfreesboro, Tennessee, investigating a development every bit as insidious as the one at Ground Zero: radical Islamists had recently gained approval to build a multi-million dollar Islamic center that would cover more than fifteen acres of land in Murfreesboro, in the very heart of the Bible Belt.

I'd been informed by local sources that in addition to a mega-mosque, a swimming pool, a gymnasium, an Islamic school, and living quarters for an imam, the center would feature an Islamic cemetery on its sprawling campus. And sure enough, shortly after arriving at the site of the future Islamic Center of Murfreesboro, or ICM, my cameraman and I found ourselves staring down at an unmarked mound of dirt covering a dead body. There was no coffin or embalming—just a corpse buried in the dirt in accordance with Islamic law, or sharia. Mind you, ground had not even been broken on the ICM, and a battle over its legality was about to begin in federal court. Yet ICM members had wasted no time burying one of their own at the proposed site, despite the fact that a death certificate had not even been issued.

If you think this all sounds like a bad fit for a small, overwhelmingly Christian town in the shadow of Nashville, you'd be right. But not to worry: according to ICM spokeswoman Camie Ayash, the burial was approved by Rutherford County and Murfreesboro city officials and conformed to all necessary health guidelines.[1] As recently as 2007, Ayash, a white convert to Islam, was serving time in federal prison for grand theft.[2] So she may not be a paragon of truth, but in the case of the unmarked grave, sadly, she was on point. The coffin-less Islamic burial at the ICM site, like the mosque itself, had indeed been green-lit by county officials, to the great dismay of many locals with whom I spoke.

In fact, the Rutherford County Commission took just seventeen days to approve the entire ICM project, despite the fact that other religious facilities in the region—mostly churches—have had to wait up to a year and a half and clear numerous hurdles before being approved.[3] But the mammoth, 52,000-square-foot site where the new ICM will stand received almost instantaneous approval. This clearly stemmed from a tendency we see time and again in similar cases around the country, be it mosque-building or installing Islamic prayer rooms in public airports: PC-addled local officials, fearful of being labeled "racist" or "Islamophobic," succumb to pressure from area Muslims and rush to show their boundless tolerance and respect for Islamic values.

Incidentally, I say "new" ICM because its members already owned a mosque in town, a few miles away at the original Islamic Center of Murfreesboro. That site was much smaller, befitting the size of ICM's membership, which consists of no more than 250 families. Yet mosque leaders claimed their modest congregation needed bigger digs. And boy, did they get them: the new and improved ICM, once complete, will be one of the largest mosque complexes in America.

You would think such a massive facility would warrant healthy discussion among local residents before being given the go-ahead. But county commissioners didn't even open the topic up for debate, and no public forum was held until *after* the mega-mosque had been approved. Once locals got wind of the project, they held large protests in front of the county courthouse demanding answers, while action groups pleaded with local leaders to look into the funding sources and ideology of the mosque's backers—all to no avail. (Sound familiar, New Yorkers?)

I interviewed Rutherford County mayor Ernest Burgess, who told me that the ICM received no special treatment and that the county had also welcomed Buddhist and Hindu temples in the past. I then pointed out the obvious: Buddhists and Hindus aren't seeking to end our way of life as we know it, while untold millions of Muslims are. Big difference.

I pressed Burgess further, asking whether he knew about the rampant Saudi funding and Muslim Brotherhood penetration of U.S. mosques. The Brotherhood, as we'll see shortly, is the granddaddy of them all when it comes to Islamic supremacist groups.

"I'm not informed about that, I don't have any evidence," he stammered.

"Don't you think you should be informed, though?" I countered. "This is kind of a big deal, right?"

"As a basic citizen, I should be informed about every issue that I can be," Burgess replied lamely. "But I can only enforce the rules and regulations that the state of Tennessee and the United States and Rutherford County have authorized me to enforce."[4]

Before my cameraman and I departed his office, Burgess—who had likely never picked up a Koran in his life, let alone read one—asked me how to tell whether a Muslim was radical; this from a man who had just helped push through a mega-mosque that will, without a doubt, irrevocably change the character of an all-American town. If only Burgess had shown such curiosity earlier in the process, he may have found some interesting tidbits about the folks behind the ICM that would indisputably qualify them as radical—and then some.

Indeed, the mayor and county commissioners would have discovered that the ICM sponsored a vicious anti-Israel rally in downtown Murfreesboro in January 2009 at which protestors shouted the Islamic exaltation "Allahu Akhbar," or "Allah is Greatest," as speakers demonized the Jewish state. In what I'm sure was just a happy coincidence, video of the rally was later removed from YouTube after the ICM gained approval to build their facility. Sounds pretty radical to me, Mr. Mayor. So does the fact that a member of ICM's board and its imam Osama Bahloul are both graduates of al-Azhar University in Egypt, which is infested with anti-American and anti-Semitic conspiracy theories.

Another board member, Mosaad Rawash, was suspended briefly from the board after pro-jihad slogans and a picture of Sheikh Ahmed Yassin, founder of the Palestinian terrorist group Hamas, were found on his MySpace page. But Rawash was soon back on the board and cleared of any wrongdoing after what I'm sure was an even-handed and thorough investigation. (By that time the jihadist materials had, magically, disappeared from his site.) Then there is the literature found at the ICM, which has included pamphlets by Muslim Brotherhood-connected groups. This comes as no surprise considering ICM's official reading list presented a who's who of Brotherhood ideologues before—you guessed it—disappearing from the ICM website.

I was able to ask Imam Bahloul some pointed questions in the parking lot of the old ICM building. Refusing to appear on camera, he told me ICM members were just looking for a quiet place to worship; when pressed, he said that he condemned the actions of Hamas and of the Lebanese terrorist group Hezbollah. "For a Muslim leader to condemn those two groups is hugely significant," I told him. "Why don't you go on camera right now and tell Murfreesboro—and the world—what you just told me? I think that would go a long way toward easing concerns about the new mosque."

Bahloul declined. His insincerity was further exposed when I pointed out the ICM's reading list and asked whether he or his mosque had any ties to the Muslim Brotherhood. "They're in this country?" he asked incredulously. "I didn't know that." Another mosque spokesman laughed nervously when I asked the same question, saying the ICM had no connections to any outside organizations and that funds for its new, multi-million dollar mega-mosque were raised locally. I found this hard to believe; during my stay in Murfreesboro, I paid a visit to Friday prayers in the old ICM building. I saw cab drivers, college students, some professional types—not exactly an affluent crowd.

So where is the money coming from to fund the mega-mosque in Murfreesboro and others that are popping up around the country? The developers behind the Ground Zero mosque have still refused to disclose their funding sources, although one of them has said he would be open to taking money from Saudi Arabia and Iran, two countries that boast arguably the most fundamentalist regimes in the Muslim world (and that's saying something).[5] But what about the money for other mega-mosque projects in the works from coast to coast, in places like rural Wisconsin, southern California, northern Kentucky, and Portland, Oregon? Or recently completed, multi-million-dollar mega-mosques in Memphis, Atlanta, and Boston? By the way, did you know that Alaska recently broke ground on its first-ever mosque, a $2.9 million facility covering nearly 17,000 square feet in Anchorage?[6]

Does anyone else think this might not be a streak of coincidences? The Muslim communities mentioned above are not known for having deep pockets, to say the least. It's almost as if rich Muslim donors in Saudi Arabia, the United Arab Emirates, and other wealthy Persian Gulf states are funding a campaign to *Islamize* America. And why not? Mosque building, massive Muslim immigration, and self-segregation comprise a strategy for Islamization that has worked to perfection in Europe. Now that a sympathetic administration is in office in the United States, the time is ripe to up the ante here.

Mosque-building is a crucial component of the strategy. U.S. intelligence sources have told me that most U.S. mosques have been thoroughly infiltrated by the Muslim Brotherhood, a group that strives to establish Islamic sharia law worldwide. Moreover, according to some estimates, no fewer than 80 percent of U.S. mosques receive funding from Saudi Arabia,[7] where the official state religion is Wahhabi Islam, a medieval medley of pro-jihad, anti-Semitic, anti-Christian, and anti-Western virulence that has inspired a long line of terrorists. The dangerous malevolence of Wahhabism was exposed in a 2005 Freedom House investigative report on Saudi publications found in U.S. mosques. The report revealed that Saudi literature spread hatred for non-Muslims, advocated the murder of converts from Islam, promoted the subjugation of women, and denounced America for being un-Islamic. Calling these teachings a "totalitarian ideology of hatred that can incite to violence," the report warned that the Saudis' dissemination of this creed in America "demands our urgent attention."[8]

So that's our starting point. But before tackling the Brotherhood/Saudi nexus and sharia any further, let's take a brief tour through Islamic history to examine the roots and implications of America's current mega-mosque onslaught.

★ ★ ★

Ever since Islam roared out of the Arabian Peninsula in the seventh century to overpower a large chunk of the known world, Muslims have built mosques at the scene of their conquests. This is an acknowledged fact to which anyone with even a passing knowledge of Islamic history can attest. The Dome of the Rock, which is actually a shrine, and the nearby al-Aqsa mosque, both of which are built directly over or next to the remains of the ancient Jewish Temple in Jerusalem, are the most prominent examples. The Umayyad caliph Abd al-Malik completed construction of the large and visually striking Dome in the late seventh century on top of the Temple Mount—Judaism's holiest site—

as a message to Jerusalem's Christians and Jews that Islam would now reign supreme.

An Arabic inscription that adorns the inside of the building, directly disparaging the Christian belief in the Trinity, is telling:

> O you People of the Book! Overstep not bounds in your religion, and of God speak only the truth. The Messiah, Jesus, son of Mary, is only an apostle of God, and his Word, which he conveyed unto Mary, and a Spirit proceeding from him. Believe therefore in God and his apostles, and say not Three. It will be better for you. God is only one God. Far be it from his glory that he should have a son.[9]

Gee, that doesn't sound very tolerant. Neither does the conversion of the famous Hagia Sophia church in Constantinople—now Istanbul—into a mosque by the conquering Ottoman Turks after a long, bloody siege in 1453. Simply put, there have been many mosques built over the centuries as symbols of triumph and shows of force. I have yet to see one built as an exercise in reconciliation and interfaith harmony, as Imam Rauf, the original face of the Ground Zero mosque, so disingenuously suggests his structure will represent.

In fact, New York's Ground Zero mosque provides a good example of the fundamental *intolerance* behind the mosque-building craze. This structure is planned as a 15-story mega-mosque to be placed just two blocks from Ground Zero, in a building that was damaged by landing gear from one of the planes that slammed into the Twin Towers on 9/11.[10] While the project has provoked widespread condemnation, some influential leaders have parroted Rauf's declaration that the mosque would be a monument to tolerance. One such person is President Barack Obama who, at a White House dinner celebrating the Islamic holy month of Ramadan, assured the assembled crowd of Muslim dignitaries that allowing a $100 million monument to Islam to be built at the site where

3,000 Americans were killed in Islam's name would uphold "the writ of our Founders":

> As a citizen, and as President, I believe that Muslims have the same right to practice their religion as anyone else in this country. That includes the right to build a place of worship and a community center on private property in lower Manhattan, in accordance with local laws and ordinances. This is America, and our commitment to religious freedom must be unshakeable. The principle that people of all faiths are welcome in this country, and will not be treated differently by their government, is essential to who we are.[11]

Obama's remarks, incidentally, were delivered to an audience that included representatives of the Islamic Society of North America and the Muslim Public Affairs Council. Both groups have been linked to the Muslim Brotherhood, and ISNA was even named as an unindicted co-conspirator in the largest terrorism financing trial in U.S. history. So while they surely appreciated Obama's defense of mosque building, it's unclear how many members of Obama's audience have any real interest in religious freedom for anyone besides Muslims.

Let's look at some details Obama omitted from his speech, beginning with the Ground Zero mosque's name. It is now called Park51, but that non-descript moniker was only adopted in response to a controversy over its original name, the Cordoba Initiative. Cordoba was a Spanish city that was conquered in the eighth century by invading Muslims, who turned it into the capital of their new caliphate in Spain. As was the norm after a Muslim victory, they erected a large mosque in the city over the remains of a destroyed Christian cathedral. The vanquished, in turn, were forced to live as second-class citizens—or *dhimmis*—under Islamic rule.[12]

By 1492, the *reconquista* of Cordoba and the rest of Spain after 800 years of Muslim domination had been completed. Ever since, jihadists from Osama bin Laden to Anwar al-Awlaki have mourned the passing of Muslim Spain and dreamed of its return to the Islamic fold. The conquest of Spain—in the heart of Western Europe—represented a seminal, symbolic victory and the height of Islam's advance against the West. Again, given the background, anyone who knows a shred of Islamic history realizes that naming a mosque—in a Western country—after Cordoba is not only a thumb in the eye to non-Muslims but an unmistakable message of dominance. "We're back, you infidels—this time, for good." Could it be any more obvious?

Unfortunately, even though we are locked in an existential struggle against Islamist barbarians, the vast majority of our elected officials and liberal media mavens—many of whom support the Ground Zero mosque—don't know a shred of Islamic history. They've never read the Koran and are oblivious to the *hadiths* (the sayings and actions of Muhammad as recorded by his companions). And sadly, before Imam Rauf came along, they had never even heard of Cordoba and had no concept of its significance to Islamists; I'll even wager many of them were unaware that Spain had lived under the heel of Islam for eight centuries. ("Really? But the clubs in Madrid are so happening!") After all, they reason, the threat of Islamic terrorism and Islamist infiltration has been severely overblown by racist, right-wing fanatics for political gain.

Imam Rauf, on the other hand, is eloquent, well-dressed, and says all the right things to the cameras—now *him* they can trust. Never mind that he refuses to condemn the terrorist group Hamas, defends Iran's theocratic regime, advocates for Islamic sharia law on U.S. soil, and insists that Mid-East peace will require Israel to transform into an Arab country with a Jewish minority.[13] And forget that nineteen days after 9/11, as gray ash and smoke still rose from the remains of what was once the World Trade Center, Rauf told *60 Minutes* host Ed Bradley, "I wouldn't say that the United States deserved what happened. But the United States' policies were an accessory to the crime." He later added, "In the most direct sense, Osama bin Laden is made in the U.S.A."

No, never mind that. Rauf now tells the media he is moderate and opposed to violence, and that Islam is peace and his mosque will preach tolerance for the infidels. Why would he lie?

Since the alternative—that Rauf is not what he appears, and that Islam's core texts encourage violence and discrimination against non-believers—is too awful for the Obama administration or the *New York Times* editorial board to accept, they've decided to cast their lot with the smiling imam and hope for the best. In fact, as the Ground Zero mosque controversy exploded in the summer of 2010, Obama's State Department sent Rauf on a taxpayer-funded tour of the Middle East. Trying to quell the ensuing outrage, then-State Department spokesman P. J. Crowley called the smooth-talking imam "a moderate Muslim figure" who preaches "religious tolerance throughout the world."[14] It's unclear, however, what exactly Rauf preaches tolerance for—it sure isn't America. Aside from his insinuation of America's culpability in the 9/11 attacks, he made his views about his adopted homeland clear enough in 2005, when he declared that "the United States has more Muslim blood on its hands than al Qaeda has on its hands of innocent non-Muslims."[15]

Despite the widespread insistence that Rauf is a moderate, it seems the Ground Zero mosque project was inconvenienced by the ongoing discovery of his decidedly non-moderate views, so in January 2011 he was pushed out of the venture. His replacement, Abdallah Adhami, lasted about a month before he too left the position after reporters uncovered his own Islamic supremacist comments, including his argument that converts from Islam should be jailed. It's funny how a shrine to tolerance like the Ground Zero mosque keeps attracting these rather intolerant types.

In reality, Rauf is a master of the Islamic concept of *taqiyya*—or deception. Hence Rauf's publication in 2004 of a book called *What's Right with Islam Is What's Right with America*. Sounds innocent enough—except that the Arabic version of the book was titled, *A Call to Prayer from the World Trade Center Rubble: Islamic Proselytization [Da'wah] from the Heart of America Post 9/11*.[16] The latter title says it all: for Rauf, the 9/11 attacks were a great Islamic victory that presented an opportunity to spread Islam in America. His English-language re-working of the book title mirrored a technique that was perfected by terrorist godfather and taqiyya master Yasser Arafat: offer a peaceful, moderate message in English to clueless Western audiences, and advocate Islamic conquest while speaking in Arabic to the Muslim masses.

Taqiyya is a vitally important concept for Westerners to understand as unctuous Muslim Brotherhood spokesmen (Rauf, not surprisingly, has been linked to MB front groups)[17] vie for air-time and influence, encouraged every step of the way by a compliant political Left in both Europe and the United States. In a nutshell, taqiyya means Muslims are permitted to lie to non-Muslims if the lie furthers the cause of Islam. In Rauf's eyes, erecting a 15-story victory mosque at Ground Zero does exactly that. So he'll gladly continue to play the public role of high-minded moderate until he achieves his goal.

Unlike naïve Western infidels, Muslims around the world know their history, and they fully understand the meaning behind the Cordoba Initiative. In August 2010, as the Ground Zero mosque furor was in full swing, Abdul Rahman Al-Rashid, general manager of Al-Arabiya TV, penned an op-ed opposing the project in Lower Manhattan. He wrote:

> I cannot imagine that Muslims want a mosque on this par-
> ticular site, because it will be turned into an arena for promot-
> ers of hatred, and a symbol of those who committed the
> crime. At the same time, there are no practicing Muslims in
> the district who need a place of worship, because it is indeed
> a commercial district.[18]

Al-Rashid, whose network is not exactly a bastion of pro-Western sym-
pathies, makes a salient point. There are currently at least 200 mosques in New York City, with some 100 located in Manhattan alone. Our old friend Imam Rauf is actually the imam of another mosque just a few

blocks north of the Ground Zero site. So why are he and his cohorts so adamant that a massive mosque be built at the scene of history's deadliest Islamic terror attack, on a spot considered sacred by most Americans (but not by Rauf, who has publicly rejected the notion that Ground Zero is "hallowed ground"[19])?

To put it in terms Manhattanites can understand, it's all about location, location, location.

It's the same reason mosques are popping up throughout Tennessee, according to local counter-jihad activist Laurie Cardoza-Moore, whom I interviewed for my report about the Murfreesboro mega-mosque.

"You have Bible book publishers, you have Christian book publishers, you have Christian music headquartered here," she told me. "So this is where the Gospel message goes out. And the radical Islamic extremists have stated that they're still fighting the Crusaders—and they see this as the capital of the Crusaders."

In other words, it's a direct challenge to Judeo-Christian civilization. Throughout the West, mosques are often built right next door to, or directly across the street from, churches or synagogues. I've been to many mosques in the United States and Europe—including the new ICM structure, which is being built next to a Baptist church—and seen this phenomenon firsthand. Just for kicks, take a few minutes and check out the location of your local mosques. I guarantee that many will either be in close proximity to Christian churches or synagogues, or will occupy buildings that are renovated churches. You'll also notice that minarets at U.S. and European mosques will usually be built higher than the steeples of neighboring churches. All this is no accident. Again: domination is the name of the game, and bigger is better.

And let's debunk one more red herring about the Ground Zero mega-mosque. Its supporters scream, "It's not a mosque! It's a cultural center. There's a big difference, you hateful Islamophobic rabble." Really? Well, during the course of my investigations over the years, I've been in dozens of "Islamic centers" from coast to coast in the United States, as well as in Europe. In each instance, the centerpiece and main hub is a large, elaborate mosque.

The Muslims who worship at these facilities don't say they are going to the "Islamic center." They say they are going to the "mosque"— because that is exactly the way they view it. As Robert Spencer, director of the invaluable Jihad Watch website, has noted, most Protestant mega-churches in America also include schools and other attached facilities. Yet they are still called churches. How are Islamic centers any different? They consist of a large mosque with attached facilities. Honest Muslims will tell you they see Islamic centers as mosques—and their viewpoint on the matter is the most important.

★ ★ ★

Ex-Muslims will tell you the same thing, and much more, about what goes on inside mosques. One of the most eloquent is Sam Solomon, co-author of a handy book called *The Mosque Exposed*. Solomon, a leading expert on Islam who trained in sharia law for fifteen years before converting to Christianity, is a consultant to the British Parliament on Islamic matters. He states:

> A mosque, totally unlike a church or a synagogue, serves the function of orchestrating and mandating every aspect of "life" in a Muslim community from the religious, to the political, to the economic, to the social, to the military. In Islam, religion and life are not separate....In addition, there is no concept of a personal relationship between the person and the entity being worshiped, so "worship" itself is of a different nature than that performed in a church or synagogue....So we see that a mosque is a seat of government. A mosque is a school. A mosque is a court. A mosque is a training center. A mosque is a gathering place, or social center. It is not a place

of "worship" per se as understood and as practiced in Western societies.[20]

You can say that again. Read the following exchange I had in late 2010 during an interview with "Reza Kahlili," a pseudonym used by a former member of Iran's notorious Revolutionary Guards Corps. Kahlili joined the Guards soon after Iran's 1979 revolution, but upon witnessing the Khomeinist regime's systematic rape, torture, and execution of political dissidents, he became disenchanted enough to begin working as an undercover agent for the United States. Kahlili described his time working for the Revolutionary Guards in Europe's Muslim communities in stunning detail:

> **Kahlili:** Mosques are supposed to be a place for prayer. A place for submission to God. But they are used as a recruitment center, for backdoor meetings, transfer of arms and cash and putting together terrorist activities and I was involved in some of their meetings.
>
> **E.S.:** You made a key point, that Iran used mosques and Islamic cultural centers in the West to further its agenda. ... Could you get a little bit more specific about that? How does Iran use mosques here in the U.S. and in Europe to plot terrorism?
>
> **Kahlili:** I can tell you from experience: I was part of the operation, I was involved in the Islamic community, and I can tell you clearly that out of mosques, there was a big effort with the Afghan communities by the Iranian Revolutionary Guards members—and with Pakistanis, Turks, and others. And they would recruit from them, they would transfer cash and arms. And mosques provided a safe haven, and actually, in my view, were one of the centers of the operation. So if an intelligence agency such as the CIA infiltrates a mosque and understands that there is a specific Guards member who runs it, then actu-

ally they could be very successful in drawing a chart of all the terrorist activities in that specific region. That's how central the mosque operation was.

E.S.: And that's in Europe—you were involved in some of these operations in Europe. How about the U.S.?

Kahlili: It's absolutely the same. They recruit, they train, they sell the ideology of martyrdom, and many, many are guided and connected to terrorist groups. And you've seen this: many U.S.-born citizens, Muslims, unfortunately, have been sold this idea and are sent to al-Qaeda camps or others. But the Iranians are very active in this country through the mosques and Islamic cultural centers to make those connections and run those operations.[21]

These are jaw-dropping revelations from a man who spent years working for the most powerful and secretive arm of the Iranian regime. But I can't say I was surprised.

Several of the 9/11 hijackers met and plotted at the Taiba mosque in Hamburg, Germany. The mosque continued to churn out terrorist recruits—including a ten-man cell that traveled to Pakistan for jihadi training—until German authorities finally shut it down in August 2010.[22] A bit further north, in Sweden, a brave Stockholm City councilman named Daniel Arrpospide went undercover in one of the city's largest mosques for six months in 2010. He told a local television station about the tolerant, peaceful activities he found there, which included al-Qaeda recruitment fully endorsed by the mosque's imam: "They promise lots of money to the family if [a mosque-goer] chooses to die in the name of Allah. Targets are the unemployed, homeless people, those without a future."[23]

Arrpospide also affirmed that the topics of jihad and killing unbelievers were discussed frequently at the mosque, and he even warned of potential attacks on nuclear power plants in Sweden. Memo to the

Swedes: when a pudgy city councilman, and not Swedish law enforcement, is your best intelligence source in mosques, you may want to rethink your counter-terrorism strategy.

Ditto for the Brits, who have seen numerous terror-linked megamosques pop up across their once proud nation over the past several years. Perhaps the most notorious is one still in the planning stages: a sprawling structure that would house tens of thousands of Muslim worshippers, to be built in the shadow of the site of the 2012 London Olympics. An Islamist separatist group called Tablighi Jamaat is behind the plan, and despite being evicted from the site in January 2010, the Tablighis continue to use it as a temporary mosque and have even erected buildings on the grounds without planning permission. After all, the infidel's laws do not apply to Islamic supremacists, and as we see in the conquest of Cordoba, once Muslims claim a site, they consider it theirs forever: *dar-al-Islam*, or the land of Islam. Alan Craig, a former London city councilor who has led local opposition to the Tablighi mosque, told me that British law enforcement officials have expressed to him major reservations about the proposed structure:

> The counterterrorism commander of the London police—the Metro London police—I've spoken to them about it and they've expressed their concern. Because as they point out, during the Olympics, the roads and the railways underground will be full. But the river will give relatively easy access. The mosque site is literally right beside the river—it borders onto the river, the small river that leads into the River Thames. I know the police have been looking at this in terms of the possibility of getting ordinates—bombs and so on—up the river, onto the mosque site and into the Olympics.

Now whatever would give British authorities that idea? Perhaps Turkey's current prime minister, Recep Tayyip Erdogan, was onto something in

1998 when he publicly recited a poem including the lines, "The mosques are our barracks, the domes our helmets, the minarets our bayonets and the faithful our soldiers."[24] This ode to jihad earned Erdogan—an Islamist, anti-Israel demagogue who has nonetheless been embraced by President Obama as a moderate—a four-month prison stay for inciting religious hatred.

Speaking of incitement, it doesn't get much more blatant than what went down in Washington, D.C., over Labor Day weekend 2010. That was when an annual Islamo/leftist freak show known as the "al-Quds Day" rally came to town, featuring a rogue's gallery of Jew-hating conspiracy theorists protesting Israel's claim to the city of Jerusalem. Leading the pack was Abolfazl Bahram Nahidian, imam of the Manassas mosque in northern Virginia, which is located near the site of the legendary Battle of Bull Run. That may sound like an odd fit on the surface, but Nahidian quickly showed at the al-Quds event that when it came to "bull," he had few peers. At the rally, Nahidian claimed the 9/11 attacks were "not done by Muslims. It is done by the plot of the Zionists in order to justify, to occupy, the land of the Muslims such as Afghanistan, such as Iraq, such as Pakistan, now moving on to the rest of the areas. [The Zionists] plot and they scheme and no doubt God is plotting and scheming against them too!"[25]

When I called Nahidian to ask him about these comments, he was unrepentant, insisting the 9/11 attacks were carried out in a joint operation by the CIA, British intelligence, and the Israeli Mossad as a pretext to "plunder the wealth and the oil of the Middle East." For good measure, he added that America "created al-Qaeda and the Taliban," and that the notion that Muslim nations would ever accept Israel as a neighbor was "impossible."

I couldn't help but marvel at how closely Nahidian's comments mirrored the rhetoric of the hard Left. I was also struck by the thought that Imam Nahidian is not just a member of the Manassas mosque—he *runs* the joint. If he is that outspoken in public about his hatred for America and for Jews, one can only imagine what he tells his congregation behind closed doors.

One thing we know for certain *has* gone on behind closed doors in U.S. mosques is terror fundraising. In June 2009, a local counter-jihad activist went undercover to videotape an event held at the Masjid al-Rahman mosque in Orlando that would benefit British parliamentarian George Galloway's anti-Israel group, Viva Palestina. Galloway, a radical leftist and longtime Islamist collaborator, raised $55,000 at the Orlando mosque and $1 million worth of aid overall during his American tour, supposedly to benefit needy Palestinians in Gaza. Galloway was later shown on al-Jazeera TV presenting the funds he garnered in the United States directly to Hamas leaders at a ceremony in Gaza—in open violation of U.S. sanctions.[26]

These are not isolated incidents, as U.S. federal agents will tell you off the record. I am not saying all mosques are havens for jihadi sympathizers or terrorist fundraising and plotting. But given that enough of them have hosted such activities over the years, and that their rapid construction in the West represents a strategic display of Islamic dominance, Americans have good reason to be alarmed. Yes, Muslims have the right to build mosques in America, so long as those mosques are transparent about their funding sources and do not promote a violent anti-Western, pro-jihadist worldview. Local residents who are seeing multi-million-dollar mega-mosques erected in their communities also have every right not only to demand answers about funding sources and the ideology of the mosques' leaders (Do they recognize Israel's right to exist? Place the U.S. constitution above Islamic sharia law? Disavow Islamic supremacist groups like the Muslim Brotherhood and Islamic terrorist groups like Hamas and Hezbollah?), but to protest their construction for reasons of national security.

At the end of the day, though, the firestorms erupting across America over the construction of sprawling mosque compounds boil down to plain common sense. Average, everyday Americans realize—after 9/11, the Fort Hood massacre, and an endless barrage of homegrown jihad plots—

that a large and aggressive slice of the Muslim world is at war with the United States and seeks its destruction. Why then, they wonder, is the U.S. government not only admitting more Muslims into the United States than it did before 9/11, but allowing them to erect giant, in-your-face mosques in America's heartland where they congregate in large numbers? It is no coincidence that poll after poll show that roughly 70 percent of all Americans oppose the Ground Zero mosque. They understand what the organizers are up to and realize that the mosque complex, as some have pointed out, is indeed the equivalent of the Japanese building a towering Shinto Temple at Pearl Harbor ten years after those attacks.

Americans also realize it is horribly wrong for a U.S. president to bow to a foreign dignitary, particularly one who has been instrumental in spreading radical Islamic ideology and mega-mosque-building worldwide. But that's exactly what President Obama did at the G-20 Summit in London in April 2009, prostrating himself before the King of Saudi Arabia as cameras flashed and other Western leaders looked on in shock. Obama's shameless act of groveling, performed in one of his first forays onto the international stage, signaled that debasing America and exalting Islam would be key elements in achieving his oft-stated goal of improving America's image in the Muslim world.

The Bow sent a clear message of subservience not only to King Abdullah—a tinpot monarch presiding over a backward, Islamo/petro-dictatorship—but to Islam itself. Saudi Arabia—land of the two holiest sites in Islam, Mecca and Medina, and the birthplace of its prophet, Mohammed—is a nation with major symbolic significance to Muslims, and one of Abdullah's titles as absolute monarch is "Keeper of the Two Holy Mosques." Accordingly, he and a long line of Saudi royals have always considered themselves the global standard bearers of Islam: defenders and propagators of the faith. The Saudi government has invested untold billions of its oil wealth to spread Wahhabi Islam worldwide through the building of mosques and *madrassahs* (Islamic schools) on six continents.

Furthermore, leaked U.S. diplomatic cables have revealed Saudi Arabia is the world's largest source of funding for Sunni terrorist groups like al-Qaeda, and that Saudi officials have shown little interest in stopping the jihadi money flow. Add to this the fact that fifteen of the nineteen hijackers on 9/11 hailed from Saudi Arabia—all of them weaned on state-sanctioned Wahhabism—and Obama's bow becomes even more unforgivable. Forget presidential protocol, which was shamefully broken: the Saudi royal family is the *enemy* in the war against global jihad.

And the enemy is very big on imagery. From Riyadh to London to Jakarta and beyond, Islamists saw Obama's bow to Abdullah and smiled broadly. To them, The Bow—and the steady stream of pandering, pro-Islamic policies that have followed from the Obama White House—represented a green light to further expand their tentacles into the United States. With a sympathetic administration in office, why not go for broke and propose what not too long ago would have been unthinkable—a mosque at Ground Zero? Sure enough, Obama took the side of the Islamists and endorsed the project: just as The Bow signaled to them, early on, that he would.

No Islamist entity has seized upon the message sent by The Bow more than the Muslim Brotherhood—the first modern Islamic terrorist group and the Saudis' steadfast ally in the *mosqueing* of America. So at this point, let's undertake a brief introduction to the Brotherhood, which is the most important and influential Islamist movement in the world—yes, even more so than al-Qaeda—and which we'll be discussing frequently in this book.

★　★　★

The Muslim Brotherhood—also known as the *Ikhwan* or the Society of Muslim Brothers—was founded in 1928 in Egypt by a schoolteacher named Hassan al-Banna. A fervent Islamist with a deep-seated hatred of the West, al-Banna established the Brotherhood with the goal of re-joining the entire Muslim world—or *ummah*—into one unified, Islamic state governed by sharia law. This global Islamic state, called the *caliphate*, had ended a few years earlier with the collapse of the Ottoman Empire.

Al-Banna and his Brotherhood cohorts wasted no time getting down to the business of reestablishing it, starting at home. By 1951, with their ranks in Egypt swelled to some 2 million members,[27] Brotherhood jihadists had committed a series of terrorist attacks and assassinations of Egyptian government officials. Al-Banna himself was assassinated in 1949, and Brotherhood members were forced to flee the country when Egyptian president Gamal Abdel Nasser launched a bloody crackdown and ultimately banned the group. Most of the Brotherhood's leaders ended up in Saudi Arabia where, as we'll see, they soon forged an unholy alliance with the Saudi royals. From Saudi Arabia, many top Brothers then made their way to Europe and the United States during the 1960s and '70s—and they weren't coming for the ambience.

There are two critical facts related to the Brotherhood's impact on the West, both of which Western governments have willfully ignored in their embrace of the Ikhwan as "outreach partners." First, the Brotherhood is the dean of all modern Islamic terrorist groups, having provided the ideological inspiration and blueprint for al-Qaeda, Hamas, and many of today's most violent jihadist outfits. Hamas, in fact, is the self-described Palestinian branch of the Muslim Brotherhood. As for al-Qaeda, most of its senior leadership, including Osama bin Laden, Ayman al-Zawahiri, and Khalid Sheikh Mohammed, belonged to the Brotherhood as young men,[28] and Anwar al-Awlaki has spoken of the seminal Brotherhood ideologue Sayyid Qutb in glowing terms.[29]

Brotherhood leaders maintain that the group is non-violent. However, as exemplified by the terror campaigns the organization carried out in Egypt until Nasser's crackdown, the Brotherhood was specifically created as a terrorist organization. As noted by Brian Fairchild, a former CIA clandestine services officer and Brotherhood expert whom I interviewed in 2010, the Brotherhood "formed a nucleus with support from

Nazi Germany and the German military intelligence. And [the Nazis] actually helped create the Brotherhood's special section, known as the 'secret apparatus,' as their military terrorist wing."[30]

The Nazis, al-Qaeda, and Hamas. Boy, this Muslim Brotherhood sure keeps some interesting company.

The second salient fact about the Brotherhood is that its founding motto—the creed it lives by—is an undisguised call to establish global Islamic domination through violence. It states: "Allah is our objective. The Prophet is our leader. Qur'an is our law. Jihad is our way. Dying in the way of Allah is our highest hope."

The last time I checked, such a belief system was fundamentally incompatible with the U.S. constitution and with Western, Judeo-Christian civilization. This should be no surprise. Here is the Brotherhood's current global leader and Supreme Guide, Mohammed Badi, endorsing jihad against America in one of his weekly sermons in Egypt in September 2010:

> Resistance is the only solution against the Zio-American arrogance and tyranny, and all we need is for the Arab and Muslim peoples to stand behind it and support it. The peoples know well who is [carrying out] resistance and who has sold out the [Palestinian] cause and bargained over it. We say to our brothers the mujahideen in Gaza: "be patient, persist in [your jihad], and know that Allah is with you."[31]

Badi was just getting warmed up:

> The Soviet Union fell dramatically, but the factors that will lead to the collapse of the U.S. are much more powerful than those that led to the collapse of the Soviet empire—for a nation that does not champion moral and human values cannot lead humanity, and its wealth will not avail it once Allah has had His say, as happened with [powerful] nations in the

past. The U.S. is now experiencing the beginning of its end, and is heading towards its demise.[32]

This was no less than a declaration of war against the United States by the leader of the world's most influential Islamist movement, one that boasts affiliates in 110 countries. But I'll bet the vast majority of leaders in America's intelligence and federal law enforcement communities never heard it. How could this be, you ask? Because those leaders and their bosses in the Obama White House do not believe the Muslim Brotherhood is a threat to U.S. national security; rather, they think that since the Ikhwan does not presently engage in violence on U.S. soil, they are a moderating force. Indeed, the prevailing view among Washington bureaucrats, as we'll discuss in greater detail later in the book, is that as long as you don't strap a bomb to yourself or openly call on others to do so, you can be "engaged" through dialogue. Therefore, they believe, the Brotherhood can be co-opted as a force for good and a counterweight to the *really* bad guys like al-Qaeda.

This is an incredibly shortsighted and naïve misunderstanding of the Islamist threat—and one that has enormous implications today, as one Arab regime after another is toppled, while in nearly every country a powerful Brotherhood group watches and waits. As we've seen, the Brotherhood shares the same goals as al-Qaeda and other violent jihadist groups: the imposition of Islamic sharia law worldwide and the reestablishment of the caliphate. Yes, the Brotherhood and al-Qaeda have different strategies for getting there: al-Qaeda pursues a short-term, *win now* strategy through violence and terror, while the Brotherhood has a more patient, long-term strategy: infiltrate a society, then conquer it from within. But again, while the tactics may be different, the endgame is unquestionably the same.

So it should come as no surprise that the Brotherhood was quickly able to put aside whatever differences it had with the Saudi royal family to further its ultimate goal: the Islamization of the West. My friend

Patrick Poole, a dogged investigative journalist and one of America's top experts on the Muslim Brothers, explained the Brotherhood's baleful influence on worldwide Islam on the *Stakelbeck on Terror* show in September 2010:

> After the oil crisis in the early 1970s, that infused a lot of cash into Saudi Arabia and the Gulf States, and the Brotherhood was there to step in. They had the institutions and apparatus to be able to help with essentially the Wahhabization of global Islam over the past 40 years. And as a result of that, they were able to take that cash and move into Europe—places like Geneva, Munich—and into the United States, where they moved right into the heartland. Places like Indianapolis and Columbus, Ohio. And they've been able to spread out—as we see, even today, with this rash of mosque building. It's all being funded by Saudi and Gulf state money.[33]

So the Saudis provide the money to build the mosques, and Brotherhood operatives and sympathizers organize and facilitate the on-the-ground apparatus: imams, literature, meetings, youth groups, guest speakers, and educational seminars, all with an anti-Western, Islamic supremacist bent that pleases the financiers back in Riyadh. Nearly all of the many U.S. mosques I've visited feature pamphlets or some kind of literature by Muslim Brotherhood-connected groups like the Muslim American Society (MAS), Islamic Society of North America (ISNA), or the Council on American-Islamic Relations (CAIR). Of course, some of the literature I've obtained in U.S. mosques, including Korans, was actually printed in Saudi Arabia.

Another Brotherhood-inspired phenomenon I have seen repeatedly in my investigations, from Oklahoma to Ohio and from London to Austria, is that when a huge Islamic center is built (usually in spite of heated local opposition), it serves as a magnet for Muslims from surrounding communities. In essence, the new mega-mosque marks an area as Muslim territory. Suddenly, more and more Muslims either resettle around the new mosque or become regular commuters there. Muslim-owned shops pop up around the structure with signs written in Arabic. Women in veils and men in traditional Islamic garb become regular sights in the neighborhood. Longtime non-Muslim residents feel uncomfortable and move out, the Muslim call to prayer echoing in their ears as they depart a neighborhood they no longer recognize. More Muslims move in.

And voila! Suddenly you have a mini-Islamic enclave in your town, with the multi-million-dollar mosque serving as the centerpiece. Perhaps down the line these self-segregating Muslim areas will also become self-governing, with sharia law enforced. Many Americans can't envision this happening here, but just a few decades ago, not many Europeans could imagine such a phenomenon occurring in their cities, either. Yet that's exactly what's happening today throughout Europe, where many Muslim neighborhoods are no-go zones for the police. As we'll see in a later chapter, some Muslim areas of Great Britain even have their own fully functioning sharia courts to resolve local disputes.

All this is part of the Brotherhood's framework for the West: establish Islamic power bases over a wide geographical area, and above all, do not assimilate into the surrounding infidel culture. It's a long-term plan for domination that has been espoused by the Brotherhood's most influential modern-day figure, the radical Qatar-based cleric Yusuf al-Qaradawi (a man, by the way, whom Imam Rauf has praised[34]), who has said, "Conquest through Da'wa [proselytizing], that is what we hope for. We will conquer Europe, we will conquer America! Not through the sword but through Da'wa."[35]

Will this strategy work in places like Murfreesboro that were previously impenetrable to Islam? It will, if the Obama administration has anything to say about it. In fact, the administration feels so strongly about the matter that the Civil Rights Division of its Department of Justice filed an amicus brief in October 2010 stating its "vigorous" support of the new Islamic Center of Mufreesboro.[36] In addition to injecting itself into a local issue, the DoJ willfully ignored the long, checkered history of mosques in the West, not to mention the radical links of the ICM's board members.

That's one reason why the Muslim Brotherhood is betting that in the long run, with the U.S. government's acquiescence, its plan for the West will succeed—one mosque at a time. And as the Brotherhood now faces a strong possibility of inheriting power, perhaps even democratically, in revolutionary Middle Eastern states like Egypt, they are becoming better positioned than ever before to implement their plan.

CHAPTER TWO

DEATH BY A THOUSAND CUTS

I stood just a few feet from the men as they trampled upon the Israeli flag. First two guys, then three, then five, like sharks in the water, all jockeying for position as they tried to tear a chunk out of the Star of David. As my cameraman and I moved alongside them and filmed their outburst, I was struck by the singular focus of their rage. They weren't just stomping on the Israeli flag—they wanted to obliterate it with their feet until not a shred was left. Likewise, their chants of "Death to Israel" were delivered with pogrom levels of fervency and conviction. It was the kind of scene that plays out on a daily basis across the Middle East. Except this wasn't Tehran or Gaza—it was New York City.

The group behind the flag-stomping display calls itself the Islamic Thinker's Society, or ITS—a Queens-based collection of young, second-generation Arab and South Asian Muslims, plus a few converts, that calls for reestablishing a worldwide Islamic caliphate. It was February 2006, and I had come to New York City to watch a group of some twenty-five ITS members and hangers-on (their website had promised a much larger crowd) gather in front of the Danish Consulate, near the United Nations building on Manhattan's east side, to protest cartoons published in a Danish newspaper featuring Islam's prophet, Mohammed. By that time, the "Mo-toons" had sparked worldwide Muslim rioting that resulted in dozens of deaths in countries like Afghanistan and Pakistan, and I was curious to see the tone of the ITS protest.

For starters, I knew that the group was linked to al-Muhajiroun, a notorious pro-jihad organization in Great Britain that had been banned by the British government and seen several former members arrested on terrorism charges.[1] I had also watched clips of ITS members burning the American flag on the streets of New York during a previous rally amid shouts of "Allahu Akhbar." So at the very least, I knew that attending the ITS event in front of the Danish consulate would give me an up-close glimpse of some of New York City's most hardcore Islamists.

While the protest didn't descend into physical violence, there was no shortage of genocidal rhetoric for me to record, all delivered under the watchful eye of the NYPD, which had sent a large contingent of officers to monitor the event. One speaker warned that Denmark would soon suffer "Allah's wrath." Another broadened the message to include all non-Muslims, bellowing into a megaphone, "We are here to tell you that there is nothing you can do and that your days are numbered. . . . All of you who disbelieve: speak good, or Allah will silence you." Non-Muslims were branded as "scum" and the Danish flag stomped upon before the event reached its crescendo with the Israeli flag feeding frenzy, which is a staple of ITS rallies. I spoke to an ITS member afterward who refused to go on camera but denied any links to al-Muhajiroun—even though ITS members waved the same black flag with Arabic inscription regularly displayed at al-Muhajiroun rallies in Great Britain.

My first thought as I watched the ITS event unfold was that it was occurring just a few miles north of where the Twin Towers had fallen four and a half years earlier. My second thought was that I was quite possibly staring at a group of future Islamic terrorists. And sure enough, in the years since that February 2006 ITS rally, at least three men connected with the group have been arrested on terrorism-related charges. One NYPD intelligence analyst has said the group's "anti-Western, anti-democratic, anti-U.S., pro-al Qaeda message" makes the ITS "almost bug lights for aspiring jihadists."[2]

There are a few routes that these up-and-comers can take to receive instruction and guidance on how to aid in the "global Islamic struggle" against America, Europe, and Israel. They can become active members of an American Islamist group like ITS and stir the pot on U.S. soil, or they can travel overseas to train with al-Qaeda before returning home to plot deadly attacks. But the easiest way is simply to go online, where a fledgling *mujahid* can receive all the instruction he needs on how to turn himself into a veritable one-man jihad. A case in point is *Inspire* magazine.

A few weeks after the failed Yemen Cargo Plane Plot, al-Qaeda in the Arabian Peninsula released a new issue of its glossy online publication, describing the cost-effective operation in detail. According to *Inspire*, which is undoubtedly a hit among the teenybopper set in Gaza and Waziristan, not to mention the ITS crowd in America, "Operation Hemorrhage" cost just $4,200 to carry out, with AQAP bombmakers designing the explosives to elude airport security devices and bomb-sniffing dogs.[3] Although the magazine went on to praise the 9/11 attacks for causing massive death and carnage, it argued that the future of jihad, at least in the short term, lies in smaller, cheaper attacks like Operation Hemorrhage: "It is more feasible to stage smaller attacks that involve less players and less time to launch and thus we may circumvent the security barriers America worked so hard to erect."[4]

The author called this "the strategy of a thousand cuts." And based on what we've seen unfold over the past three years, al-Qaeda has found a winning approach. "How could you say their strategy is working?" you might counter. "It's been ten years and we still haven't been hit with another 9/11. Admit it, Stakelbeck: we're winning this war!"

How wrong you are. Although al-Qaeda admittedly has failed to duplicate the kind of history-altering destruction we witnessed on 9/11 (though not for lack of effort), in the jihadists' eyes, the past few years have brought some major successes. But before reviewing them, we need to examine a few recent developments within al-Qaeda that have signaled a new direction for the organization.

For starters, al-Qaeda's hierarchy has reluctantly accepted the fact that post-9/11, apocalyptic attacks will be extremely difficult to pull off. This is due to three main factors. First, intelligence services around the world have stepped up their game considerably over the past decade, gaining a firmer understanding of the threat and doing a much better job at surveillance and information sharing. Second, many of al-Qaeda's trusted funding sources have dried up since 9/11 due to a global crackdown on terrorist financing. This makes it difficult to conduct large-scale, 9/11-style operations or to acquire weapons of mass destruction, a long-held al-Qaeda goal.[5] Last, large attacks take a great deal of planning. September 11 took five years to plot and carry out, while the 1998 Africa Embassy bombings took at least three years—and remember, these attacks occurred when America's guard was *down*.

The post-9/11 world is a much trickier beast for a terrorist group to navigate, but al-Qaeda had been slow to accept this reality in the years immediately following its greatest triumph. After all, it set the bar extremely high on 9/11, which established a standard for economic, psychological, and physical devastation that is difficult to surpass. What do you do for a follow-up to the most destructive terrorist attack in modern history? While attacks on the mass transit systems of Madrid in 2004 and London in 2005 were acceptable, al-Qaeda's brain trust felt that its encore on U.S. soil had to be massive. Whether by weapons of mass destruction, a dirty bomb, or another round of multiple airplane hijackings, the next attack had to be as big as or bigger than 9/11. The group had a fearsome reputation to uphold in America, and killing a hundred people with a bomb on a train just wouldn't do. Thousands of casualties, mass paranoia, and economic collapse were the only acceptable outcomes.

That's one reason al-Qaeda's second-in-command, Ayman al-Zawahiri, called off a planned cyanide gas attack against the New York City subway system in 2003—he felt that the plot, which likely would have killed hundreds, simply would not cause enough casualties or make a big enough splash.[6]

Al-Qaeda would surely not call off that attack today, as evidenced by a foiled 2009 plot to bomb that same New York City subway system. The main foot soldier in that scheme was 25-year-old Afghan native Najibullah Zazi, who had been recruited by al-Qaeda in Pakistan.[7] A trusted intelligence source told me the feds were late to the game in uncovering the Zazi plot, and that New York dodged a bullet only because the aspiring terrorist got cold feet at the last second and was then arrested. Whatever the case, al-Qaeda's lowering of the bar with the Zazi plot revealed a bit of desperation.

For ten years, the organization has released countless audio tapes and videos threatening devastating new attacks against the United States that would rival 9/11. Thankfully, as of this writing, this has not materialized. That marks an entire *decade* of boasts and threats by al-Qaeda's hierarchy against America—with nothing to show for it. They came close in 2006 with an intricate plot to hijack ten transatlantic airliners traveling from Britain to the United States and blow them up in midair, but the plan was ultimately foiled.

If you talk a big game but fail to back it up, eventually people begin to tune you out—and that applies to Islamists like anyone else. Our what-have-you-done-for-me-lately culture demands instant results, and with al-Qaeda downsizing its ambitions, others in the jihadist world are eagerly filling the void. We have Iran threatening the West, vowing to wipe out Israel, and feverishly trying to develop nuclear weapons. After going toe-to-toe with Israel in 2006, Iran's proxy, Hezbollah, plunged Lebanon into crisis by bringing down the Western-backed government and maneuvering its chosen candidate into the position of prime minister. Then there are the Turks, led by their fiery Islamist president, Recep Tayyip Erdogan, who sent a flotilla of Hamas supporters to stage a violent confrontation with the Israeli Navy. And of course, from Egypt to Tunisia to Libya and beyond, you have the Muslim Brotherhood and other Islamist groups seeking to capitalize on political instability and usher in new Islamist states.

These actions have made Iran, Hezbollah, and Turkey the toast of the Islamist world and, for many, the vanguard of the global jihad. Al-Qaeda, however, resents the growing primacy of Iran and Hezbollah. They are the standard bearers of Shia Islam, a sect al-Qaeda regards as heretical (though it will still cooperate with either entity to target Israel and the West). Simply put, al-Qaeda's hierarchy knows that it has to do something to stay relevant and maintain its jihadi street cred among young Muslims worldwide, especially after it stood on the sidelines and watched impotently as a new mass movement formed in Egypt and, within weeks, overthrew a secular government that al-Qaeda itself had tried for years to dislodge. Now similar events could unfold in Yemen, Libya, and elsewhere. But with 9/11-style attacks a difficult proposition in the short term, how can al-Qaeda regain its cachet? Mumbai provided the blueprint.

As the Mumbai massacre unfolded over Thanksgiving weekend 2008, it became clear we were seeing the next stage of Islamic terrorism. Ten young Pakistani men—each armed with assault rifles and bombs— fanned out across the Indian city of Mumbai and engaged in a murder spree that killed 175 people and wounded more than 300. Among the slaughtered were Rabbi Gavriel Holtzberg and his six-months-pregnant wife, Rivka Holtzberg, who were murdered along with four other hostages after the jihadists stormed a Jewish center in downtown Mumbai. The dead bodies showed signs of torture. Indian intelligence later revealed that the attackers were "told by their handlers in Pakistan that the lives of Jews were worth 50 times those of non-Jews."[8]

The assailants were directed throughout the attack via satellite phones by members of the Pakistan-based, al-Qaeda-linked terrorist group Lashkar-e-Taiba.[9] They were disciplined and well-trained (probably by

Pakistan's notoriously corrupt and Islamist-ridden Inter-Services Intelligence, or ISI)[10] and formed a tight paramilitary unit that initially surprised and overwhelmed Indian police and counter-terror forces. Incidentally, an American Muslim of Pakistani descent, David Coleman Headley, was later convicted of aiding and abetting the Mumbai attackers. Headley had traveled five times from America to India to scout out potential targets for Lashkar-e-Taiba.[11]

The Mumbai operation presented an appealing package to the jihadist world. It garnered massive media coverage and dominated the international news cycle for nearly a week. It was cheap, low-tech, and didn't take much manpower to pull off, yet it still caused immense carnage and crippled the world's second-largest city for days. It also created the kind of psychological terror and economic damage that Islamic terrorist groups yearn for, and showed how a major city could be completely unprepared for a coordinated onslaught by jihadi foot soldiers.

Think back to the fall of 2002, when two devout Muslims known as the "Beltway snipers" killed ten people and created havoc across the Washington, D.C. area for weeks. Now multiply those two terrorists by five, equip them with explosives to go along with their assault rifles, and drop them downtown in a sleepy, mid-sized American city like Des Moines or Boise at lunchtime. We'll take for granted that they have trained with al-Qaeda in the tribal regions of Pakistan or some other foreign terrorist safe haven, that they have spent months surveilling their intended targets, and that they are fully prepared to die to achieve their mission. Is America ready for that? Major cities like New York, Chicago, or Los Angeles would clearly be far better equipped to deal with such a scenario, and New York in particular has a top-notch counter-terrorism team. But even those cities would suffer significant casualties due to the sheer suddenness and randomness of a Mumbai-style attack.

And what about middle America? How many lives would be lost, how much devastation would ensue, before a ten-man team of well-armed, well-trained jihadists could be subdued in a city like Columbus,

Ohio? Local police would take them on at first. The FBI, SWAT, and potentially even the National Guard would later rush to the scene. Eventually the situation would be brought under control—but not before many people were killed and countless more wounded.

But forget about a ten-man team—what about a single committed jihadist acting all by his lonesome? It doesn't take a brain surgeon to walk into a shopping mall during the Christmas shopping season, yell "Allahu Akhbar," and mow down a few dozen people with an assault rifle and grenades. Remember, Nidal Malik Hasan murdered thirteen people and wounded thirty in just ten minutes using nothing but two hand-guns—and that was at Fort Hood, where he was surrounded by highly trained military personnel. Let's be honest: Americans are psychologically unprepared right now to live under the kind of threat environment that Israelis have gritted through for decades, where the next danger is always just around the corner and may be sitting next to you with a bomb under his jacket at your child's playground.

★   ★   ★

America's unpreparedness, both psychologically and in terms of contingency planning, is one reason the world's most notorious terror-ist organization has conducted a tactical shift over the past three years, turning to something I call the "Chip Away" strategy. For the moment, al-Qaeda has readjusted its plan for the United States, lowering the bar a bit, so to speak—aiming for smaller-scale attacks that occur with greater frequency, rather than waiting for years to pull off the next Big One.

While lacking the symbolism and history-altering qualities of 9/11— the kind of effect al-Qaeda craves—these smaller attacks, if carried out steadily, can "chip away" at a society's confidence and security. There is a growing fear among the U.S. intelligence community that this is pre-cisely the new prototype for al-Qaeda: small, grassroots, and inexpensive, with individuals or tiny splinter groups executing attacks. And while al-Qaeda unleashes a series of smaller-scale assaults that keeps America off balance, it continues to plot larger, more long-term attacks that would dwarf 9/11.

The question as to whether al-Qaeda's hierarchy—a prideful bunch, to say the least—has come around to endorsing the Chip Away strategy was put to rest in March 2010 by American-born al-Qaeda spokesman Adam Gadahn, who issued a videotape extolling Nidal Malik Hasan and his killing spree at Fort Hood, perhaps the most notorious Chip Away attack. Gadahn is close to al-Qaeda's hierarchy in the tribal regions of Pakistan, and his statement provided valuable insights into the group's current thinking:

> The Mujahid Brother Nidal Hasan used firearms in his assault on Fort Hood, but the fact is, today's Mujahid is no longer limited to bullets and bombs when it comes to his choice of a weapon. As the blessed operations of September 11th showed, a little imagination and planning and a minimal budget can turn almost anything into a deadly, effective and convenient weapon, which can take the enemy by surprise and deprive him of sleep for years on end.
>
> ... When the time came to pick his target, the Mujahid Brother Nidal chose carefully, looking for a target with which he was well acquainted, a target which was feasible and a target whose hitting would have a major impact on the enemy.... [A]s you start to make your plans, you shouldn't make the mistake of thinking that military bases are the only high-value targets in America and the West. On the contrary, there are countless other strategic places, institutions and installations which, by striking, the Muslim can do major damage to the Crusader West and further our global agenda and long-range strategic objectives.

We must look to further undermine the West's already-struggling economies with carefully-timed-and-targeted attacks on symbols of capitalism, which will again shake consumer confidence and stifle spending. We must keep in mind how even apparently unsuccessful attacks on Western mass transportation systems can bring major cities to a halt, cost the enemy billions and send his corporations into bankruptcy. We must erode our cowardly enemy's will to fight by killing and capturing leading Crusaders and Zionists in government, industry and media.... We should look for targets which epitomize Western decadence, depravity, immorality and atheism, targets which the enemy and his mouthpieces will have trouble trying to pass off to the conservative Muslim majority as illegitimate targets full of innocent people.[12]

Bear in mind that Gadahn's statements are issued in English and targeted specifically to a Western audience. The message is clear: *Rise up, young American Muslims, and wage jihad now, in any way you can. And hey, even if you fail, the mere attempt could still spread panic and disorder.*

Today, any Muslim can take part in the jihad and strike a powerful blow against non-Muslims. The aforementioned *Inspire* magazine, which intelligence officials believe is published by an American citizen living in Yemen named Samir Khan, has made this abundantly clear. The Web-based al-Qaeda glossy regularly provides terror tips for aspiring Western jihadists. One article, titled "The Ultimate Mowing Machine," recommends driving a four-wheel drive pickup truck into a crowd of people to act as a "mowing machine, not to mow grass but mow down the enemies of Allah." The author may have been inspired by Mohammed Taheri-Azar, the Tar Heel Terrorist who drove his SUV through a crowd of students in a 2006 jihadist attack on the campus of the University of North Carolina at Chapel Hill.

Another *Inspire* article calls for killing U.S. government workers through firearms attacks on crowded restaurants in Washington, D.C. "Targeting such employees is paramount," the article states, "and the location would also give the operation additional media attention." Perhaps the ultimate *Inspire* how-to piece, though, came in the inaugural issue: it was called "Make a Bomb in the Kitchen of Your Mom."[13]

So we have al-Qaeda's chief English-language spokesman and its leading publication both publicly endorsing Chip Away attacks on U.S. soil. It's the kind of scenario that Attorney General Eric Holder says keeps him "up at night."[14] Obama administration officials see clearly the coordinated shift in terrorist tactics. Yet their public response, from the president on down, has been to ignore the obvious pattern and treat each attempted Chip Away attack as a one-off fluke carried out by an "isolated extremist." Such attacks, Obama and his cabinet assure us, have nothing to do with the true teachings of Islam and are condemned by Muslims worldwide.

If only that were true. The following list of the most prominent Chip Away attacks and plots on U.S. soil since 2009, including the U.S. government's response to each, shows a risible pattern of dishonesty from the Obama administration, reflecting a profound lack of seriousness and understanding when it comes to the jihadist threat.

THE FORT HOOD SHOOTINGS: NOVEMBER 4, 2009

U.S. Army Major Nidal Malik Hasan shoots more than forty people, killing thirteen of them, including a pregnant women, in a terrorist rampage on a military base in Fort Hood, Texas. He is shot and left paralyzed during the attack and now awaits sentencing. Witnesses say that Hasan, a U.S.-born Muslim of Palestinian descent, shouted "Allahu Akhbar" before opening fire on the soldiers, who were preparing to deploy to Iraq and Afghanistan.[15] It is later revealed that prior to the shootings, he had exchanged e-mails with al-Qaeda cleric Anwar al-Awlaki. Following the slaughter at Fort Hood, Hasan is praised on jihadist websites as a hero and role model by Awlaki and others.

Talk about the Chip Away blueprint. An Islamic jihadist who is a U.S. citizen patiently climbs the ranks of the U.S. Army. When the time is right, he carries out a murderous, low-tech attack that shakes the military—an institution that, for Islamists, symbolizes America's supposed war on Islam—to its foundation.

It was a massacre and massive security breach that should never have happened. Once Hasan's superiors got wind of his undisguised pro-jihad behavior prior to the shootings, his military career should have come to a swift and unceremonious end. It was impossible to miss the warning signals. Hasan did everything but parade around the base wearing a T-shirt that read, "I am an Islamic terrorist." He was, however, captured on surveillance video on the morning of the attacks wearing full Islamic garb at a local convenience store, so he wasn't far off.[16]

And that was just the tip of the iceberg. Here are some further clues, evident to anyone with the slightest understanding of Islamic terrorism, that Hasan was on the road to jihad:

• Shortly after the attacks, some of Hasan's former classmates at the Uniformed Services University of the Health Sciences described him to *Time* magazine as an America-hating Islamist who had no business in the U.S. military. One described him as a "ticking time bomb":

> "We asked him pointedly, 'Nidal, do you consider Shari'a law to transcend the Constitution of the United States?' And he said, 'Yes,'" a classmate told TIME.... "We asked him if homicidal bombers were rewarded for their acts with 72 virgins in heaven and he responded, 'I've done the research—yes.' Those are comments he made in front of the class." But such statements apparently didn't trigger an inquiry. "I was astounded and went to multiple faculty and asked why he was

even in the Army," the officer said. "Political correctness squelched any opportunity to confront him."[17]

What a shame—because as the *Time* article describes, there were plenty of opportunities to confront Hasan, who was widely regarded by his superiors as a lazy, below-average performer:

> "He wore his rigid Islam ideology on his sleeve and weaved it throughout his coursework," says the third classmate. "He would be standing there in uniform pledging allegiance to the Koran."
>
> The third classmate says he witnessed at least three oral presentations by Hasan over the course of a year that focused on the morality of Muslims, war and justification for suicide bombers. "People were giving presentations on air quality or water quality, but he'd be full of psychobabble about how the persecution of Muslims justifies suicide bombers," the officer says. After a while, Hasan's classmates "would just roll our eyes saying, 'Here we go again.'"[18]

One can only guess his colleagues' reaction when their resident Islamist was later promoted to the rank of major—or when he was ordered to deploy to Afghanistan to assist the United States in what he openly viewed as a war against Islam.

• Hasan carried business cards that bore the jihadi inscription SoA, or "Soldier of Allah." The cards' green and white design matched the colors of Islam. They did not mention his U.S. military rank.[19]

• The FBI intercepted at least ten e-mails Hasan had sent to Awlaki, the American-born al-Qaeda recruiter who's had a hand in several home-grown jihad plots. In the e-mails, Hasan gushed that he couldn't wait to join Awlaki in the afterlife, and asked the terror cleric questions about jihad and suicide bombings.[20] Incredibly, a joint terrorism task force convened prior to the Fort Hood attack concluded that Hasan's outreach to Awlaki was—brace yourself—part of his research as a psychiatrist. The task force never opened any sort of in-depth investigation, and never passed the e-mails on to the Department of Defense.[21]

Awlaki, interestingly enough, was imam of the notorious Dar al-Hijrah mosque in Falls Church, Virginia, in 2001, when he presided over the funeral of Hasan's mother.[22] In the aftermath of the jihadist rampage in Texas, he referred to himself as Hasan's "confidant," calling the Fort Hood killer "a hero" and "man of conscience who could not bear living the contradiction of being a Muslim and serving in an army that is fighting against his own people."[23]

• In those e-mail exchanges Hasan also wrote, "My strength is my financial capabilities." Federal investigators have disclosed that Hasan donated $20,000 to $30,000 a year to Islamic "charities" overseas, a method that has been used time and again to raise funds for terrorism.[24]

Hasan's repeated pro-jihad statements, his relationship with Awlaki, and for crying out loud, his shouts of "Allahu Akhbar" as he was gunning down U.S. troops in cold blood lead to only one conclusion: Hasan was a jihadist who carried out the worst Islamic terrorist attack on U.S. soil since 9/11. Yet as of this writing, more than a year after the Fort Hood attack, the Obama administration has yet to use the words "Islam" or "terrorism" when referring to Nidal Hasan and Fort Hood.

But Department of Homeland Security chief Janet Napolitano, speaking from a conference in—of all places—the United Arab Emirates, did utter the word "Muslim" in reference to Nidal Hasan's actions: she warned against "anti-Muslim sentiment" and declared that Hasan "does not represent the Muslim faith."[25] Yes, ten years after 9/11, Napolitano and her compadres on the Left are still more concerned about an imaginary anti-Muslim backlash than they are about real-life Muslim terrorists.

As for her religious ruling that Hasan does not represent Islam, it's a shame that Napolitano is a woman; otherwise, the Grand Mufti of Saudi Arabia might have made her an honorary sheikh.

True to form, in January 2010 the Department of Defense issued the results of an internal investigation into the Hasan case that completely ignored his well-documented jihadist ideology and correspondence with Awlaki. In fact, the 86-page report did not mention Islam at all, nor did it even mention Hasan by name.[26] No, in a stunning display of intellectual cowardice, Pentagon bureaucrats just couldn't bring themselves to admit what motivated Hasan to murder thirteen of his fellow soldiers. The rampant political correctness of today's U.S. military was epitomized by the Army's top officer, General George Casey, who appeared on CNN shortly after the Fort Hood attack and fretted that speculation over Hasan's jihadist motivations could cause a backlash against Muslim soldiers.[27] He went further on NBC's *Meet the Press*, saying, "Our diversity, not only in our Army, but in our country, is a strength. And as horrific as this tragedy was, if our diversity becomes a casualty, I think that's worse."[28]

Really? Does Casey truly believe that having a few less Muslims in the military is a bigger tragedy than the slaughter of thirteen U.S. soldiers who were needlessly ripped from their families forever? In one fell swoop, Casey showed he is unfit to lead the Army in an existential struggle against global Islamism. With men like him running the show, is it any wonder Hasan was promoted through the ranks despite his jihadist inclinations? Hey, having a Muslim major showed the diversity and tolerance of the U.S. military, and the brass couldn't afford to lose him, especially at a time when we are trying to win those ever-elusive Islamic hearts and minds abroad.

In early 2011, a Senate committee released a blistering report deeming the Fort Hood massacre to have been preventable. Not only did Department of Defense officials fail to recognize Hasan's obvious Islamist tendencies, the committee found, but in the name of multiculturalism they actively covered them up. "Rather than discipline or discharge him,

Hasan's superiors sanitized his personnel evaluations so that evidence of his radicalization was praised as research on terrorism and Islam," the committee's leaders, senators Joseph Lieberman and Susan Collins, wrote in the *Washington Post*.[29] As the *Wall Street Journal*'s Dorothy Rabinowitz noted, "In November 2010, each branch of the military issued a final report on the Fort Hood shooting. Not one mentioned the perpetrator's ties to radical Islam. Even today, [the Senate committee report] reminds us that DoD still hasn't specifically named the threat represented by the Fort Hood attack—a signal to the entire Defense bureaucracy that the subject is taboo."[30]

Because Hasan is a Muslim, firing or demoting him could have provoked the dreaded accusations of "Islamophobia" and "racism" against the military, shouted from the rooftops by CAIR and other Islamist pressure groups. No, it would all have been much too messy and inconvenient. Better to look the other way as the seeds for jihad—in the form of the quintessential Chip Away attack—were planted on U.S. soil. If the American people ask why Hasan did what he did, keep them in the dark. Tell them he was just a lone wacko who snapped, and not part of any larger jihadist movement or new terrorist strategy. Move along, folks, nothing to see here. That is the unspoken but undeniable bedrock of the Obama administration's counter-terrorism policy.

THE TIMES SQUARE PLOT: MAY 1, 2010

An astute food cart operator notices a smoking SUV parked in New York City's Times Square on a warm, crowded Saturday evening. The car is packed with bags of fertilizer, gasoline, propane, firecrackers, and alarm clocks, comprising a lethal homemade bomb that would be catastrophic if detonated among the thousands of people in Times Square. The would-be bomber, a 30-year-old Pakistani-American named Faisal Shahzad who recently became a U.S. citizen, is arrested and later sentenced to life in prison on terrorism charges.

Shahzad, an MBA and married father of two who lived with his family in the Connecticut suburbs, was the face of this plot.[31] But its genesis is found in the tribal regions of Pakistan, where Shahzad had trained in bomb-making with the Pakistani Taliban.[32] Pakistani authorities detained at least eleven men in connection with the attempted Times Square bombing, including a former Pakistani Army major who had been in phone contact with Shahzad on the day of the incident.[33]

Although Shahzad had been on a U.S. government travel-lookout list from 1999 until 2008 and had been on the Joint Terrorism Task Force's radar since at least 2004,[34] he was apparently not being monitored by U.S. authorities at the time of the attempted bombing. This would likely explain how he gained U.S. citizenship in 2009, how he moved freely between Pakistan and the United States during his jihadist training, and how he boarded a flight at New York's JFK Airport two days after planting the bomb, nearly escaping to Dubai.[35]

Based on the timeline of events, it appears the Obama administration ceased surveillance of Faisal Shahzad that had begun way back in the latter days of the Clinton administration. Memo to the Obamis: any U.S. citizen—particularly a Muslim male under the age of thirty-five—who takes trips to Pakistan, Somalia, or Yemen for months at a time should be monitored and questioned vigorously when he returns to America. Let's be realistic. In the current threat climate, there is no compelling reason to travel to these al-Qaeda strongholds unless you are a) from there and visiting family, or b) doing some kind of government consulting or contracting work. All three countries are impoverished, jihad-plagued war zones that are unwelcoming to Westerners. The lure for a young American Muslim like Shahzad to visit a place like Pakistan's tribal regions is obvious: it is the epicenter of the global jihad, the location of countless terror training camps, and the seat of power for al-Qaeda and the Taliban.

If there were any doubts as to why Shahzad, who cited the ubiquitous Anwar al-Awlaki as one of his inspirations,[36] would have traveled to Pakistan, his behavior at his sentencing put them to rest. As *ABC News* reported, "Shahzad, wearing a white prayer cap, said 'Allahu Akbar' after hearing the sentence, and said he would sacrifice a thousand lives for Allah. 'War with Muslims has just begun,' said Shahzad, who then predicted that 'the defeat of the U.S. is imminent, God willing.'"[37]

As in the case of Nidal Hasan, the facts show that Faisal Shahzad was an Islamic terrorist, one who nearly pulled off a lethal Chip Away attack at a highly visible American cultural landmark.

So how did the Obama administration respond to the Shahzad plot? At a press briefing two days after the incident, White House press secretary Robert Gibbs mumbled, stumbled, and refused to use the appropriate word until asked point-blank if Shahzad was a terrorist: "I think anybody that has the type of material they had in the car in Times Square, I would say that that was intended to terrorize, absolutely. I would say whoever, whoever did that would be categorized as a terrorist, yes."[38]

How else would you describe an Islamic fanatic who tried to kill hundreds, potentially thousands, of people at Times Square with a car bomb? Gibbs' natural reaction should have been a firm, "Yes, this was clearly an Islamic terrorist act." Instead, we got ten seconds of hemming and hawing in which the word "Islamic" was never mentioned.

It was the same story with Homeland Security chief Janet Napolitano. The day after the attempted attack, she said on ABC—twice—that it was just a "one-off" event.[39] The fact that Shahzad had international jihadi links and was trained by the Taliban in Pakistan for his mission in New York City was apparently no big deal to Big Sis.

Likewise, PC-addled attorney general Eric Holder could not bring himself to utter the words "radical Islam" during his testimony before the House Judiciary Committee following the Times Square incident. The now infamous YouTube clip shows Holder putting himself through contortions to avoid directly answering Texas congressman Lamar Smith's persistent questioning as to whether radical Islam played a part in the Shahzad case and others like it.[40] Here's part of the exchange:

Smith: But radical Islam could have been one of the reasons [why Shahzad tried to bomb Times Square]?

Holder: There are a variety of reasons why people—

Smith: But was radical Islam one of them?

Holder: There are a variety of reasons why people do these things. Some of them are potentially religious-based—

Smith: But all I'm asking is if you think among those variety of reasons, radical Islam might have been one of the reasons that the individuals took the steps that they did.

Holder: You see—radical Islam—I think those people who espouse a version of Islam that is not—

Smith: Are you uncomfortable attributing any of the actions to radical Islam? It sounds like it.

Holder: No, I don't want to say anything negative about a religion…

Doggedly refusing to concede the obvious, Holder capped his cringe-worthy display by playing armchair imam, telling Smith that Anwar al-Awlaki "has a version of Islam that is not consistent with the teachings of it."

And what exactly are those teachings, Mr. Attorney General? Since you speak so confidently about what Islam is all about, please inform us what research you've done on this topic. And no, Googling a random, peaceful-sounding Koranic verse for use in one of your pandering speeches to Muslim Brotherhood front groups does not count.

Sadly, Americans who were rightly curious about the motivations behind Faisal Shahzad's attack on Times Square wouldn't find answers from the Obama administration. New York City mayor (and notorious panderer to Islam) Michael Bloomberg had a unique take though, pinning the plot on "maybe a mentally deranged person or somebody with a political agenda that doesn't like the [Obama] health care bill or something."[41]

Mind you, Bloomberg said this with a straight face.

LITTLE ROCK JIHAD: JUNE 1, 2009

In an act of homegrown Islamic terrorism that received minimal coverage by the mainstream media (imagine that), a Muslim convert named Abdulhakim Muhammad shoots two U.S. soldiers who are taking a smoke break in front of a recruiting center in Little Rock, Arkansas. One of the soldiers is seriously wounded and the other, 23-year-old Private William Long, is killed. Muhammad—formerly known as Calvin Bledsoe—had spent sixteen months cavorting with jihadists in the al-Qaeda hotbed of Yemen before returning to the United States and murdering Private Long.

Upon his arrest shortly after the shootings, Muhammad reportedly tells police he wanted to kill as many Army personnel as possible. The small arsenal found in his car at the time of his arrest—including 562 rounds of ammunition, two assault rifles, and two pistols—certainly didn't hurt his cause.

Federal officials say Muhammad used Google Maps to scope out military recruiting centers in several states before settling on the Little Rock location. He also considered hitting Jewish facilities, a Baptist Church, a daycare center, and a post office.[42]

Shortly after his conversion to Islam, Muhammad—who was raised Christian in his hometown of Memphis—traveled to Yemen, supposedly to teach English and learn Arabic. His busy itinerary also included joining al-Qaeda in the Arabian Peninsula, marrying a Yemeni woman, and spending time in jail for overstaying his visa and possessing a fraudulent passport.[43] U.S. authorities, understandably concerned, asked the Yemeni government to deport Muhammad back to America. The Yemenis complied, and upon his return to the United States four months before slaughtering Private Long, Muhammad became the subject of a preliminary investigation by the FBI's Joint Counter-Terrorism Task Force.[44]

Nevertheless, he was able to stockpile a small arsenal and eventually open a barrage of gunfire on a U.S. military recruiting center, apparently right under the FBI's noses. Muhammad's track record raised so many red flags you'd think the feds were monitoring his every move. Yet, like in the cases of Nidal Hasan and Faisal Shahzad, you'd have thought wrong.

In a letter to the judge hearing his case, Muhammad wrote that his attack represented "a Jihadi Attack on infidel forces" that was "justified according to Islamic Laws and the Islamic Religion. Jihad—to fight those who wage war on Islam and Muslims."[45] In Muhammad's view, that would mean the U.S. military. It is a recurring theme in every homegrown jihad case I investigate: U.S. troops are viewed as the living, breathing symbol of imperialist, Crusader aggression against Muslims, and need to be punished accordingly.

There was a telling side note to Muhammad's case. Just one day before Muhammad's premeditated, Islamically inspired murder of a brave U.S. serviceman, a notorious late-term abortion provider named George Tiller was gunned down during Sunday services at a Kansas church. It was a heinous crime worthy of strong condemnation. But to witness the spontaneous outpouring of grief from the Obama administration, you'd have thought Tiller, arguably America's most infamous abortionist, was Mother Theresa incarnate.

The president felt compelled to issue a Rose Garden statement just hours after Tiller's death, professing that he was "shocked and outraged."[46] His Department of Justice followed suit, releasing its own same-day statement decrying the "abhorrent act of violence" against Tiller, vowing to guard against similar acts of mayhem, and even promising to send federal marshals to protect abortion clinics nationwide.[47] They were no doubt concerned that a wave of suicide bombings by fundamentalist Christians acting in Jesus' name was imminent. Remember, for the Left, the next Eric Rudolph or Timothy McVeigh, two psychopaths whose actions transgressed Biblical Christianity and who were universally denounced by Christians, is always lurking right around the corner—as opposed to Islamic jihadists, who have actually spent centuries rounding the corner in waves.

In contrast to the administration's immediate wailing over Tiller's death, it took President Obama two days to get around to issuing a statement saying he was "deeply saddened" over Abdulhakim Muhammad's jihadist murder of Private Long.[48] No "shock" or "outrage" like there was with Tiller—just deep sadness, like when the family pet dies. And of course, no mention of Islam or Islamic terrorism was anywhere to be found. And why would there be? After all, Abdulhakim Muhammad and the scores of others like him are just isolated extremists who have distorted the true teachings of Islam, or so the Obama administration would have us believe.

★ ★ ★

We'll discuss some other Chip Away attacks in later chapters, notably the November 2010 attempted Christmas tree bombing in Oregon. But we can't end our discussion without awarding to the Obama administration a dishonorable mention for "Worst Government Reaction to a Chip Away Attack," for its handling of the "Underwear Bomber," Umar Farouk Abdulmutallab, on Christmas Day 2009. Before attempting to ignite explosives hidden in his pants aboard Northwest Airlines Flight 253, Abdulmutallab, who was on a no-fly list, paid $2,381 in cash for a one-way ticket.[49] Despite those red flags and his own father's warning to the CIA that his son was a terrorist threat,[50] Abdulmutallab was permitted to board the Detroit-bound flight, where he proceeded to set fire to his pants in hopes of setting off an explosion that would have brought down the plane and killed everyone on board. Fortunately, as he tried to detonate his explosives, he was seized and restrained by other passengers.

True to form, President Obama waited three days until commenting on the failed attack—and when he did, he branded the Underwear Bomber "an isolated extremist."[51] What kind of "extremist," Mr. President? Hindu? Buddhist? Mormon? That question was never answered. Worse still, at the time of his statement, President Obama had to know that Abdulmutallab had trained with al-Qaeda in Yemen and been men-tored by—you guessed it—Anwar al-Awlaki.[52] Yet Obama's modus operandi remained defiantly in check: *Move along folks, nothing to see here. Just an isolated case, a random wacko. No larger, more pervasive threat associated with any particular religion.* And if you're worried about Abdulmutallab's breach of our national security, don't be: according to our fearless Homeland Security director, Janet Napolitano, despite the near-downing of Flight 253, "The system worked."[53]

If "the system" consists of a terrorist bringing explosives onto a plane, setting fire to his clothes and to a wall of the plane, and then being tack-led by civilian passengers, then yes, the system worked to perfection.

★　★　★

The fact that we have not seen more successful Chip Away attacks on U.S. soil can be attributed mainly to superior work by federal and local law enforcement, coupled with great intelligence and a healthy dose of luck. On that last point, there have been several near-misses. One particularly nasty plot in 2005 involved a group of jihadists using firearms and explosives to attack military and Jewish sites in Los Angeles on the four-year anniversary of 9/11. The scheme, hatched by a group of Mus-lim inmates inside California's New Folsom State Prison, may well have succeeded had one of the participants not dropped a cell phone during a gas station robbery, leading investigators to uncover the larger plan for jihad in L.A.[54]

In the future, we may not be so fortunate. Other than random screen-ing and bag searches in a handful of cities, mainly New York City and Washington, D.C., security on America's railways is almost nonexistent. About 15 million unscreened passengers board trains and subways each day across the United States.[55] What's to stop a terrorist who has managed to slip under the radar of law enforcement (Faisal Shahzad, anyone?) from donning a backpack full of explosives, boarding a train, and blowing himself up? Ditto for other soft targets, like schools, stadiums, and shopping malls. If attacks came against such venues in waves, how would we stop them?

"Chip Away" has not succeeded in Israel, where Palestinian jihadists spent decades refining the strategy, culminating in the second intifada of 2000–2002. The Israelis, always innovators in the security and counterterrorism fields, have successfully adapted their approach to deal with the Chip Away threat. More important, the Israelis have proven time and again that they are a gutsy, proud, and resilient people who refuse to succumb to terrorism. For that same reason, it's a safe bet the Chip Away tactic would not succeed in the United States in the long term. In addition to our own penchant for adaption and innovation, Americans are still, at our core, a tough, resilient, patriotic people who place God and country first. We are also a people who possess the right to own firearms and will fight to defend what is ours, in spite of the weakness shown by our current leadership.

But could today's post-Christian, coddled Western Europe—with its lack of cultural confidence and large Muslim populations—withstand an onslaught of Chip Away terrorism without turning to draconian counter-measures, particularly in these shaky economic times? We almost had our answer in the fall of 2010, when details emerged of a major al-Qaeda plot to carry out Mumbai-style attacks in Western Europe. A trusted intelligence source told me there were at least twelve teams of well-trained jihadists in place, ready to carry out commando-style raids in multiple European cities.[56] Authorities hoped to foil the plot by publicly exposing it, and thankfully, no attacks have materialized as of this writing, though it is unclear whether the terrorists are still in place.

What is clear is that al-Qaeda has, out of necessity, changed the game, at least for the short term, and moved to smaller scale operations focusing more on economic and psychological terror rather than widespread destruction. If Obama administration officials refuse to admit that this shift in tactics is more than just a string of isolated cases, or to acknowledge the religious-ideological motivations of the Muslim attackers, Americans may have to learn about Chip Away the hard way.

CHAPTER THREE

SOUTHERN INHOSPITALITY

"I don't have any cell phone reception out here. How about you?"

"No. Looks like we're on our own. Except for this guy."

My friend and colleague, terrorism expert Daveed Gartenstein-Ross, tapped his foot against the skeleton of what used to be a mid-sized animal, sprawled out on the ground beneath us.

For the next thirty seconds or so, as we stretched out and breathed in some fresh air, my eyes never left the animal's lifeless skull, which stared back at me from a bed of tangled weeds. Amid a palpable strain in the air, we piled back into our minivan along with our cameraman and pushed on down a deserted country road into one of the most rural areas that I—an admitted city slicker—had ever been in my lifetime.

We had left the offices of CBN's Washington, D.C. bureau that morning to investigate an Islamic compound that—according to sources—lay smack dab in the middle of nowhere. They weren't lying. Red House is a no-stoplight town located deep in southern Virginia—Charlotte County to be exact—about ninety-five miles southwest of Richmond and not far from the North Carolina border. It had been a four-hour car ride from

D.C., and by this point we had rehearsed our game plan backward and forward. Nevertheless, as we prepared to enter the town of Red House, we touched base with each other one last time.

For starters, we knew the group that owned and occupied the compound, a radical Islamic sect called Muslims of America (MOA), had a long history of violence on U.S. soil. During the 1980s, MOA members firebombed Hindu and Hare Krishna temples and assassinated two rival Muslim leaders. Federal raids on the group's Colorado compound in the early '90s turned up bombs, automatic weapons, and plans for terrorist attacks, and additional MOA members have been arrested since 9/11 on weapons charges.[1] Many in the group are hardened ex-convicts and, according to local sources in Red House, are known to train with firearms at the compound. In fact, I had been told by locals prior to our trip that an armed guard manned a tower at the entrance of the community at all times. I had even seen footage of another investigative team being threatened by MOA members and then having their car attacked with blunt objects as they sped away from the property.

MOA consists overwhelmingly of African-American converts to Islam. I had been informed that members were none too fond of whites—particularly nosy white journalists like the three of us, who turned up on their property asking questions. Add our affiliation with an "infidel" Christian TV network into the equation, and you had a recipe for serious danger.

But our cameraman—who we'll call Mike—didn't perceive any danger. As we sat parked on the side of the road about a half-mile from the compound, he laughed off my warnings to exercise extreme caution on the shoot. "C'mon, they're not gonna do anything," he said with a wave of the hand. "You're being paranoid. We'll just walk into the compound and tell them we're journalists. They'll talk to us, trust me."

I tried to hide my aggravation with Mike, who was a great guy and a superb cameraman, but a novice in covering terrorism. "Let me put it this way, Mike," I answered. "We're in the middle of nowhere, unarmed, with no cell phone reception. We're not black and we're not Muslims. Every grown man in the compound probably owns at least two guns. And if they want to, they can just shoot us and bury us out in the woods somewhere."

My thoughts turned for a moment to our encounter with the animal skeleton. "If we go up there and they tell us to leave, then we leave, no questions asked," I said. "Who knows, we might not even get past the guard. Our trip may have been a waste of time."

I planned to put together an investigative report about MOA for CBN's flagship program, *The 700 Club*. I knew all along we might embark on the eight-hour round trip excursion to Red House only to come back empty-handed. But as someone who covers Islamic terrorism and jihad for a living, I had to at least *try* to see the place for myself.

Muslims of America, according to a 2006 Department of Justice report, has some 3,000 members nationwide and owns and operates up to thirty-five such compounds in rural areas across nineteen states, including Georgia, Alabama, South Carolina, Tennessee, and Texas.[2] The group's compound in upstate New York, located at the foot of the Catskill Mountains, is called, aptly enough, "Islamberg." Covering seventy acres of land, the compound is reportedly MOA's largest. But since the Red House locale was the closest to my D.C. home base and had quite a dubious reputation of its own, we decided it would be our best bet. Now Mike and I needed to get on the same page—fast.

"I think you're both going overboard," offered Daveed, as always, a cool head and voice of reason. "Erick, this group knows it's being monitored by law enforcement, and the last thing it wants is the kind of attention three missing journalists would bring. People know we're here."

Indeed, we had informed local authorities that we would be visiting the compound.

"All that said," he continued, turning to Mike, "these guys are not the Boy Scouts, and they're armed. We can't just walk in there with a video camera and start asking questions. We need to be careful and have some tact."

Daveed, a former Islamist who, in his Muslim days, had interacted closely with al-Qaeda-linked jihadists, serves as a counterterrorism consultant for law enforcement and the U.S. military. His firsthand knowledge of the subject matter has made him a welcome collaborator on several of my homegrown jihad stories, and MOA was undoubtedly one of our most intriguing investigations to date.

Our drive into Red House revealed a dusty, dilapidated little town whose better days were far behind it. Except for the occasional passing pickup truck or suspicious granny peering at us from a front porch, the place seemed abandoned. A few shack-like houses were scattered along the main road into town, where we stumbled upon the MOA compound.

Based on the phone conversations I'd had with locals before my trip, I was anticipating something like a scaled-down al-Qaeda training camp, complete with obstacle courses and shooting ranges in plain view.

Instead, there were rows of run-down trailers separated by laundry-filled clotheslines. A small group of women and children milled about outside; all of them, including the kids, wore ultra-conservative Islamic garb that covered most of their bodies. For the moment, there was not a man in sight. But there was indeed a guard tower at the compound's entrance, albeit empty and only a few feet above ground level. A large, green "Muslims of America" sign stood below the tower, and several "No Trespassing" signs hung from fencing that enclosed the sprawling, 40-acre community. To my amusement, there was also an American flag hanging from a pole planted in front of the compound. It was added, according to a local source, after 9/11, when many Islamist groups in the United States were donning a patriotic veneer to deflect newfound attention from the authorities. Located at the compound's entrance was perhaps the most telling symbol of MOA's purpose, showing why the group's ownership of an abundance of land across rural America had so aroused my alarm. It was a street sign that looked much like any other except for one major difference: this one bore the name of a man with longstanding ties to global Islamic terrorism.

Sheikh Gilani Lane was named in honor of Sheikh Mubarak Gilani, the founder of Muslims of America and a man whom MOA members follow with messianic fervor. MOA has close ties to a violent Pakistani Islamist group, also founded by Gilani, named Jamaat al-Fuqra. According to a 1999 U.S. State Department report on terrorism, al-Fuqra "seeks to purify Islam through violence."[3] Sheikh Gilani serves as al-Fuqra's and MOA's ideological bedrock; his images and messages dominate the MOA website. He founded the group during a visit to Brooklyn in 1980, encouraging his pupils—mostly African-Americans—to move to rural areas and establish Muslim communes free of Western decadence. Shoe bomber Richard Reid and Beltway sniper John Allen Muhammad are rumored to have been among his followers.[4]

Gilani also trained jihadists to fight against the Soviets in Afghanistan during the 1980s,[5] and he attended a 1993 terrorist conference in Sudan that included members of Hamas, Hezbollah, and yes, Osama bin Laden himself. According to a *Weekly Standard* account of the conference, "In the evening, large crowds regaled the assembled jihadists with chants of "Down, down USA! Down, down CIA!" and (in Arabic) "Death to the Jews!"[6] As if that weren't enough, American journalist Daniel Pearl was on his way to interview Gilani in Karachi, Pakistan in 2002 when he was kidnapped by jihadists and brutally murdered.[7] The sheikh denies any connection to Pearl's killing, but suspicion of his involvement is understandable: in 1990, for instance, Gilani produced a video called "The Soldiers of Allah" in which he instructs his American followers in tactics including guerilla warfare, murdering enemies, hijacking cars, kidnapping, weapons training, and explosives.[8]

Prior to our trip to Red House, I spoke to "Mustafa," a former MOA member who fled the group and now fears for his life. He told me he and others had lived in Pakistan and were trained in paramilitary tactics by Gilani and the Pakistani military for several months.[9] According to Mustafa, Gilani runs MOA with an iron fist from Lahore, Pakistan, and members almost literally worship him; they believe he is a direct descendant of Islam's prophet Mohammed. Moreover, like the founder of Islam, Gilani reportedly kept several wives—including some black American converts—at his opulent residence in Lahore.

"He's the leader of the group," Mustafa said of Gilani. "He's a former member of the Pakistani military. His father was one of the founding fathers of Pakistan. He has great connections to Pakistani intelligence, the ISI."

Given the history of corruption and pro-jihad sympathies among Pakistan's military and intelligence services, Mustafa's account of Gilani's connections within those two entities did not surprise me.

He went on to tell me that Muslims of America serves as a cash cow for Gilani and for Jamaat al-Fuqra. Each member is required to send 30 percent of his or her income to Gilani in Pakistan. The group even has a treasurer that checks members' pay stubs.

"[Sheikh Gilani] said that the 30 percent is money that God has chosen to take from you," Mustafa recounted. "And if you spend that 30 percent you are stealing from God. The money got to Pakistan through the [MOA] elders who traveled to Pakistan. They carried cash with them or they sent it Western Union. Since there's Americans under Gilani's rule who live in Pakistan, it's like from one American name to another American name and it's never linked to Gilani at all."

Sheikh Gilani uses these American dollars to help fund the Taliban and other terrorist groups, according to Mustafa. Group members hand deliver thousands in cash at a time to Gilani in Pakistan. Mustafa said the money is "earned" by MOA members through illegal means, and that male members often set up kiosks at local shopping malls or on the street to hawk their wares.

"A lot of the guys will do bootlegging—you know, it's all illegal—videotapes, CDs, clothing," Mustafa explained. "The counterfeiting comes in with the bootlegging. It's all counterfeit movies not sanctioned by Paramount or MGM or things like that—they're not legitimate."

Now, as Sheikh Gilani Lane loomed before us, I replayed my conversations with Mustafa in my mind—he had confirmed that all MOA members possessed at least one gun—and tried to summon any important details about the compound that we may have missed.

Mike, however, was in no mood for baby steps. "Let me out," he ordered. "It's nothing but a bunch of women and children in there. I want to go get some footage." We reluctantly agreed to let the old pro go and prayed silently to ourselves that no one would come charging out of the compound once they saw a white man with a $20,000 camera filming their private property. In the meantime, Daveed and I brainstormed about what I would say when I taped my report from beneath the Sheikh Gilani Lane street sign.

Since we were constantly glancing over our shoulders to make sure Mike wasn't dodging bullets as he filmed, I didn't have much time to be clever or creative. Instead, I kept it simple, attempting to paint a picture for viewers of the jarring contrasts at work in Red House: on one hand, you had an overwhelmingly Christian, dirt-poor, southern town. On the other hand, you had a sprawling compound filled with radical, well-armed Muslims who had dedicated their lives to a terror-linked Pakistani cleric. "Red House, Virginia is as rural as it gets," I began as Mike's camera rolled. "There are no traffic lights, and the only signs of industry are a pair of convenience stores. So when a street sign popped up here named after a radical Pakistani sheikh—along with men and women dressed in traditional Islamic garb—locals took notice."

Just as I finished speaking, a carload of African-American women and children came driving out of the compound. We waved hello, and the car stopped at the entrance. A veiled woman in the passenger seat stared out at us bemusedly.

"Hi," I said as I approached the car. "My name is Erick Stakelbeck. We're with CBN News in Washington. We'd love to interview one of your spokespeople for a story we're working on. Is there anyone around who we could speak to?"

The woman seemed unfazed. Strange visitors bearing notepads or video cameras and questions about the goings-on inside the compound had become more common since 9/11.

"The guy you want to talk to isn't here," she replied. "But if you go inside and ask, someone will help you."

With that, she turned to the woman driving and said something. They immediately sped away before I had a chance to thank them. Daveed, Mike, and I looked at each other. "You guys ready?" I asked. Both of them nodded, and we entered the compound.

★   ★   ★

You might be shocked that a compound like the one in Red House exists in rural America. After all, we're not talking about Afghanistan, Yemen, or Somalia—we're talking Dukes of Hazzard country. As I write these words, I can just hear our enlightened Left's indignant response: "We'd believe it if you found white supremacist rednecks and far-right militia types setting up a backwoods shooting range and railing against the government. But sprawling camps filled with Islamic jihadists (er, 'violent extremists'), just a few miles from the local Wal-Mart? Stakelbeck, you're an alarmist fearmonger and an intolerant Islamophobe. Anyway, there are no Muslims in the South."

Oh no? Have you heard about the $10 million al-Farooq Masjid mega-mosque that opened in 2008 in Atlanta?[10] Or what about Abu Mansoor al-Amriki (formerly Omar Hammadi), the Alabama-bred kid who has become a leading spokesman for the al-Qaeda-linked Somali terror group al-Shabaab? And have you checked out the demographics lately in Tennessee? About twenty years ago, following the first Gulf War, Nashville was designated by the U.S. State Department as a "gateway city" for Iraqi refugees fleeing Saddam Hussein's regime.[11] In the ensuing two decades, those gates were opened to Muslims from Iraq as well as other countries—because our government elites aren't satisfied to see Islam only spreading in major cities like New York, Detroit, and Chicago. No, the residents of America's Christian heartland must also learn to be "tolerant" and "accepting" of Islamic culture, and open their long-established communities to a way of life that is completely antithetical to their values. Whether they want it or not, it will be rammed down their throats with bureaucratic efficiency, and their neighborhoods and towns will be changed irrevocably. Forget about waking up to the sounds of the rooster crowing, Farmer John. The call to prayer billowing from the local mosque will be your new alarm clock.

A 2008 survey showed the percentage of non-Christians in Tennessee's population tripled from 1 percent in 1990 to 3 percent in 2008.[12] The greater Memphis area is now home to an estimated 10,000 to 15,000 Muslims, and local Islamic leaders put the number of Muslims in Nashville at around 20,000.[13] It's tough to verify those numbers, but spend a few days on the ground in Nashville and in nearby towns in middle Tennessee like Murfreesboro and Shelbyville, as I have, and the growing Islamic influence is unmistakable—from shops to schools to restaurants to, of course, the shiny new multi-million-dollar mega-mosques.

As we discussed in chapter one, this trend comports with a specific agenda: Islamists are taking the fight directly to what they view as the heart of American Christendom. What better way to show Allah's dominion over infidel land than to build giant victory arches in the form of sprawling Islamic centers?

If the current Muslim influx continues, terrorist recruiters overseas may begin to take Tennessee's nickname, "The Volunteer State," quite seriously. And if the case of Abdulhakim Muhammad is any indication, they've already begun. Muhammad, as you'll recall, is the Little Rock jihadist who murdered a U.S. soldier and seriously wounded another in a 2009 attack on an Army recruiting center—and he was born and raised in Memphis.

★ ★ ★

But back to those U.S.-based jihadi compounds. Their genesis dates back to late 1999 and early 2000, when a Seattle native named James

Ujaama attempted to enlist some powerful foreign connections to help him set up a terror training camp in rural Bly, Oregon. Ujaama, an African-American convert to Islam, was an associate of the notorious London-based cleric Abu Hamza al-Masri, a jihadist firebrand who is currently imprisoned in Britain on terrorism charges. U.S. authorities are still seeking al-Masri's extradition to this country to face charges over his role in attempting to set up the Oregon terror training camp.

The purpose of the camp was to school aspiring holy warriors from the United States and Great Britain in the finer arts of hand-to-hand combat and automatic weapons skills in preparation for joining the jihad in Afghanistan.[14] According to a fax sent by Ujaama to al-Masri, Oregon was a "pro-militia and fire-arms state" where a little gunplay out in the woods wouldn't raise eyebrows. Al-Masri sent two of his cronies, including convicted terrorist Haroon Rashid Aswat, to scout out the Bly locale in the fall of 1999. Aswat engaged in firearms training with Ujaama and his cohorts during his month-long stay at the Bly ranch, but was ultimately turned off by the amateurish operation he found there. He returned to London, and Ujaama's grand plan to establish an international jihadi training hub in southern Oregon subsequently fizzled out.[15]

Other terror cells, however, have taken advantage of the vast rural expanse of the continental United States. The so-called Virginia Jihad Network featured eleven men training for jihad in a wooded area near Fredericksburg, Virginia—about an hour's drive south of the nation's capital—in 2000 and 2001. After using paintball to simulate battlefield combat, members of the group traveled overseas to fight alongside the Pakistani terrorist group Lashkar e-Taiba against Indian forces in Kashmir. Other members made their way to Pakistan after the 9/11 attacks in an attempt to join the Taliban and fight against U.S. troops in neighboring Afghanistan.

Ultimately, thirteen men were convicted in connection with the Virginia case. One of them was a white convert to Islam named Randall Todd "Ismail" Royer, a former employee of both the Council on American-

Islamic Relations (CAIR) and the Muslim American Society (MAS)—two groups that, as we'll see, have been embraced by successive U.S. administrations despite their radical connections and pro-terrorist track records. Royer and several of his fellow cell members worshipped, it should be noted, at the Dar al-Arqam Islamic Center in Falls Church, Virginia, just miles from the White House. No reason to be concerned or anything, though. Again, just a merry band of isolated Taliban wannabes who just so happened to be fanatical, well-trained, and within spitting distance of the Pentagon and Capitol Hill.

The Fort Dix Five were another recent, homegrown Islamic terror cell that trained for jihad by playing paintball in a secluded area, this time in Pennsylvania's Pocono Mountains. The five young Muslim men (anyone sensing a pattern here?) were convicted in 2009 of plotting to storm New Jersey's Fort Dix and massacre U.S. soldiers.

No region in America, however, presents the perfect storm of gun culture, rural expanse, and growing Muslim populations quite like the South. In that sense, the strange case of a jihadist named Daniel Boyd may be a harbinger of things to come.

★ ★ ★

Willow Springs isn't Mayberry—but it's close. This sleepy North Carolina hamlet, population 11,576, is nestled in the rolling countryside outside of Raleigh, just a stone's throw from North Carolina State University. A drive past the well-kept cul de sacs and freshly mowed lawns that dot rural Willow Springs reveals scenes from a simpler time. Old folks stroll hand in hand while young children ride bikes together in the streets. Churches are filled on Sundays and neighbors look out for one another.

Clad regularly in fundamentalist Muslim garb, Daniel Patrick Boyd and his family were not your typical Willow Springers. Boyd wore a long, Islamic-style beard and his wife was often seen wearing an all-encompassing, black burqa that left only her eyes visible. If this were a liberal Hollywood production, frothing fundamentalist Christian neighbors would have ridden the Boyds out of town on a rail, hanging their cat from a tree for good measure. But reality has a way of shattering liberal stereotypes. I found that Boyd and his family were not only accepted by their Christian neighbors, they were wholeheartedly embraced. Strangely enough, Daniel Boyd, despite his present jihadist beliefs, actually had an all-American upbringing familiar to many folks in Willow Springs.

Raised Episcopalian in suburban Washington, D.C., the fair-haired Boyd played defensive line for his state champion high school football team and was reared by a Marine father who earned four Purple Hearts. Engaged to his high school sweetheart in a region brimming with job opportunities, Daniel Boyd had a bright future. But his life took an unlikely turn in 1988, when the 17-year-old made a fateful decision that would lead to his eventual arrest on terrorism charges two decades later. Daniel Boyd converted to Islam.

Boyd's parents had divorced when he was a teen. His mother soon remarried a devout Muslim lawyer named William Saddler, who made a profound impact on Daniel and his brother. Both young men embraced Islam with a fervor that led them to the notorious tribal regions of Pakistan and Afghanistan shortly after high school graduation. And the two white, suburban teens certainly didn't travel halfway around the world to a godforsaken backwater for the scenery. Once they arrived in Afghanistan, the Boyds linked up with Islamic "mujahedeen" fighters who were battling Soviet occupying forces. Years later, Boyd would boast to fellow worshippers at his Raleigh Islamic Center about his days spent waging jihad against Soviet infidels in the mountains of Afghanistan. He was building the "street cred" that would enable him to assemble an eight-man Islamic terrorist cell in the Raleigh area that sought to attack U.S. military installations.

Boyd first captured U.S. media attention years earlier, in 1991, when he and his brother were arrested in Peshawar, Pakistan, after allegedly robbing a bank. Boyd was convicted by an Islamic court and sentenced to have his right hand and left foot amputated according to Islamic sharia law. (This is the same type of legal "verdict," by the way, that U.S.-based Islamists would like to see enforced here via sharia.) The U.S. State Department got involved in Boyd's case, and a Pakistani appeals panel eventually tossed out the verdict against him and his brother. Boyd soon returned to the United States and settled in Willow Springs with his wife, Sabrina—his high school girlfriend who had since converted to Islam and followed Daniel to the wilds of Afghanistan.

It's no surprise that Boyd found it difficult to suppress his hunger for jihad upon returning to the United States. After spending years fighting in a foreign terrorist hotbed alongside battle-hardened jihadists, it wasn't like Boyd could easily transition into a 9-to-5 gig at the local gas station. A Muslim friend of the Boyd family told me Daniel had an insatiable appetite for jihad and talked about it all the time. He found the American South to be the perfect place to pursue his "hobby."

And why not? Land is plentiful in Old Dixie, including lots of remote, potential training grounds allowing for plenty of cover to fire weapons, conduct drills, and plot. And in most rural southern areas, guys owning several guns, God love 'em, just go with the territory. Another reason the South is attractive for jihadists (and which may stun the deans of the mainstream media) is that the people are, well, downright tolerant— perhaps self-consciously so, given the region's checkered history of race relations. As anyone who has recently spent even a few days in places like Arkansas and Tennessee can tell you, this is not your granddaddy's South—yet old stereotypes and outdated media narratives die hard. The Klan is now a decrepit, vanishing punch line, and I can say from firsthand experience that blacks and whites co-exist more harmoniously down South than in Philadelphia, New York City, or Washington, D.C., the three "enlightened" liberal cities in which I have spent my entire life.

In the case of Daniel Boyd, the devout, friendly people of the South welcomed him and his Muslim family. In fact, I found that Boyd's overwhelmingly Christian neighbors adored him. He was seen as a leader, a pillar of his quiet suburban subdivision, where a lake resting behind his well-kept single home added to the tranquility. I spent some time in Willow Springs interviewing Boyd's neighbors shortly after he and two of his sons were arrested on terrorism charges in July 2009. One close neighbor, a woman in her late thirties, told me the Boyds formed "the biggest welcoming party in the neighborhood" when she moved in, and that they were full of "kindness" and "empathy." She nervously fingered a cross around her neck and shot glances at her young daughter as she described how Sabrina Boyd had "helped her through a tough time" in her life. A practicing Christian, she had engaged in some friendly religious debates with the Boyds, but said they never tried to press their Islamic beliefs upon her. She also said she found the terrorism charges against Boyd and his boys hard to believe. As for the huge weapons cache that authorities found hidden beneath Boyd's home, she had no idea.

Across the street, a grungy young guy with a ponytail took time from working on a car in his driveway to adamantly declare Daniel Boyd's innocence. He said that young people like him considered Boyd the neighborhood "advice-giver," a father figure in whom they could confide. He added that Boyd helped steer him back on the right path after he ran away from home. Like the other neighbor, this young guy, who looked like he just strolled out of a Marilyn Manson concert, maintained that Boyd never tried to impress his Islamic beliefs upon anyone. Yet it was obvious that he deeply admired Boyd, and he may not have been completely forthcoming with me.

Indeed, as I conducted more interviews in and around Willow Springs, a fuller and much less flattering portrait began to emerge of Daniel Boyd than the one presented by his trusting neighbors. In the course of my investigation, I learned that Boyd took the Koranic justification for lying to non-believers and the Islamic doctrine of "taqiyya," or deception, quite literally.

On my first day in Raleigh, I visited a strip mall in nearby Garner, North Carolina, where Boyd had owned an Islamic store that also served as a gathering place for local Muslims. The store—which sold Muslim garb and halal meats—was unsuccessful, and Boyd closed it down after less than a year. It was replaced by a thrift shop whose owner, Ramona McWhorter, told me she believes Boyd stole several storage shelves from the property months after he had vacated it.

According to McWhorter—and corroborated by an independent witness—Boyd entered the property illegally through the back entrance one day shortly before his arrest in July 2009, probably using a spare key he had kept. He casually loaded several storage shelves into his truck and drove away. One wonders if the shelves helped store the weapons cache in the ditch he had dug out beneath his home.

Boyd's Pied Piper act with local youths was most effective at the Raleigh Islamic Center, which he attended for a time. Before leaving the mosque, apparently because it was not extreme enough, he was able to recruit an eight-man crew of impressionable young Muslim men— including his two sons—whom he would later lead in weapons training in the remote countryside of Caswell County, North Carolina. Their ultimate goal, according to the federal indictment against them: attack a U.S. military facility in Quantico, Virginia, and kill as many U.S. soldiers as possible. The indictment stated that Boyd had also traveled to the Gaza Strip with one of his sons in 2006 in order to link up with Palestinian jihadists. He was denied entry by Israeli authorities upon a return visit in 2007 and detained for two days.

As more details emerged, it became obvious that the Boyd cell wasn't just some hackneyed, country-bumpkin affair. Almost one year after Boyd's July 2009 arrest on terrorism charges, authorities uncovered an overseas connection to his jihadist cell, revealing that it had international clout and backing.[16] The link comprised a co-conspirator in Kosovo who was providing funding and working on grander plots outside his country along with Boyd and the other defendants. The damage Boyd's cell eventually intended to inflict was global, to be done in cooperation with the jihadist movement in Kosovo.[17]

So what, if anything, did Boyd's fellow mosque-goers at the Raleigh Islamic Center know about his activities, and when did they know it? Did the Muslim community in Raleigh realize that Boyd was consulting with international jihadists, planning terrorist attacks, and recruiting followers? The pro-jihad worldview of Daniel Boyd could not have been a secret to them. Some would say he wore his intentions on his sleeve. One man who frequented the Raleigh Islamic Center told me he voiced concerns about Boyd but was ignored. I also spoke to a regular at the mosque who said it was "hard to argue with anything that is in the indictment" against Boyd and the other cell members, noting that Boyd spoke "openly" and often among fellow Muslims about the need to wage violent jihad. The source described Boyd's views about U.S. involvement in Iraq and Afghanistan and about the Israel-Palestinian conflict as "very strong." Much like the grungy neighbor, young Muslims from dysfunctional backgrounds at the mosque gravitated to Boyd and looked up to him, enthralled by his tales of fighting alongside the Afghan mujahedeen.

According to my source, not all Muslims at the Raleigh Islamic Center agreed with Boyd's viewpoints, and there were some arguments. But he noted that American Muslim communities in Raleigh and elsewhere are fiercely insular and often enforce a "code of silence" when it comes to fellow believers. This trend toward self-segregation is exactly the blueprint that Islamist groups like the Muslim Brotherhood encourage for Western Muslims, as we saw in chapter one.

At least one local Muslim apparently assisted the FBI in bringing down Boyd's southern-fried terror cell, and that is encouraging news. But the fact remains that Boyd, who is now awaiting sentencing after pleading guilty to conspiracy charges, was able to build an eight-member team—right under the noses of Raleigh's Muslims—that was allegedly training for attacks both overseas and on U.S soil.

The Boyd case shows that the U.S. government should consider any American Muslims who fought in Afghanistan during the 1980s and early '90s—alongside men who would later form the vanguard of al-Qaeda—not as washed-up adventurers, but as serious security risks. It is unclear when exactly Daniel Boyd entered federal authorities' radar screen. What is clear is that for Boyd, jihad was not a passing fancy that could be discarded in favor of the NASCAR-and-BBQ culture of rural North Carolina. As increasing numbers of young American Muslims return to the South and elsewhere from time spent in terrorist training camps overseas, U.S. officials would do well to consider Daniel Boyd a cautionary tale.

★ ★ ★

In the case of Muslims of America, any lessons the feds learned during the height of the group's terrorist activities in the '80s and '90s have apparently been forgotten. As we walked up the gravel road and entered the Red House compound, I braced myself for physical confrontation and, frankly, almost expected it. Since there were just three of us without so much as a butter knife on our persons, I didn't like our odds. We parked our van strategically near the entrance to enable a quick getaway. But as we moved closer to the columns of run-down trailers, we saw no one. All the women and children we had seen earlier had apparently disappeared inside the trailers. Was this some sort of ruse to draw us in?

As a slender black man in his mid-40's emerged from one of the trailers and began to walk toward us, I knew we were about to get our answer. He wore a skullcap and loose fitting Islamic clothes, and did not look like someone preparing for conflict. He stopped about three feet in front of us and asked, a bit warily, "Can I help you?" Introducing myself and my two colleagues, I told the man we were from CBN News and would love to interview someone from the compound concerning reports of MOA's ties to terrorism. His response was simple but firm. "We're not doing any more media, because we're always misrepresented," he replied. "Sorry you came all the way down here, but we can't help you. Have a good day." His look told me the matter was not open for debate, and as

I gazed around at the trailers that surrounded us on all sides, I was in no mood to push my luck.

We thanked him and headed back to the van as he watched our every step. Breathing a collective sigh of relief, we pulled away and began chatting about the footage we had captured. And just like that, our much-anticipated visit to the MOA compound was over—but not without a final, unnerving incident. As we drove away, I noticed in the rearview mirror that a car we had seen parked at the compound was behind us, creeping ever closer to our van. I alerted Mike, who was driving, and he stepped on the gas. The car, which was driven by two black men in Islamic garb—obviously MOA members—followed on our heels for another half mile before abruptly turning around and heading back toward the compound. Message received: we shouldn't think about coming back.

★   ★   ★

My investigative report about Muslims of America, featuring footage of our trip to the Red House compound, aired in September 2007. My goal was to raise awareness about the group and the threat posed by its thousands of radical, well-armed members scattered across multiple rural compounds nationwide. MOA's history of violence and its open allegiance to a jihadist Pakistani sheikh should be enough to warrant steady surveillance and the occasional raid by federal authorities, not to mention the fact that ex-cons are likely bearing firearms at its compounds, violating state and federal law. But it's unclear how closely these compounds are being monitored. Some federal law enforcement officials have assured me MOA is on their radar screen, but others tell me MOA compounds are a potentially lethal powder keg—possible mini-Wacos—that the feds have all but ignored.

Which is it? It's tough to say, although a video I found on MOA's website was certainly not encouraging. It featured the former head of

South Carolina's FBI branch—yes, the state's top federal law enforcement official—speaking at a Muslims of America-sponsored event in 2004 honoring "diversity." It was an ironic topic, given that the audience was almost exclusively Muslim.

That event, it must be noted, occurred under the Bush administration. Today, with the Obama administration and its relentless push to charm Islamists here and abroad, MOA is no doubt riding even higher. The group's website is much more comprehensive than it was just a few years ago, and I've picked up copies of its official newspaper, *The Islamic Post*, at Muslim stores around Washington, D.C; predictably, it's filled with anti-American and anti-Semitic conspiracy theories. At the end of the day, MOA has a good thing going in rural America—particularly in the South—and its leaders know it.

Other Islamic jihadist groups, however, have had once-successful southern operations thwarted in recent years. One of the most notable cases was a cigarette smuggling ring masterminded by the terrorist group Hezbollah out of Charlotte, North Carolina, that raised millions for terrorism overseas.[18] Another example was a Hamas fundraising operation outside of Dallas, Texas, that turned into the largest terrorism financing trial in U.S. history: the now infamous Holy Land Foundation case, which saw several U.S.-based Muslim Brotherhood members sentenced to prison terms.[19] So a sliver of hope remains that MOA will one day receive its comeuppance, although under the Obama administration it is more likely to receive encouragement as a "moderating force" in American Islam, with perhaps some million-dollar grants to build new madrassahs on MOA compounds.

As for the good people of the South? Well, they'll just have to learn to stop worrying and start loving Islam.

CHAPTER FOUR

SOMALI AMERICA: BLACK HAWK NOW

We were on the lookout for Somalis.

Not Somali pirates or AK-47-toting, feudal warlords. And not on the dusty, chaotic streets of Mogadishu. No, my cameraman and I were looking for Somali chicken pluckers. And we were doing it in the heart of the Bible Belt.

Government bureaucrats and social engineers: delight in what you have wrought.

We had traveled to Shelbyville, Tennessee, to investigate a large influx of Somali Muslims into what had been your typical, sleepy southern hamlet—that is, until a few years ago, when waves of Somalis began arriving in Shelbyville from other U.S. cities (a so-called "secondary migration") to take jobs at the local Tyson Chicken processing plant. It wasn't long before the Somali population there had gone from zero to as many as 1,100. For a small, agricultural town of only 17,000, where the walking horse industry is king, that is a very sizable—and noticeable—occurrence.

The Somalis arrived faster and in greater numbers than Shelbyville—economically depressed and with limited resources—could adequately handle. The assimilation process, to no one's great surprise, has not been smooth, and the problems extend far beyond the usual language and communication barriers that most immigrants experience. Shelbyville is also home to a sizable Hispanic population that, after some initial problems, has blended into the fabric of the town relatively well over the past two decades. The Somalis, however, have proven quite a different story.

Back home, the Somalis lived in near Stone Age conditions; many had never even used a toilet or running water. If getting used to their American amenities was difficult for them, the sight of women covered in all-concealing Islamic garb had an even more jarring effect on their new, Christian neighbors. This was middle Tennessee, in the shadow of the country music capital of the world, Nashville, and just a stone's throw from that decidedly un-Islamic landmark, the Jack Daniels distillery. It doesn't get more southern or more traditional Americana. So the culture shock, needless to say, was mutual.

Yet as I stood on Main Street on a sunny Friday afternoon, watching a steady stream of residents shuffle in and out of a local bank, I realized there was one thing everyone in Shelbyville could get behind, regardless of their background: payday. Locals had told us a crowd of Somalis begins arriving at the bank at around 3:00 p.m. on Fridays, looking to cash their checks from the nearby Tyson plant. I intended to secure a few on-the-fly interviews with them, first to ask how they were adjusting to life in Shelbyville, and second, to gauge how seriously they took their Islam. I had heard concerns that Islamic radicalism could take root in Shelbyville's Somali community, and based on rumblings out of other U.S. cities like Minneapolis—where a number of Somalis had recently been arrested on terrorism charges—I was alarmed. I saw Shelbyville as a perfect place to lay low and plot in secret, much like I saw in Willow

Spring, North Carolina, and other rural, southern areas that have been used as bases for Islamic jihadists.

As the Somalis began arriving at the bank, I saw that the majority were women covered from head to toe in burqas, with only their eyes visible. They became angry at the sight of my cameraman and shouted at us in a Somali dialect as they rushed into the bank, small children in tow. Several carloads of Somali men arrived soon after and eyed us suspiciously. They, too, wanted no part of us and rushed in and out of the bank, despite my friendly invitations to chat.

One guy in his early twenties did stop and linger, intrigued by the TV camera that was trained on him. While he declined to appear on camera, he briefly shared his thoughts with me on life in Shelbyville. "The people seem very nice," he said in halting English. "But I am lonely. I miss Somalia." He added that he didn't associate with anyone in town aside from his fellow Somalis. He then shot a few nervous glances back at his friends, who were waiting for him in a car parked by the curb, and announced he had to leave. I gave him my business card and told him to call so we could talk further. He never called, and I never did get to have any kind of meaningful interaction with Shelbyville's extremely insular Somali community, despite repeated efforts. Neither, I soon found out, had most Shelbyvillians.

"They've had an impact here. Unfortunately, it's not been a good impact," said Brian Mosely, a reporter for the *Shelbyville Times-Gazette* newspaper.

Shortly after my arrival in Shelbyville, I spent an afternoon getting the lay of the land from Mosely, who won an award from the Associated Press in 2008 for a series of articles he wrote about the town's Somali population. He said that other than going to work at the Tyson plant or using local stores, the Somalis rarely emerged from the apartment complex where a majority of them lived in a run-down section of town. Their self-segregation and indifference to the norms of their new community had not endeared them to locals.

"I found that there was just an enormous culture clash going on here," Mosely said as we sat in at the local courthouse, an old building that felt straight out of Mayberry. "The Somalis were—according to a lot of the people I talked to here—being very, very rude, inconsiderate, very demanding. They would go into stores and haggle over prices. They would also demand to see a male salesperson, [they] would not deal with women in stores."

Sounds like a unique brand of southern etiquette—as in southern Somalia.

Mosely, who was born and raised near Shelbyville, said the problems extend to local schools, where male Somali students refuse to speak to female administrators. Perhaps they learned this demeaning attitude toward women at the local Somali mosque, which has become a central gathering place for the refugees, with about 100 of them converging there each day for prayer, according to Mosely. Since it's human nature to cling to the familiar when in unfamiliar surroundings, many Somalis in Shelbyville, unsurprisingly, have decided to stick with what they know—and that's Islam. It's not a comforting thought for Shelbyvillians, given that Muslims in the West who become "more religious" have recently shown a nasty tendency to drift into jihad.

"We're talking about people who have not had any experience with Western civilization," Mosely explained. "They don't know the language. Things like running water are a miracle to some of these folks.... You don't take people from a totally alien culture, put them into a community, and then say, 'Alright, you must get along.'"

Of course you don't. Nevertheless, it's becoming the norm in communities across the United States. As I continued watching the surreal scene of faceless, shapeless, burqa-clad women walking into the bank in downtown Shelbyville alongside good ol' boys in American flag t-shirts—neither side looking particularly comfortable with the arrangement—I couldn't help but wonder how all this had happened. I soon learned that the growing Somali population in Shelbyville and other

U.S. cities could be traced back to a deeply misguided U.S. State Department program that has increased the Islamic terrorist threat to the United States incalculably.

★ ★ ★

Ask most Americans what they know about Somalia and they will likely respond with three words: *Black Hawk Down*. That 1993 incident, which inspired a bestselling book and a hit Hollywood film, represented one of the most frustrating, painful, and ultimately heroic episodes in the history of the American military. Eighteen U.S. servicemen were killed and more than seventy-five were wounded after a raid to capture two senior henchmen of the Somali warlord Mohammed Farrah Aidid turned into a massive firefight that raged through the streets of Mogadishu for nearly an entire day.[1] Thousands of heavily armed Somalis—including civilians, Aidid militiamen, and yes, Islamic jihadists—cornered a team of U.S. Special Forces soldiers in a cramped section of the city. Meanwhile, Somali militiamen used rocket-propelled grenades to shoot down two U.S. Black Hawk helicopters, and the lifeless bodies of U.S. soldiers were subsequently mutilated and dragged through the streets by a frenzied Somali mob. Broadcast internationally, these images shocked, appalled, and infuriated Americans. Weren't these the same downtrodden, starving Somalis that our entire military presence in Somalia was dedicated to feeding? And this is how we were repaid?

Looking back, perhaps the incident in Somalia should not have been surprising. Over the past thirty years or so, when a majority Muslim country has been in trouble—whether the result of a natural disaster or internal repression or unrest—the United States has frequently lent a hand, financially and often militarily as well. From Lebanon and Somalia, to Kuwait and Iraq, to Bosnia and Afghanistan, from earthquakes in Pakistan and Iran to tsunamis in Indonesia, America—more than any nation on earth, including the oil-rich Saudi kingdom—has been there to help Muslim peoples.

Our reward has been ever greater anti-American vitriol and increased international terrorism against U.S. interests. And if you think American generosity to Muslim nations will be returned in kind the next time, God forbid, some natural disaster hits our shores, keep dreaming, you foolish infidel. In the eyes of many Muslims, we are "kaffirs"—unclean unbelievers—cursed in this life and the next and not worthy to breathe the same air as Muslims, let alone merit their assistance.

With such a mindset, is it any wonder that Somalis would turn violently against U.S. troops—a Christian crusader force on Muslim land, and a living symbol of the greedy Western oppressor of Islamic and brown-skinned peoples everywhere? This narrative has long been pushed by Osama bin Laden and Ayman al-Zawahiri, so it also came as no surprise when bin Laden admitted in later interviews to helping fund and train Aidid's forces for their assault against U.S. troops in Mogadishu. In his book *Holy War Inc.*, journalist Peter Bergen, who has met and interviewed bin Laden, writes:

> In 1993, one of bin Laden's military commanders, Muhammed Atef, traveled twice to Somalia to determine how best to attack U.S. forces, reporting back to bin Laden in Sudan. An Al-Qaeda mortar specialist was also dispatched to the country. ...A U.S. official told me that the skills involved in shooting down those helicopters were not skills that the Somalis could have learned on their own.

So the Battle of Mogadishu had, in at least some capacity, al-Qaeda fingerprints, according to bin Laden himself. In the end, the greatest impression that al-Qaeda gleaned from the events of October 3 and 4, 1993, was not of the bravery and fighting skills of the U.S. military, epitomized by a group of severely undermanned and outgunned Special Forces soldiers killing, by most estimates, upwards of 1,000 enemy fighters in a legendary display of battlefield courage and proficiency. No, what bin Laden took from the Battle of Mogadishu, he would later say, was that the United States is a "paper tiger" that would cut and run rather than stand and fight. He was referring to President Clinton's hasty withdrawal of U.S. forces from Somalia in the wake of the battle. As we'll hear from a former bin Laden associate in a later chapter, al-Qaeda's view of the United States as a paper tiger was later reinforced on several occasions during the Clinton administration, emboldening the terror group as it planned the 9/11 attacks.

To say that Americans were left with a bad taste in their mouths following the Black Hawk Down incident would be an understatement. Somalia, which has not had a functioning central government since 1991, was rightly viewed as a backward, violent, and barbaric place that was hostile to America and to Judeo-Christian, Western values. And today, eighteen years after the Battle of Mogadishu and in the wake of two decades of non-stop war, famine, lawlessness, and crushing poverty, Somalia is frequently referred to as the most dangerous place on earth.

These days, large swaths of the country—including Mogadishu—are ruled by an Islamic terrorist group called al-Shabaab (*The Youth*), which has aligned itself with al-Qaeda and pledged allegiance to Osama bin Laden. Like clockwork, al-Shabaab has made sharia the law of much of the land, predictably resulting in stonings, beheadings, amputations, the degradation of women, and bans on music and TV. In addition, the group claimed responsibility for a July 2010 suicide bombing in neighboring Uganda that killed seventy-eight people who were watching a World Cup soccer match.[2] This attack, combined with al-Shabaab leaders' repeated threats against Israel and the United States, shows that the jihadist militia's ambitions now extend outside the Horn of Africa.

Under the Shabaab's guidance, several terrorist training camps are currently operating in Somalia and have attracted scores of Western Muslims, including Americans. The most notorious of these jihadists is an Islamic convert from small-town Alabama named Omar Hammami. Now known as Abu Mansoor al-Amriki, Hammami is the son of a Caucasian mother and Syrian father who was raised in his mother's southern Baptist faith until turning to Islam in high school. He grew increasingly radical and ultimately traveled to Somalia in 2006, where he has now become a top military commander and recruiter for al-Shabaab.

His main value to the group, though, is as a propagandist. He has appeared in several slickly produced al-Shabaab videos—including one showing him leading fighters into battle against a hip-hop beat—encouraging Western Muslims to leave the comforts of home behind for the noble, romantic life of a *mujahid*, or holy warrior, in Somalia. Hammami's pale skin, fluent English, and use of hip-hop terminology have had their desired effect, inspiring young Islamists in the U.S. like Zachary Chesser, a 20-year-old white convert to Islam from Virginia who idolized Hammami and re-posted his videos online. Chesser was arrested at New York's Kennedy Airport in July 2010 while boarding a plane to Africa to join al-Shabaab.

The jihadi onslaught in Somalia, combined with the continued proliferation of gangs, warlords, and piracy on Somali soil, has created a hellish state of affairs that comes as no surprise to anyone who watched the events of October 1993 unfold. Yet while most Americans decided back then they wanted to stay as far away from Somalia as possible, the U.S. government thought it would be a grand idea to bring a slice of Somalia to the American heartland. Other Western governments have followed in kind, dismissing the obvious perils of allowing waves of largely uneducated, third-world Muslims from a primitive tribal culture to settle in advanced, industrialized, non-Muslim societies.

Over the past twenty years, the Somali population in the United States, Canada, and Europe has gone from virtually zero to being one of the fastest growing immigrant blocs in the West. Their numbers are steadily increasing in far-flung places that, like in the case of Shelbyville, may surprise you. For example, it is no great shock that there are, according to some estimates, up to 250,000 Somalis living in the Islamo-asylum haven of Great Britain, a country that seems hell-bent on committing national suicide.[3] But who would have predicted back in 1993 that more than 50,000 Somalis would settle in Sweden?[4] Or that more than 25,000 Somalis would lay down roots in Norway,[5] and another 20,000 in the Netherlands?[6] How about close to 17,000 Somalis living in Denmark?[7]

It seems that frigid, remote Scandinavia—where suicidal, open-door immigration policies for Muslims are every bit as prevalent as in Great Britain—suits warm-blooded Somalis just fine. The same goes for Canada, where close to 40,000 Somalis currently reside (although unofficial estimates place that number much higher).[8] And it doesn't get more far-flung than Australia, yet some 20,000 Somalis have settled Down Under in recent years, with 10,000 alone living in Melbourne, a city that boasts one of the world's largest concentrations of Somalis outside of Africa.[9]

In the United States, where their population now numbers some 200,000 thanks to a State Department refugee resettlement program, Somalis have settled in cities from coast to coast since first arriving in large numbers in 1992.[10] That they reside in Atlanta, Seattle, San Diego, Boston, Denver, Washington, D.C., and Los Angeles comes as no great surprise. But the fact that the frozen tundra of Minneapolis/St. Paul has become the undisputed mecca of Somali America, with some 100,000 Somali residents, is telling.[11] So, too, are the large Somali influxes to Portland, Columbus, Cedar Rapids, Nashville, and Lewiston, Maine. These are all small and mid-sized cities that, until recently, had little experience with immigration, let alone of the third-world, Islamic variety—that is, until our government's irrepressible social engineers decided it would be prudent not only to inundate traditional "gateway" cities like New York and Los Angeles with Muslim immigrants, but to spread the wealth, as their current boss might say, to flyover country.

As a result, a southern, Bible Belt city like Nashville has become a kind of mini-Ellis Island, with tens of thousands of Somalis and Iraqi Kurds being directed there by the State Department in recent years. This has spawned a new reality that has "culture clash" written all over it.

Government officials, however, don't bother taking into account pesky distractions like the potential for social unrest or refugees' lack of adaptability when deciding who to resettle and where to resettle them. Their single-minded goal seems to be placing Muslim refugees in as much of the United States as possible, encompassing every region of the country, regardless of its predominant ethnic, religious, or economic makeup. Ironically, in its quest to bring sharia to America, the Muslim Brotherhood pursues this very immigration strategy.

This means no longer will large, diverse metropolitan areas like New York City or Los Angeles, with long histories of absorbing immigrants, be the default landing points for government-sponsored Islamic refugees. While some may settle in large cities initially, after a few months in America they are free to move around and resettle wherever they please. These "secondary migrations" have seen droves of Somalis pick up and move, suddenly and en masse, to sleepy small towns like Shelbyville and Lewiston. They are often drawn by work opportunities and cheap housing, which sounds like the American dream in action—until you see the statistics showing that Somali unemployment and illiteracy rates are through the roof across the United States, with taxpayers footing the bills for the inevitable welfare checks.

In March 2009 Senate testimony about al-Shabaab recruitment in America, the Deputy Director of Intelligence at the National Counterterrorism Center, Andrew Liepman, painted a bleak picture of Somali prospects in the United States:

> Compared to most Muslim immigrants to the U.S., many Somalis—seeking refuge from a war-torn country—received less language and cultural training and education prior to migration. Despite the efforts of Federal, State and local government and non-governmental organizations to facilitate their settlement into American communities, their relative linguistic isolation and the sudden adjustment to American society many refugees faced has reinforced, in some areas, their greater insularity compared to other, more integrated

Muslim immigrant communities, and has aggravated the challenges of assimilation for their children.[12]

Hello, Shelbyville! Liepman continued,

> According to data from the most recent census, the Somali-American population suffers the highest unemployment rate among East African diaspora communities in the United States, and experience significantly high poverty rates and the lowest rate of college graduation. These data also suggest that Somali-Americans are far more likely to be linguistically isolated than other East African immigrants.[13]

For the State Department, the solution to this failed sociology experiment is obvious: more Somalis, of course. While State may not control secondary migration, it does decide who gets to enter the country since it, after all, runs the refugee resettlement program. The way it all works is quite simple. The refugees are chosen from UN camps in their home countries—UN involvement being the first red flag that something is not right with the program. They undergo four days of "cultural orientation" and are then on their way to America. Just like that. This means, in some cases, that a nomadic Somali Muslim tribesman who has never seen a toilet, a light bulb, or running water is suddenly plopped down into middle America and expected to make do for himself. The federal government contracts with social welfare groups like Catholic Charities at the local level to help the refugees find apartments and jobs and generally ease their transition. But after a few months, they're on their own and free to move.

A spokesman for the State Department's Bureau of Population, Refugees and Migration told me in an interview that the program, which is a billion-dollar annual enterprise funded by taxpayers, specifically targets refugees from Africa, the Middle East, and Southeast Asia—Islamic strongholds all.[14] The thinking here is that if the United States continues to help Muslims, they will begin to like us—even though, as mentioned previously, all existing evidence points to the contrary. "It's one of the best facets of America, that we are a very generous, hospitable country," the spokesman said, noting that a number of Iraqi Christians have also been resettled in the United States in recent years.

Amen to that last point: I support an influx of Iraq's beleaguered Christian minority—which is being systematically exterminated by Islamic jihadists—into the United States. Of course, Iraqi Christians do not follow a religious-political system that commands them to wage jihad, slay Christian and Jewish infidels, and impose sharia law until the Day of Judgment comes. Muslims, however—at least those who take their Islam literally, and many Somalis do—follow such a system. Nevertheless, they receive red carpet treatment from the U.S. government.

In fact, the Somali presence in the United States has exploded since 9/11, and is slated to expand further. Here are the figures from the invaluable Refugee Resettlement Watch website on the number of Somali refugees admitted to America, beginning ten years ago:[15]

2001: 4,940
2002: 242

The huge dip here shows that the government momentarily wised up after 9/11—but only momentarily, as the annual number of Somali refugees admitted to the United States increased by over 14,000 between 2002 and 2004 alone. Bear in mind also that each Somali family in America has, on average, six children. Here are the figures for the ensuing years:

2003: 1,708
2004: 12,814
2005: 10,101
2006: 10,220
2007: 6,958
2008: 2,523

We see a big dip in 2008, likely due to massive fraud that was uncovered in the family reunification, or P-3, portion of the resettlement program. In a bombshell revelation, the State Department admitted that up to 80 percent of the African refugees that were granted entry to America between 2003 and 2008—tens of thousands of them—had falsely claimed to have family members who were already here. Were any of the Somalis that fraudulently exploited the program covert al-Shabaab operatives aligned with al-Qaeda? Were any of them pirates, warlords, or participants in the Black Hawk Down incident? If the State Department knows, it isn't saying.

And apparently, it isn't too concerned, as the number of Somali refugees is now back on the rise, with a combined 9,073 Somalis admitted in 2009 and 2010 despite the family reunification travesty and the growing menace of Islamic jihadism emanating from Somalia, courtesy of al-Shabaab.

Under President Obama, who has made Muslim outreach a top priority, the number of Somali refugees promises to increase further. Obama announced in September 2010 that the ceiling for refugees in 2011 would be the maximum currently allowed under the resettlement program: 80,000.[16] Of that number, well over half will hail from Muslim countries, including Somalia. But don't worry: that same State Department spokesman said all necessary precautions are taken to ensure that Islamic jihadists are not among the new arrivals, assuring me that State "work[s] closely with the Department of Homeland Security to make sure we vet people coming here. Especially since 9/11, it's very important."

I would say so, and forgive me if I'm a bit uneasy that the same administration that failed to connect the dots at Fort Hood and with the Christmas Day underwear bomber is in charge of detecting potential Somali terrorists. And sure enough, even the most cursory investigation shows that, despite the supposedly rigorous screening process for refugees, an alarming number of Somalis in America are turning to terrorism and jihad. Minnesota, take a bow.

★ ★ ★

For someone arriving at the departure gate of an air terminal, there are few scenes more disconcerting than seeing a dozen men performing Islamic prayers in front of the building. In a post 9/11-world, it's an unfriendly reminder of the jihadist danger that might be lurking on the plane you're about to board. So it was with great interest that I observed the concerned expressions worn by pedestrians arriving at Minneapolis-St. Paul International Airport one afternoon in June 2007, as a group of Somali Muslim taxi drivers performed prayers next to a fleet of parked cabs. While some prayed, others sat on the curb and ritually cleansed their feet from water bottles as they readied to face Mecca. It was a public and brazen display of Islamic supremacism, yet the cabbies were none too happy that my cameraman and I had decided to film it. Some shouted at us angrily and others hopped in their cabs and sped away. Unfortunately for them, we had been cleared to film at the airport—but the rules are a mere trifle to the Somali cabbies, who operate a whopping 75 percent of the airport's 900 or so cabs.

Indeed, I'd come to the Twin Cities, home to the nation's largest Somali population, to report on the widespread refusal of Somali cabbies at the airport to transport passengers who had alcohol in their possession. *So you've just arrived in Minneapolis from out of town and want to take a nice bottle of wine from the duty-free store to your parents' house for Christmas dinner, eh? Forget about it, infidel.* Alcohol is *haram*—forbidden—in Islam, and in the Somali cabbies' view, to merely transport it in their cars is a grave sin. The same goes for transporting seeing-eye dogs for blind passengers, since dogs are viewed as filthy by Muslims and were detested by Islam's prophet, Mohammed, according to Islamic tradition.

Since most non-Muslims don't share these hang-ups about booze and dogs, the Somali cabbies were effectively practicing religious discrimination, not to mention imposing sharia law, in their own creative way. It was no coincidence, then, that they had been emboldened to turn away passengers with alcohol by a fatwa issued by the local chapter of the Muslim American Society, or MAS, that commanded as much. MAS is an American arm of the Muslim Brotherhood that is devoted to imposing sharia law far and wide—and the Somali cabbies got the memo. Thankfully, their efforts at making the Twin Cities' airport sharia-compliant seem to have failed for the moment, as the Metropolitan Airports Commission eventually ruled that a cabbie's license can be revoked for thirty days for refusing to pick up a passenger for any reason, with a second refusal bringing a two-year revocation.

Nevertheless, Somali Islamists are making great strides elsewhere in Minneapolis-St. Paul, where their pressure campaigns have led to the installation of ritual foot-washing basins at some local universities and the continued operation of a taxpayer-funded Islamic public school in suburban St. Paul, called the Tarek ibn Zayad Academy, that even the Muslim-coddling ACLU has accused of Islamist indoctrination. In addition, Minneapolis Somalis form a powerful voting bloc that was critical in electing America's first Muslim congressman, Democrat Keith Ellison, a Muslim Brotherhood favorite who swore his individual oath of office on a Koran.

But the most notorious contribution by Somali Islamists in Minneapolis has been to the global jihad. U.S. officials say that since 2007, at least twenty young Somalis from the Twin Cities area have traveled back to their homeland to fight alongside the terrorist group al-Shabaab in its jihad campaigns against both internal rivals and soldiers from neighboring Ethiopia, which occupied Somalia from 2007 until 2008. In the process, these Somali-American terrorists have no doubt received invaluable jihadi training from their Shabaab overlords that, as FBI director Robert Mueller pointed out in 2009, "raises the question of whether these young men will one day come home, and, if so, what they might undertake here."[17]

The potential magnitude of this danger became clear in October 2008 when Shirwa Ahmed, a Somali-born Minneapolis resident, became the first successful American suicide bomber. Ahmed, a naturalized U.S. citizen, drove a car filled with explosives into a government compound in northern Somalia, killing himself and twenty-nine others. Ahmed and his family had arrived in Minneapolis in 1996 courtesy of—you guessed it—the State Department's refugee resettlement program. Mueller said shortly after the suicide bombing that Ahmed "was radicalized in his hometown in Minnesota."[18] Of course, that didn't stop Mueller and the Bureau from shipping Ahmed's remains home to Minneapolis for an Islamic burial on the U.S. taxpayers' dime. As for a potential radicalization spot, a great deal of suspicion has surrounded the Abubakar as-Siddiq mosque in Minneapolis, which Ahmed and several other Shabaab wannabes had attended before trekking to Somalia in pursuit of their seventy-two virgins. (The mosque's imam, predictably, has denied any involvement.) Sure enough, at least six of them have been killed, including a white convert to Islam who had had hooked up with Somali radicals in Minneapolis.

The prospect of battle-hardened Somali jihadists carrying U.S. passports is a nightmare scenario for U.S. intelligence officials; one former federal investigator told me in late 2010 that Somalis have moved to the top of the list of potential threats to the American and Canadian homelands. It's not hard to see why:

- In August 2010, the Department of Justice indicted fourteen people from Minnesota, Alabama, California, and Ohio on terrorism charges for allegedly providing financial and material support to al-Shabaab.
- In Columbus, Ohio, Somali Islamists allegedly waged an intimidation campaign against a moderate Somali mosque whose leaders spoke out against the Shabaab. Moreover, a former Columbus resident was killed in Somalia in 2009 while serving as a commander for the terror group.
- Another Somali native, an 18-year-old who lived in Seattle, joined Shirwa Ahmed among the ranks of American suicide bombers when he blew up himself and seventeen African Union peacekeepers in Somalia in 2009.

And Somali Islamist mayhem isn't limited to the Western Hemisphere:

- Five al-Shabaab sympathizers of Somali and Lebanese descent were arrested in Australia in 2009 for plotting to attack an army base in Sydney.
- A Somali with al-Qaeda links was charged with attempted murder in a 2010 attack on cartoonist Kurt Westergaard in Denmark. The 75-year-old Westergaard had depicted Mohammed with a bomb in his turban in one of the Danish Mohammad cartoons that had provoked deadly rioting throughout the Muslim world in 2006. Since any depictions of Mohammed are a dire offense under sharia, Westergaard's would-be assailant felt compelled to break into the cartoonist's house wielding an axe and a knife, looking for blood. Westergaard, who was at home with his 5-year-old granddaughter, narrowly escaped into a panic room he had installed in his home due to repeated death threats by jihadists.

In the June 2009 issue of *New English Review* magazine, counter-jihad activist Jerry Gordon outlined a chilling scenario of a Mumbai-style attack being carried out on U.S. soil by Somali-American terrorists:

> Such attacks could be perpetrated by homegrown Jihadis like those naturalized American Somali youths, alleged to have "disappeared" to join Al Shabaab militia groups in Somalia. Those returnees could constitute cadres to train fellow American Somali youths. They could orchestrate swarming attacks against public facilities in this country using so-called low-tech means: cheap weapons and pickup trucks. These possible swarming attacks could be devastating "mini-9/11 events." Deadly scenarios might include simultaneous attacks against

exposed queues of customers at so-called "big box stores" especially on high sales days like Black Friday, the start of the Christmas holiday retailing season.

Gordon's article was proven prescient on Black Friday—November 26, 2010—when a 19-year-old Somali-American named Mohamed Osman Mohamud was arrested after attempting to detonate what he believed was an explosives-laden van at an annual Christmas tree lighting ceremony in Portland, Oregon. Mohamud, who was snagged through an FBI sting operation (undercover agents had supplied the phony explosives), told the feds he was aiming to murder as many people as possible—and indeed, such an attack would have potentially killed thousands. He yelled "Allahu Akhbar" and tried to kick agents and police as he was taken into custody. He also made a pre-attack video in which, dressed in al-Qaeda-type garb, he denounced America and extolled jihad.

These and other facts of Mohamud's case no doubt left government officials scrambling for answers. Up until his arrest, their scant public comments about the Somali terror threat in America focused on Ethiopia's occupation of Somalia or various social ills as the prime motivators for Somali radicalization. Yet in Mohamud's case, he had never traveled to Somalia or made contact with al-Shabaab (although he did reach out to terrorists in Pakistan's tribal regions). An engineering student at Oregon State University, he was, by most accounts, well-adjusted to American life and fairly normal, at least on the surface. So forget about social ills. At the end of the day, what has motivated Mohamud and all the other Somali jihadists to emerge from American cities is Islamist ideology, plain and simple.

★   ★   ★

To the average American, the arrival of tens of thousands of Somali Muslims on the taxpayers' dime represents a looming cultural and national security disaster—and an expensive one to boot. Yet average

Americans are no more shaping such policies in Washington than average Europeans are influencing them in their continent's capitals. Resettling Somali refugees, not only to major urban centers but to the very heart of America and of European nations, furthers the goal of a multicultural utopia that has long been the dream of academic and government elites on both sides of the pond. After all, these elites believe, no culture is superior to another, and spoiled, sheltered Westerners will be enriched by pre-dawn calls to prayer blaring through their windows from the local mosque, or by the sight of their Somali next-door-neighbors slaughtering a goat in their backyard according to Muslim tradition. Or perhaps they'll be enlightened by news of local Somali girls being subjected to female genital mutilation, a hellish ritual widely practiced in Somalia that sees part or all of the external genitalia hacked off.

You don't like it, you bitter, guns-and-religion clinger? Too bad. And hey, the elites reason, in the very least, the new arrivals will provide cheap labor and take on undesirable jobs like chicken plucking. In the case of Europe, home to rapidly aging indigenous populations with fertility rates well below replacement level, Somali and other Muslim immigrants can also help replenish a shrinking workforce and enable Europeans to retire in comfort. Or so the elites' thinking goes. But what happens when the new arrivals refuse to assimilate and instead demand religious and cultural accommodation, or worse, turn against their adopted countries and embrace jihad?

In Shelbyville, as of this writing, there have been no documented cases of local Somalis turning to terrorism. Demands for accommodation, on the other hand, are already a Somali-American tradition, and Shelbyville is no different. The Tyson Chicken processing plant that employs many of the town's Somalis stirred national controversy in 2008 when it dropped Labor Day as a paid holiday in favor of the Muslim holiday Eid al-Fitr. This shameless kowtow to Islam was later reversed amidst a huge outcry, but the writing is on the wall for Shelbyville: things will have to change now that the Religion of Peace is in town.

That suits the folks in the refugee industry, from the State Department on down, just fine. A representative from the Tennessee Office of Refugees summed up their line of thinking when I asked her thoughts on the Somali influx into the town. "I think that Shelbyville ... needs to look at it as a learning opportunity," she replied. "And a chance to get to know someone that is really different from you and to learn from them. And I think that they would find some really interesting people."

Perhaps even the next Shirwa Ahmed or Mohamed Osman Mohamud.

CHAPTER FIVE

FREAKS, GEEKS, AND JIHADIS

As I slipped off my shoes and stepped into the mosque, all conversation ceased.

A black man in flowing Islamic garb had been teaching the Koran to a group of younger men sitting on the floor in one corner of the room. Now they just stared coldly at the tall, white infidel in a suit standing in their midst. So did the others, mostly Middle Easterners, who were milling around the place.

Their eyes said it all: *another bigoted FBI agent has come to harass the Muslims.*

But as they saw my cameraman wheel his gear into the room behind me, a look of annoyed recognition came to their faces, and they began to file silently out of the room. *Another bigoted TV station has come to make Muslims look bad.*

It was October 2005, and I had come to the Masjid An-Nur mosque, near the campus of the University of Oklahoma in Norman, to try to solve a growing mystery. A few weeks before, an OU engineering student named Joel Hinrichs had committed suicide on campus. The method he used was unique, to say the least: the 21-year-old blew himself up while sitting on a bench 200 yards from a stadium packed with 84,000 football fans watching OU play Kansas State on a Saturday night. Shattering windows on campus, the blast emanating from the bomb in his backpack was audible inside the noisy stadium.[1] The explosives consisted of triacetone triperoxide, or TATP, the same highly volatile substance favored by Islamic terrorists such as the July 7, 2005 London mass transit bombers, "Underwear Bomber" Umar Farouk Abdulmutallab, and the would-be "Shoe Bomber," Richard Reid.

To this day, it is unclear whether Hinrichs planned to enter Memorial Stadium. Since he obviously isn't available for questioning and the feds have been elusive about his case, we'll probably never know. Perhaps it was all just an unfortunate coincidence that the young man was prowling outside a jam-packed football stadium with a bomb in his backpack. But I doubt it. Although Hinrichs was not captured on any surveillance cameras, one government intelligence analyst told me that he believed Hinrichs intended to head into the game but was probably inhibited by the sight of stadium security guards conducting bag searches. Moreover, a top Norman police official revealed that Hinrichs had been spotted fiddling with his backpack while sitting on the bench. He believed Hinrichs accidentally detonated the bomb in that spot, saying, "I think he got a little bit cocky and it went off."[2]

This begs an obvious question: if Hinrichs didn't mean to set the bomb off on the bench, just where did he plan to do it?

In the days and weeks following the blast, it was hard to believe the insistence of school officials and federal investigators that this was just a run-of-the-mill suicide. Led by OU president David Boren, a former Democratic senator and governor of Oklahoma, authorities calmly reassured OU students and the local and national media that Hinrichs was a classic, depressed loner with no plans to hurt anyone but himself. So what was their message for the 84,000 unsuspecting football fans and additional passers-by situated a stone's throw from the scene of Hinrichs' suicide bombing? *Well, uh, these things happen.*

Except that they don't. Needless to say, detonating a powerful back-pack bomb in a public place is not a common way for a guy to off himself.

Undaunted, the mainstream media—eager, as always, to avoid any discussion that might reflect poorly on Muslims—quickly swallowed the flimsy explanations and rejected local reports that Hinrichs was a white convert to Islam. Yet I and a handful of other journalists could not ignore the glaring truth that Hinrichs' method of self-murder was awfully similar to that used by Islamic terrorists—right down to the large quantities of bomb-making materials that investigators found in his apartment as well as his proximity to a major civilian target at the time of the blast.[3] I also couldn't shake the fact that older photos of Hinrichs showed him clean-shaven, while before his death he sported an Islamic-style beard. And all that brings us back to Norman's Masjid An-Nur mosque.

I'd spent three days around Norman visiting the scene of the bomb-ing, interviewing Hinrichs' acquaintances, and scoping out the apartment he had lived in just one block from the Masjid An-Nur mosque with, interestingly, a Pakistani Muslim roommate. On my last day in town, I received an intriguing tip. Local sources put me in touch with someone who claimed to have seen Hinrichs several times at the mosque. When I met with this witness, blurring her face on camera for her safety during our interview, she was adamant about what she had observed:

> I did see Joel [Hinrichs] on several occasions outside of the mosque, actually, in the parking lot of the mosque. It wasn't in the yard, it wasn't behind the fence, it was always in the parking lot when I would see him. And there was one time when I passed him, actually, on the sidewalk. As soon as I saw the picture of Joel Hinrichs on TV, not the clean-shaven one, but the one with the beard, I knew immediately that that was the gentleman I had seen on several occasions.

With no evident axe to grind, this woman spoke confidently as she described in detail when and where she saw Hinrichs. So I headed to the Masjid An-Nur mosque along with my cameraman to get some answers.

After the chilly reception, we were approached by mosque spokesman Mohamed Elyazgi. We shook hands and exchanged pleasantries—and then things went quickly downhill. Before I could even ask a question, Elyazgi began complaining about CBN's "anti-Muslim" coverage. We went back and forth a bit as Elyazgi, with barely disguised disdain for me, tried to explain away Islam's obvious terrorism problem and disputed my well-proven assertion that the vast majority of today's terrorist acts are committed by Muslims.

A Libyan native, Elyazgi has been known to keep some interesting company. His former business partner, Mufid Abdulqader, was one of several U.S.-based Muslim Brotherhood operatives convicted in the landmark Holy Land Foundation terrorism financing case. Abdulqader received twenty years in prison for raising funds for Hamas[4] and just so happens to be the half-brother of Khaled Meshaal, the terror group's so-called "political leader." Incidentally, both Abdulqader and Elyazgi have worked for the Oklahoma Department of Transportation—helping, no doubt, to keep the Sooner State's roads safe and sound.[5]

The Masjid An-Nur mosque, like Elyazgi, has some dubious connections. Al-Qaeda operative Zacarias Moussaoui, who was convicted of helping to plot the 9/11 attacks, worshipped there while living in Norman in 2001.[6] His presence doesn't seem to have left a lasting taint locally—as of this writing, the Islamic Society of Norman is planning to build a new, expanded mosque on the site of the existing one, at an estimated cost of $750,000.[7] Strike another one for Islam in America's heartland.

While Mohamed Elyazgi never raised his voice during our encounter, he did become slightly agitated when I asked about Moussaoui, who he claimed had little contact with fellow mosque-goers. Elyazgi became more upset when I began to press about Joel Hinrichs. "The first time we've seen his picture is when the news and the media put his pictures in the papers and on TV," he told me. "Other than that, we've never seen him here." When I countered that an eyewitness told me she had repeatedly seen Hinrichs at the mosque, Elyazgi gave the same response—he'd never seen Hinrichs there, and neither had any of the other congregants. Our interview ended soon after.

Before leaving Norman, I headed over to a local feed store and confirmed reports that Joel Hinrichs had stopped there in the days before his death to inquire about purchasing ammonium nitrate fertilizer—the same substance used in the 1995 bombing of the Federal Building in nearby Oklahoma City. If Hinrichs wasn't looking to harm anyone but himself, as Boren and the FBI had suggested, why would he look into buying a substance that can potentially take down an entire building? And if authorities knew from the beginning that Islam played no role in Hinrichs' actions, then why were at least seven members of OU's Muslim community either detained or questioned following Hinrichs' suicide?[8]

Regardless, the FBI's official verdict was that Hinrichs was not a terrorist, and that he had no outside help, nor any involvement with terrorist organizations.[9] Yet I got a different take from two government intelligence analysts who spoke to me on condition of anonymity. Both classified Hinrichs' suicide as an attempted act of terrorism and believed he was indeed a Muslim convert. One opined that Hinrichs was a seriously disturbed individual who was attracted to Islamic jihadism simply because it was the darkest thing available, and that he may have self-radicalized over the Internet.

The fact that Hinrichs was a deeply troubled loner is undeniable. He'd been picked on as a boy and had struggled with depression throughout his life, and his father said Joel had a lifelong difficulty relating to and interacting with other people. Nevertheless, he was an excellent student, even a National Merit Scholar.[10] But the questions remain: was Hinrichs a homegrown Islamic terrorist, and did Oklahoma University football fans narrowly avoid falling victim to the first successful suicide bombing on U.S. soil since 9/11?

Hinrichs' profile—emotionally disturbed, brainy white kid from middle-class Colorado Springs—certainly doesn't fit most people's image of a jihadist. And that's part of the problem. If academically gifted, mentally unbalanced Joel Hinrichs was indeed acting in the name of Allah on that fateful October night in 2005, he would have had plenty of company. Increasingly, terror recruiters are connecting with psychologically unstable people, usually through the Internet, and helping to transform them into the unlikeliest of jihadis. As a result, the terrorists next door are now taking up more real estate than ever before.

★ ★ ★

In recent years, social outcasts have increasingly found appeal in Islamism. They might be lonely nerds, love-starved women, ex-cons, or people who grew up in abusive families. Some are white converts to Islam, others are African-American or Hispanic. All have one thing in common: they find a meaning and purpose in the jihadist cause that they previously lacked in life. In the old days, they may have joined a cult, hooked up with a street gang, or listened to the darkest form of heavy metal music. But with the advent of the Internet came a sudden host of causes and interests that an angry, disturbed, or alienated person could latch on to simply by clicking a mouse. Some have gone out searching for answers and acceptance on the Web and found Islam's rigid system of absolutes to be anchors in what had previously been chaotic, aimless lives.

A more fundamental transformation occurs when they learn about the Koran-mandated duty to wage jihad against all non-Muslims and to completely subjugate the world to Islam. For the first time in what they themselves often view as their wretched lives, these misfits become part of something bigger, something that matters—a powerful, world-changing movement. Overnight, one can go from being a friendless sad sack or a directionless street thug to being a member of the ummah, or global Islamic community, simply by entering a jihadi chat room or sharing an al-Qaeda video on YouTube. For an ex-con or a lonely, tormented soul who blames his failures and unhappiness on a U.S. system and society that has done them wrong, aiding and abetting America's enemies in a jihad against that very power structure is a perfect way to gain revenge.

Furthermore, for many young, radicalized converts, Islamism is the new rebellion—dangerous, scary, dark, and forbidden. Some have referred to this appeal as "Jihadi Cool."[11] You want to upset your parents and rebel against authority? Forget drugs, graffiti, stealing a car, or shaving your hair into a spiked orange mohawk. These days, it doesn't get much edgier than hooking up online with a hip-hop loving British kid who's secretly communicating with al-Qaeda leaders—and who just happens to be planning to blow up some subway cars in London. Forget the Bloods and Crips—it doesn't get more "gangsta" than al-Qaeda. And unlike most gangs, the jihadist movement has a clear, well-defined goal: the reestablishment of a global Islamic caliphate and the imposition of Islamic sharia law on one and all. The global jihad also has no shortage of inflammatory rallying cries: Palestine, Kashmir, Chechnya, Bosnia, Iraq, Abu Ghraib, and Guantanamo Bay, just to name a few.

You can almost hear the seductive whispers of the Islamo-pimps and martyrdom-pushers as they beckon to a lost, angry American over the Web:

America—the country that has failed you personally and spread misery throughout the world—is waging a genocidal war against peace-loving, impoverished Muslims and must be stopped. Only through Islamic unity and jihad can this be accomplished, and thus can peace, justice, and equality be established at last in a wicked world. Join our cause, my eager young convert, and you can help change the world. Oh, and if you blow yourself up and take a few infidels with you, you'll drink the choicest wine and cavort with seventy-two virgins in the afterlife. See you in Waziristan in two weeks—pack light.

The narrative of Muslims as *oppressed underdogs standing up to the evil American hegemon* resonates with outcasts who've been left in the dust while the "cool kids" have all the fun and get the girls.

This is unfair, they say to themselves. *The whole system is rigged against me. Why not turn it upside down and actively work to destroy it? Then I'll finally end up on top as an integral part of a new order, a triumphant Islamic wave. Or in the very least, I'll blow myself up and go to heaven, away from all these miserable fools for good. Hopefully, I'll take a few of them with me.*

Yes, the scary quiet kid with the distant stare, bad acne, and *Ozzfest* t-shirt that sat next to you in biology class is now a prime candidate to carry the banner of Islamic jihad. Ditto the thuggish troublemaker who was in and out of juvenile hall throughout high school. Thanks to the Internet, they can now reach out and touch an Islamic terrorist halfway across the world. And once they're in the jihadist fold, most Americans will never see them coming. The following are some real-life examples of this threat, which will become increasingly familiar in the near future.

THE METALHEAD

> Your failure to heed our demands and the demands of reason means that you and your people will—Allah willing—experience things which will make you forget all about the horrors of September 11th.
>
> —Adam Pearlman Gadahn[12]

The date was May 29, 2007, and the bespectacled, bearded terrorist in the white turban was on a roll. Pointing at the video camera for emphasis and speaking in strangely accented English, he was clearly relishing his status as al-Qaeda's chief spokesman to the West. Only twelve years prior, Adam Pearlman Gadahn—grandson of a Jewish Zionist—had been living on a goat farm in rural California and writing reviews for death metal publications.[13] But by the time his threat of new "horrors" was broadcast worldwide, Gadahn was known as "Azzam the American" and had risen to become a senior operative for al-Qaeda as well as its media advisor and chief English-language propagandist. Since 2004, Gadahn has regularly appeared in the group's video releases to threaten mass bloodshed against the country in which he was born and raised. In 2006, he became the first U.S. citizen to be charged with treason in half a century. Most likely based in Pakistan's tribal regions along with the rest of al-Qaeda's hierarchy, he is now one of the most wanted men in the world. In short, he's a long way removed from his days as a chubby, homeschooled headbanger. So what on earth happened here?

Gadahn was raised a Christian by ex-hippie parents on a goat farm in rural California. His father, ironically, made a living as a *halal* butcher, slaughtering farm animals in an Islamically correct manner and supplying them to a Muslim food market in downtown Los Angeles.[14] The young Gadahn was homeschooled by his parents and took part in Christian homeschooling support groups. He's written that he eventually grew to loathe "fundamentalist Christianity" and became deeply immersed in death metal, an extreme subculture of heavy metal music that features violent, overtly Satanic lyrics sung through guttural growling. Gadahn was hooked, even contributing music reviews and artwork to a death metal publication called *Xenocide*.[15] Gadahn, a self-described "revolting geek" whom friends in the death metal scene recall as highly literate and intelligent,[16] later wrote of his musical fixation:

I had become obsessed with demonic Heavy Metal music, something the rest of my family (as I now realize, rightfully so) was not happy with. My entire life was focused on expanding my music collection. I eschewed personal cleanliness and let my room reach an unbelievable state of disarray. My relationship with my parents became strained, although only intermittently so. I am sorry even as I write this.[17]

Gadahn eventually moved into his grandparents' home, where he had ready access to the Internet. While surfing the Web and looking to fill what he described as a "void," he discovered Islam.[18] Soon it was out with his long, heavy metal hair and in with a flowing Islamic beard—from one extreme to another. After his conversion to Islam in 1995, Gadahn fell under the sway of a group of hardcore jihadists at the southern California mosque where he worshipped. He was an apt pupil, and before long was assaulting a mosque leader whom his radical circle considered too moderate. Gadahn was arrested and pleaded guilty to misdemeanor assault and battery.[19] By 1998, with the sponsorship of two of his jihadi friends from the mosque, he left for Pakistan. Other then one brief trip back to California a few months later, he has remained in Pakistan ever since, working his way through the ranks of al-Qaeda to become one of the organization's most recognizable figures. Adam Gadahn, described by one former friend as socially inexperienced, withdrawn, and lonely in his headbanger days, has found his voice as "Azzam the American," one of al-Qaeda's public faces.[20]

THE EX-CON

"He seemed like such a nice young man."

I was standing outside a run-down apartment building in run-down Decatur, Illinois, speaking with a neighbor of accused terrorist Michael Finton, also known as "Talib Islam." That neighbor and others expressed shock that their fellow tenant, a tall, lanky redhead with polite manners, stood accused of plotting to blow up a federal building and the offices of a Republican congressman in nearby Springfield, Illinois.

Others were more evasive. When I popped into the nearby fish-and-chicken takeout joint where Finton had worked as a 29-year-old fry cook prior to his arrest, I was told that the store was "under new management" and that they didn't know Finton. I got the message. After all, what business would want to be associated with a man like Finton, who authorities say parked a truck filled with what he believed to be a large quantity of explosives outside a crowded federal building and tried to detonate it remotely with a cell phone? Unfortunately for Finton—and fortunately for federal workers—the explosives were fakes supplied by a federal agent posing as an al-Qaeda operative. Finton was arrested at the scene and now sits in a prison cell awaiting trial.

Where did it all go wrong for Finton, and how did a fry cook in a decaying mill town in rural Illinois end up on the fast track to jihad? Searching for answers, I travelled to Decatur in November 2009, shortly after Finton's arrest made national headlines. I discovered that warning signs of a budding jihadist were evident in the pale-skinned redhead who, according to his acquaintances, was prone to denouncing America for ostensibly victimizing Muslims.[21] As for the small mosque he attended in town, it was locked, with the lights off, when I tried to enter on a Tuesday afternoon. Similarly, my phone calls went unanswered, although leaders of the mosque, which primarily caters to immigrants from Pakistan and India, did issue a statement condemning Finton's actions.[22]

The best clues concerning Finton's conversion to Islam and subsequent radicalization derive from his own statements and from federal documents. Finton described himself to co-workers at the fish-and-chicken shop as a troubled youth who ran away from foster care.[23] After being expelled from high school in Warren, Michigan, for fighting with a teacher, he eventually moved to Illinois, where he was sentenced to twelve years in prison in 1999 for aggravated robbery and aggravated battery.[24]

Like a growing number of jihadists in the United States and Europe, Finton converted to Islam in prison. He was released early in 2006, and later described his pre-Muslim days on his MySpace page: "There was a time when looking inside of myself only brought forth darkness. Everybody liked me, yet I hated myself. People thought I was smart, and reasonably good-looking, but to me, I was a moron, and a freak."[25]

Finton's self-loathing seems to have quickly been cured by his turn to Islam. Suddenly, he was part of a global jihadist movement in which he had the power, in his mind, to change world dynamics. He told undercover

FBI agents that he hoped his acts of terror in Springfield "would cause American troops to be pulled back out of Afghanistan and Iraq,"[26] and that he would rather die as a martyr for Islam than live in the United States.

Even before taking matters into his own hands in Springfield, however, Finton clearly longed to join the jihadist cause. He had sent letters to imprisoned American Taliban John Walker Lindh; although authorities have never revealed the contents, the subject probably wasn't prison food. Still more alarming, in March 2008 Finton received $1,375 from a man in Saudi Arabia, later sending that same amount to a travel agency and making his way to Saudi Arabia for a one-month stay.[27] The nature of Finton's conversation with his Saudi contact, named "Asala Hussain Abiba" in court documents, and who they met with in Saudi Arabia have yet to be disclosed.[28] It's clear, however, that Finton was so taken with the desert kingdom that he talked of moving there and starting a business.[29] But ultimately, he decided on a different course—he struck a blow for jihad by trying to massacre his countrymen here in the United States.

THE PROBLEM CHILDREN

Twenty-four-year-old Carlos Almonte and 20-year-old Mohamed Mahmood Alessa had made up their minds: they were going to Somalia to join the al-Qaeda-linked terror group al-Shabaab and kill as many infidels as possible. One of their heroes, al-Qaeda cleric Anwar al-Awlaki, had recommended Somalia in his sermons as an ideal spot to wage jihad. Like so many homegrown American terrorists do when Awlaki speaks, Almonte and Alessa listened—intently.[30] Then they took action. Heading to Somalia, the two were arrested in June 2010 while boarding a flight at New York's Kennedy Airport. They now await trial on terrorism charges.[31]

In conversations secretly recorded by an undercover New York police officer, the pair discussed killing U.S. troops and beheading non-Muslims.[32] "I wanna, like, be the world's known terrorist," Alessa boasted in one conversation, saying of Fort Hood shooter Nidal Hasan, "I'll do twice what he did." It was not idle talk. Alessa and Almonte simulated firefights by playing paintball, practiced hand-to-hand combat, and bought military gear. They also joined a gym to lift weights because, Alessa reasoned, "Stronger muscles means bigger muscles which means killing more non-Muslims."[33] Almonte and Alessa supplemented their physical training by downloading the sermons of al-Qaeda leaders—especially Awlaki—and watching jihadist videos over the Internet.

The pair, born and bred in the North Jersey suburbs, initially seemed more likely to become involved in a street gang than in international terrorism. Almonte, raised Catholic in a Dominican family, began to find trouble during his senior year in high school. He was arrested three times in less than four months for, variously, taking a knife to campus, punching someone in a supermarket parking lot, and drinking beer in a park. In short, Almonte appeared destined for the life of a common street punk—until he heard someone preaching about Islam at a New Jersey shopping mall. Intrigued, he began frequenting local mosques and eventually became a Muslim. He met Mohamed Alessa in 2005 while hanging with a group of troubled young Arabs in North Jersey who called themselves the "Arabian Knights." The two quickly became inseparable.[34]

Alessa's lifelong history of anti-social behavior makes Almonte's look tame by comparison. The son of a Palestinian father and Jordanian mother, Alessa had such an explosive temper and acid tongue that he was seeing a psychiatrist and was placed on medication by the age of six. Over the years, his proclivity for fighting and verbal threats forced him to change schools at least ten times, yet he refused the advice of his parents and friends to go back to therapy.[35] He entered the Department of Homeland Security's radar screen around 2006 after threatening to blow up two public high schools that he attended and menacing students and staff.[36]

Alessa, raised Muslim, was not very religious when he met Almonte, but that quickly changed. The two grew matching Islamic-style beards and seemed to feed off each other. In 2007, they traveled together to Jordan in a failed attempt to link up with al-Qaeda and enter Iraq. Their inability to join the jihad early on seems only to have upped their motivation. By the time of their arrests in 2010, Alessa and Almonte knew exactly what they wanted to do with their lives—and it didn't involve car theft, vandalism, or drug dealing. The two former hoodlums had found the ultimate *thug life* in the form of Islamic terrorism.

★   ★   ★

Adam Gadahn, Michael Finton, and the Jersey jihadis were all social misfits who converted to Islam and used the Internet to further their crash course in jihad. Terrorist recruiters overseas are having a field day connecting with similar outcasts through social networking websites and video sharing sites like YouTube. They've taken to the Web, in part, because mosques, where potential recruits would normally be sought out, are now under increased scrutiny by federal and local law enforcement. U.S. counterterrorism officials are well aware of the online trend, but their tracking abilities are at times hampered by privacy laws and constitutional concerns.[37] Navigating the massive scope of the Internet is another obvious hurdle.

As a result, the online push is proving a big winner for the jihadist movement. According to a September 2010 study conducted by the Bipartisan Policy Center's National Security Preparedness Group, "[I]n 2009 at least 43 American citizens or residents were charged or convicted of terrorism crimes in the U.S. or elsewhere, the highest number in any year since 9/11."[38] No fewer than eleven major Islamic terrorist plots were hatched in 2009 alone on U.S. soil. Two were successful: the jihadi rampage at Fort Hood and the murder of U.S. military recruiter Private William Long in Little Rock, Arkansas. The rapidly increasing pace of homegrown jihad continued in 2010, with at least twenty-four convictions or arrests of U.S. citizens and residents for terrorism crimes.

A review of the various indictments and complaints against the defendants in each of these cases reveals the central role of the Internet, both in the radicalization process and in establishing contact with jihadists abroad.

A prime example was the case of five young American Muslims who left their homes in the Washington, D.C. suburbs in November 2009 and headed to Pakistan to wage jihad against U.S. troops. One was a Howard University dental student; all were seemingly well-adjusted American citizens. Yet they made contact with a Taliban recruiter via YouTube, exchange coded e-mail messages with him over a period of months, and journeyed overseas intending to kill U.S. soldiers in Afghanistan.[39] The five were then arrested by Pakistani authorities and sentenced to ten years in prison each, to be served in Pakistan.[40] The ease with which these Americans established a relationship with a terrorist recruiter through the Web shows, once again, why this method has become such an attractive option for al-Qaeda and its ilk.

The five would-be jihadists apparently met at an Alexandria, Virginia mosque run by the Islamic Circle of North America (ICNA), a Muslim Brotherhood-connected group that peddles Islamic supremacist materials.[41] Notably, Alexandria is just a short drive from Falls Church, Virginia, the former stomping ground of none other than Anwar al-Awlaki. From January 2001 until March 2002, Awlaki served as imam of the Dar al-Hijrah mosque in Falls Church, just outside the nation's capital, where he mentored two of the 9/11 hijackers.

Before we delve any further into the world of homegrown jihadi geekdom, we should examine Awlaki's life and times in order to better understand the charismatic cleric whose sermons and writings have galvanized everyone from freaks and geeks to honors students into joining the global jihad.

★ ★ ★

Although Awlaki is now based in Yemen, where he helps lead al-Qaeda in the Arabian Peninsula, he is, in fact, a New Mexico-born U.S.

citizen who attended Colorado State University. His fluent English and grasp of U.S. culture and norms are a major reason why he is so appealing to young, Western Muslims—particularly recent converts—who don't speak Arabic and have never been overseas. And unlike Adam Gadahn, al-Qaeda's other English-speaking mouthpiece, the 40-year-old Awlaki is an imam who teaches at length from the Koran and the Sunnah and is viewed by Islamists as a major religious authority.

A veteran al-Qaeda-linked terrorist named Saad al-Faqih spoke to me of the much younger Awlaki in reverent tones. "I highly recommend that you read him in English," al-Faqih gushed. "He is a jewel for you. He is very impressive and sophisticated, very linguistic. He is very powerful. His message is that America must change its entire foreign policy." He paused for a second and added, "You cannot defeat him."

Al-Faqih's accolades are common among Islamists; Awlaki has been dubbed the "Bin Laden of the Internet,"[42] and due in large part to his massive online presence, U.S. intelligence officials tell me they now consider him the world's must influential jihadist, surpassing even bin Laden himself. As described in chapter two, al-Faqih was in direct contact with both Fort Hood shooter Nidal Hasan and the Underwear Bomber, Umar Farouk Abdulmutallab, in the run-up to their respective terrorist acts. He's also served as inspiration for Times Square bomber Faisal Shahzad and a host of other recent, homegrown Islamic terrorists. For his troubles, in 2010, Awlaki became the first U.S. citizen to be placed on the CIA's target-for-assassination list.[43]

It was a stunning turn of events, considering that just eight years prior Awlaki had been an honored guest at U.S. government functions. In 2002, Awlaki conducted a prayer service at the U.S. Capitol for the Congressional Muslim Staffers Association.[44] If it unnerves you that an al-Qaeda terrorist with 9/11 links led prayers inside the U.S. Capitol just months after the attacks, consider this: Awlaki was also a guest at a Pentagon luncheon, again, just a few months after 9/11.[45] The fact that Awlaki had been interviewed by federal agents four times in the eight days following the 9/11 attacks apparently didn't raise any red flags among our military brass.[46] After all, Anwar al-Awlaki was a well-known local moderate and decidedly *mainstream*—at least, according to his resume.

However, by the time Awlaki was being feted around Washington in 2002, he had already blamed the 9/11 attacks on Israel, endorsed Palestinian terrorism against Israeli civilians, defended the Taliban, and referred to the 9/11 hijackers as "victims."[47] All this was public information, but conducting a quick Google search is apparently beyond the capabilities of Congress or the Pentagon.

Awlaki's facilitation of Islamic terrorism on U.S. soil stretches back at least to 2000. It was then, while serving as imam of a San Diego mosque, that he acted as "spiritual adviser" to two of the 9/11 hijackers, Nawaf al-Hazmi and Khalid al-Mihdhar, and held lengthy, closed-door meetings with the pair. Awlaki was also in contact with a third hijacker, Hani Hanjour, who visited al-Hazmi and al-Mihdhar frequently in San Diego. Unsurprisingly, members of the FBI and the 9/11 Commission, as well as participants in a Congressional inquiry, believe that Awlaki played a significant role in the 9/11 attacks.[48]

When Awlaki left San Diego for northern Virginia in 2001 to take over as imam of Dar al-Hijrah, al-Hazmi and Hanjour followed. The men rented an apartment not far from Falls Church and attended Awlaki's sermons at Dar al-Hijrah.[49] But not to worry: the mosque's Muslim Brotherhood-connected leaders to this day insist they had no idea back then about their popular young imam's terror ties or his fervent desire to destroy America.[50]

★   ★   ★

Although Awlaki left Falls Church in 2002, spending the obligatory (for jihadis) two years in London before settling in Yemen, he is still quite popular among northern Virginia's Muslim community—and not just over the Internet. I discovered this firsthand when I paid a visit to the largest Islamic supermarket in the Washington, D.C. area. That store, Halalco, is also located in Falls Church, about a mile from the Dar al-Hijrah mosque. But Halalco is much more than a supermarket. In addition to *halal* meat and various delicacies from the Middle East and South Asia, the store carries a large selection of Islamic books, recordings, and clothing. I received a tip from a federal law enforcement source in 2009 that among Halalco's titles were a litany of Muslim Brotherhood, anti-Semitic, and pro-jihad works. Sure enough, I found exactly that in multiple visits to the store over a period of months.

Books by revered Muslim Brotherhood ideologues Sayyid Qutb and Yusuf al-Qaradawi and by convicted terrorist Abu Hamza al-Masri could be found on the shelves, while an entire section of CDs was devoted to the sermons of Sheikh Khalid Yasin, an American-born, pro-terror cleric who has described the beliefs of Christians and Jews as "filth."[51] Halalco was also stocked with a number of anti-Semitic tracts, including *The Protocols of the Elders of Zion*, a notorious nineteenth-century forgery out of Tsarist Russia. Simply put, these are the types of books and recordings that provide a gateway into Islamic radicalism—and they're right at the fingertips of northern Virginia's large Muslim community, courtesy of Halalco. No wonder a number of young Muslims from that region—like the five described earlier in this chapter—have been arrested on terrorism charges since 9/11.

By May 2010, I had compiled enough radical materials at Halalco to produce an exposé for CBN News. As I entered the store, cameraman in tow, I was stopped dead in my tracks by a large display that I had not seen in my previous visits—shelves featuring dozens of CDs and DVDs by none other than Anwar al-Awlaki. Coincidentally or not, just one day before, Awlaki had released a video recording calling for the murder of American civilians.[52] Yet there I stood, staring at a prominent display of the al-Qaeda cleric's collected works, just a few miles from the White House.[53]

I grabbed one of the DVDs and asked a nervous-looking young clerk if I could speak with the store's owner. He disappeared for a few moments and returned with a middle-aged man who identified himself as a store manager. He eyed my colleague's video camera warily as I showed him the Awlaki DVD and asked for the owner. "I will check and see if he will talk to you," he said. "Come back tomorrow."

When we returned to Halalco the next day, the Awlaki display had been taken down. After telling us the owner had agreed to talk to us, the manager from the previous day disappeared to go find him. Fifteen minutes passed as my cameraman and I—the only ones not wearing Muslim garb among the dozens of people milling around the packed store—took in the usual hostile glares. Just as I began to wonder if we were being set up, an older man with short white hair and a flowing white beard came walking toward us, followed by the manager.

"Hello," said Abdul Mateen Chida with a nervous smile. "I am the owner of the store. Let's go into the other room and talk." The manager departed, and Chida led my cameraman and me into a small meeting room near the store's entrance. As we sat down across from each other at a table, I asked permission from Chida to record the interview. He consented, and I went to work.

"What happened to the big Anwar al-Awlaki display?" I asked. "It was just here yesterday, now it's gone."

Chida stammered that he had decided it was probably not a good idea to be hawking the wares of a wanted al-Qaeda terrorist who had just called for the murder of American civilians.

"So you just came to this realization yesterday?" I countered. "Awlaki has been in the news for months for his involvement in terrorism. Be honest: If I had never come in here and noticed that display, would it still be up?"

Chida hesitated for a moment then conceded, with a defeated look on his face, "It is possible." But he denied that exposure to the materials sold at Halalco could inspire young Muslims to commit violence. This contradicted the testimony of Awlaki himself, who said of the Muslim Brotherhood ideologue Sayyid Qutb's writings, which were also sold at Halalco, "Because of the flowing style of Sayyid I would read between 100 and 150 pages a day. I would be so immersed with the author I would feel Sayyid was with me ... speaking to me directly."[54]

Halalco's displaying of Awlaki's CDs and DVDs was comparable to, say, a German-American restaurant peddling the speeches of Nazi propagandist Josef Goebbels during World War II. Yet according to Chida, selling Awlaki's sermons was just a way to make a few bucks—after all, "They were very good sellers." To put it in perspective, that means that until CBN exposed Halalco, the recordings of a wanted al-Qaeda terrorist who has declared war on America were selling like hotcakes among northern Virginia's Muslim community—just minutes from Washington, D.C.

Mr. President, we have a problem.

★   ★   ★

In the course of my investigations, I've discovered that Islamist materials like those sold at Halalco are readily available in Islamic bookstores throughout the United States. Indeed, pop into your local Muslim shop in New York City, Los Angeles, Chicago, or Dearborn, Michigan, and you may be surprised at what you find. For our freaks and geeks, however, who are often a homebound, anti-social lot, nothing beats the convenience and anonymity of the Internet. How else can a homely white woman like Colleen LaRose, living in the rural suburbs of Philadelphia, communicate with jihadists around the world and become a terrorist recruiter?

The 46-year-old LaRose, blonde-haired and blue-eyed, is a far cry from the usual profile of an Islamic terrorist, at least on the surface. That fact, plus her U.S. citizenship and passport, was what made her so appealing to the jihadist movement. Going by the monikers "Jihad Jane" and "Fatima LaRose" in her online postings, LaRose is now in federal custody awaiting sentencing after pleading guilty to providing material support to terrorists and other charges. Specifically, she recruited men and women in the United States, Europe, and South Asia to "wage violent jihad," according to her indictment. She also solicited funds for terrorists online—where she frequently contributed jihadist videos and messages to YouTube and MySpace—and attempted to arrange the murder of Swedish artist Lars Vilks, who had drawn a picture depicting the Islamic prophet Mohammed's head on the body of a dog. With the encouragement of her online jihadi community, LaRose even traveled to Sweden herself to track Vilks in 2009.[55] In perhaps the least surprising nugget to emerge in LaRose's case, authorities have investigated whether there was a link between her and Anwar al-Awlaki.[56]

It's unclear when Jihad Jane, who stands 4-feet-11-inches tall and weighs barely over 100 pounds, converted to Islam. But she had a troubled past. At the age of sixteen, LaRose, a junior high dropout, was briefly married to a 32-year-old man. She divorced and remarried, only to see her second marriage dissolve after ten years.[57] During that time, she bounced around several Texas towns and was arrested for writing bad checks and driving while intoxicated.[58] She eventually ended up living with a boyfriend in Pennsylvania where, depressed over her father's death, she tried to commit suicide in 2005.[59] LaRose apparently buried herself in her computer not long after and became attracted to the jihadist cause online.

There, she made contact with another baggage-laden white woman who had drifted into the dark world of jihad. Jamie Paulin-Ramirez hailed from Leadville, Colorado, a tiny town in the Rocky Mountains where she worked as a medical assistant. By the time she was thirty-one years old, the tall, blue-eyed blonde had already been married four times and had a 6-year-old son who had no contact with his father. In spring 2009, Paulin-Ramirez, described by her mother as a "very insecure, unhappy person that was just looking for something to hang on to," announced to her family that she had converted to Islam.[60]

She began spending more time on the computer and dressing in full Muslim garb that covered everything but her eyes. Then suddenly she disappeared, along with her young son, whom she now called "Wahid." It seems that Colleen LaRose had invited Paulin-Ramirez online to join a terrorist training camp in Europe. Paulin-Ramirez agreed and traveled to Ireland, where she married an Algerian jihadi she'd met on the

Internet and became pregnant with his child. All this was no surprise to Paulin-Ramirez's brother, who later told a local television station, "Any man that came along in my sister's life, she kind of followed like a lost puppy."[61]

Unfortunately, her newest squeeze was also a terrorist. On March 10, 2010, he and Paulin-Ramirez, along with five others, were arrested by Irish police in connection with a plot to kill Lars Vilks, whom Colleen LaRose had also targeted. As of this writing, Paulin-Ramirez is awaiting sentencing after pleading guilty to conspiring to provide material support to terrorists.

★ ★ ★

The lesson driven home by the Jihad Jane and Jihad Jamie cases, along with many others, is that Islamic terrorists are doubling their efforts to recruit disaffected, vulnerable, and quite possibly, mentally unstable U.S. citizens via the Internet. If these troubled outcasts are, say, two white, blonde-haired women like LaRose and Paulin-Ramirez who are capable of slipping detection in Western countries, even better. Had they not been lured in by Islamic extremism, the "Jihadi Chicks" likely would have found some other form of excitement among the endless array of choices presented in cyberspace. But they and a growing number of others like them have been seduced by the message of jihad—suckered in by online sweet talk and a sense of belonging, then quickly radicalized.

With each new arrest of an American Muslim terrorist, the Obama administration warns the American people that there is a growing threat posed by homegrown "violent extremists." Yet the administration's main solution to this problem is reaching out to groups intimately connected to the Muslim Brotherhood, the world's preeminent Islamic supremacist group, in hopes they will be a moderating force in America's Muslim communities. This suicidal strategy involves allowing Brotherhood-linked elements to build more mosques, which will only serve to radicalize more American Muslims, especially impressionable recent converts. Indeed, other than pandering to the Brotherhood at home and other Islamist elements abroad and praising Islam at every available public opportunity, members of the Obama national security team are at a loss as to how to tackle the growing jihadist phenomenon.

Realistically, at the end of the day, there is probably little that can be done to prevent a downtrodden freak or geek from logging on to the Internet, stumbling upon a jihadist website, and being drawn in by an Anwar al-Awlaki sermon. The easy answer would be to continue to shut down jihadi websites wherever they are found, and to continue to monitor social networking sites like Facebook, MySpace, and YouTube, as well as online chat rooms, that are utilized by terrorist recruiters. The more difficult answer is that both Democratic and Republican lawmakers will have to take a long, hard look at why a religion they've branded as peaceful, tolerant, and loving seems to attract so many violent, intolerant, and hateful individuals.

CHAPTER SIX

LONDONISTAN: A CAUTIONARY TALE

I instantly decided not to sit by the window.

Saad al-Faqih—a man with suspected ties to Osama bin Laden and the global al-Qaeda network—had just informed me that he was being targeted in an assassination plot. And I was standing in his home.[1]

"You just missed the British authorities," al-Faqih casually mentioned to my cameraman Ian and me as he led us into his living room. "They had stopped here to warn me about a plan to kidnap and kill me. The Saudis are behind it. It's not the first time."

That would explain the "CCTV" signs dotting the exterior of al-Faqih's well-kept home, located in a quiet corner of northwest London. The signs were a warning to potential intruders that security cameras were monitoring their every move.

Al-Faqih had already informed us that, since we were with a Christian TV network, he would not appear on camera. Eying us suspiciously as we entered his home, he made clear from the outset that he was only speaking to us because a mutual contact had recommended us highly. The initial tension eventually eased, but not before al-Faqih left the room twice to make phone calls. As my colleague and I overheard him speaking animatedly in Arabic, I envisioned us in a starring role in an al-Qaeda snuff video. But during the course of our nearly two-hour conversation with al-Faqih, jihadi gunmen never did burst through the door—although, judging by what I'd seen in London up until that point, I can't say I would have been surprised if they had.

I'd gone there with the goal of interviewing the worst of the worst: the most notorious of the city's seemingly endless supply of Islamist ideologues. My intent, first and foremost, was to shine a light on the insanely permissive situation in the city that British writer Melanie Phillips has aptly dubbed "Londonistan," where wanted Islamic terrorists walk the streets as free men and even receive welfare benefits from the British government. Secondly, I wanted Britain's descent into jihadist madness and dhimmitude to serve as a cautionary tale for an American audience that was gradually seeing its own country move in the same suicidal direction under the Obama administration.

In Saad al-Faqih—who, according to the U.S. Treasury Department, has maintained associations with the al-Qaeda network since the mid-1990s and has had direct contact with Osama bin Laden[2]—I had found the perfect case study.

Given that we were guests in his home, al-Faqih's quick admission that he had been marked for death by the Saudis was certainly unnerving, yet not surprising. A former medical surgeon, the 54-year-old Saudi native now makes a living—on the Web and in media appearances—as one of the world's most outspoken critics of the House of Saud. Viewing the Saudi royal family as corrupt, insufficiently Islamic pawns of the West, al-Faqih wants to see the Saudis' radical Wahhabi regime deposed (by peaceful means, he insists) and replaced with an even more extreme Islamic government. The Saudi royals are none too fond of al-Faqih's activities, and have been pressuring Great Britain for years, unsuccessfully, to deport him back to Saudi Arabia—where his treatment, needless to say, would be a bit less hospitable than what he found in England.

"The Islamic state I envision for Saudi Arabia will not be like the Taliban," he told me over Arab tea in his sparsely furnished living room. "Saudi officials say our movement wants to take the country back to the seventh century. That is not true. We are pioneers of using modern technology."

A look of self-satisfaction crept across his face as he folded his legs Arabic-style beneath his traditional, one-piece dishdasha. "Our use of technology," he offered, "is much better than the Saudi government's.... We have informants at every level of the Saudi government."

At first glance, it would seem that al-Faqih's self-professed mastery of the Internet and Web networking has created more problems than benefits for him and his London-based group, the Movement for Islamic Reform in Arabia (MIRA). He was designated by both the United States and the United Nations as a global terrorist in 2004, in large part due to his operation of a website that, according to the U.S. Treasury Department, was utilized by Islamic extremists "to post al Qaida-related statements and images... intended to provide ideological and financial support to al-Qaida affiliated networks and potential recruits."[3]

Among the charges against Saad al-Faqih is that he paid for a satellite phone used by Osama bin Laden in the 1998 Africa embassy bombings. According to the PBS program *Frontline*, "Saad says he's never met bin Laden, but he is connected somehow. For one, the satellite telephone that bin Laden allegedly used to plan the Nairobi and Dar es Salaam bombings was purchased from a merchant in Columbus, Ohio, on Saad's own credit card."[4]

Al-Faqih became visibly irritated when discussing his terrorist designation in the United States with me, blaming it on the Saudi lobby in Washington, D.C. "Saudi agents put that material on the sites," he said of the al-Qaeda propaganda that was featured on his websites. "They would then call the media to tip them off. I challenge anyone to find a single sentence on my website that calls for or glorifies violence."

Yet prior to my meeting with al-Faqih, a trusted intelligence source that worked on the U.S. government's case against him confirmed to me that al-Faqih had direct links to al-Qaeda, characterizing the Saudi exile as "bad with a capital B." So when al-Faqih began to open up to me about the inner workings of the world's most notorious terrorist organization, I sat in rapt attention.

"Al-Qaeda consists of three circles," he began. "The first and central circle is made up of the real al-Qaeda team who have given homage to Osama bin Laden or other leaders." Foremost among this group, he explained, would be the members who have been with al-Qaeda since its beginnings in the late 1980s.

"Inside the second circle are those who have trained with al-Qaeda but have not formally been accepted into the organization," al-Faqih continued. "This group is bigger than the first circle." This would most likely mean jihadists who have trained with al-Qaeda in Pakistan or elsewhere and then returned to their native countries replete with new-found expertise in terrorist tactics.

The third and largest circle, according to al-Faqih, consists of Muslims who are "ready to join al-Qaeda and are looking for the means to enroll in the group." Those are the homegrown jihadis, the self-starters and lone wolves, who have no direct links to al-Qaeda but are inspired by the group and its message. As we've seen, there is no shortage of this sort on U.S. soil.

Al-Faqih believes al-Qaeda is the vanguard of Muslim resistance to the West and that there is no credible alternative to bin Laden and co. "as long as there is no movement in the middle that can satisfy the Muslim world's hunger for dignity" after years of supposed humiliation by America and its allies, especially Israel.

"There has been a failure of Muslim leaders to channel their people against America," al-Faqih told me. "But bin Laden has shown that he can do it."

He watched as I scribbled furiously in my notepad.

"There will always be new recruits," he said matter-of-factly. "Al-Qaeda's structure can never collapse."

The day before my meeting with al-Faqih, I had sat down with another wanted terrorist with links to that very al-Qaeda structure. I had obtained Yasser al-Sirri's mobile phone number from one of my European contacts and had called him a few days before leaving for London. At first, al-Sirri was highly suspicious. But after I mentioned the name of my contact, he agreed to meet with me, although he still sounded a bit reluctant. I had to chuckle to myself as I hung up the phone, seeing as my conversation with al-Sirri was likely monitored by intelligence agencies on both sides of the Atlantic. Like al-Faqih, al-Sirri was the "real deal"—a wanted Islamic terrorist with ties to leading al-Qaeda members.

An Egyptian exile, al-Sirri has lived in London since 1994. Like al-Faqih, he received asylum in Britain after fleeing his native country under threat of death. In Egypt, al-Sirri belonged to Islamic Jihad, a brutal terrorist organization that seeks to impose an Islamic state in Egypt and was led by al-Qaeda's second-in command, Ayman al-Zawahiri. In 1993, al-Sirri was found guilty of participating in a failed Islamic Jihad assassination attempt against Egypt's prime minister that resulted in the killing of a 12-year-old schoolgirl. Al-Sirri was sentenced to death in Egypt for this heinous act, yet he now walks the streets of London a free man and collects welfare benefits courtesy of the British taxpayer.

Al-Sirri runs a small operation in London called the Islamic Observation Centre that he uses to announce the latest al-Qaeda messages via his sources within the group. Like al-Faqih, he has refashioned himself as an expert "analyst" of al-Qaeda, and he is quoted from time to time in the British media pontificating about the latest developments in the global jihadist movement. Many suspect that al-Sirri's little operation has done much more, however, than just document the jihad for his Islamist echo chamber.

The British government locked al-Sirri up in 1999 on terrorism charges. He was soon released and then arrested again in 2001 for allegedly helping to set up the murder of Ahmad Shah Massoud, an Afghan anti-Taliban leader who was killed by two al-Qaeda suicide bombers days before the 9/11 attacks. Al-Sirri allegedly provided the two bombers with identification that named them as journalists, thus giving them access to Massoud. Inexplicably, a British judge later cleared al-Sirri of all charges and released him, labeling him "an innocent fall guy."[5]

Although the Brits seem content to let al-Sirri operate with impunity, U.S. officials still want to get their hands on the pint-sized terrorist. The United States, like Egypt, has been trying in vain to extradite al-Sirri from Britain for years.

In 2005, he was found guilty in a U.S. federal court of relaying illegal messages to the imprisoned terrorist leader Omar Abdel Rahman, the notorious "Blind Sheikh" who masterminded the 1993 World Trade Center bombing.[6] Rahman, a close associate of Osama bin Laden and Ayman al-Zawahiri, is currently serving a life sentence in a U.S. Supermax prison in Colorado.

Liberal British judges refuse to deport murderous jihadists like al-Sirri over fears that they will be tortured back home and—don't laugh—that their human rights will be violated. Why they won't extradite al-Sirri to the United States is anyone's guess; perhaps they're afraid he'll be subjected to 4,000 calories a day, cable TV, and Korans-on-demand at that awful Guantanamo Bay prison.

What is clear is that al-Sirri maintains close ties to some very dangerous men. So as my cameraman and I waited for him to arrive for our meeting at a hotel in West London, I wondered who he might bring along. Perhaps he would be joined by Abu Qatada, al-Qaeda's spiritual leader in Europe, who was granted asylum and welfare benefits in Great Britain and had been photographed with al-Sirri on a London street in 2008.[7]

Alas, al-Sirri showed up alone. Short, slightly built, and sporting a long beard dyed red with henna in the tradition of Islam's prophet, Mohammed, al-Sirri wore a Palestinian-style scarf, or keffiyeh, draped over his shoulders. His eyes scanned the hotel lobby nervously until I waved, and he approached us. Having assumed I was a print journalist, he had not realized our interview would be conducted before a TV camera. Nevertheless, as his eyes continued to dart around the room, he consented to sit down with me for an on-camera discussion. We adjourned to a small conference room in the hotel, and just like that, I had secured wanted terrorist Yasser al-Sirri's first appearance on a U.S. television network.

"The British government knows about my activities, my situation," al-Sirri told me. "Everything is clear and I have done nothing to break the law." Denying any wrongdoing, he blamed the British tabloid media for creating a false impression of him. He also, predictably, blamed America.

"Many times the American government uses the wrong people for spies or to get intelligence information," he claimed. "Some people do business with the FBI [or] CIA and give them wrong information and sometimes the wrong decision is made."

Speaking softly in halting English, al-Sirri did not make for great TV. I had read interviews with him from the 1990s and 2001 in which he quite openly supported jihad.[8] But as we sat together in 2010, he had clearly learned to speak more carefully, lest British officials suddenly wake up and deport him back to Egypt. The only time al-Sirri did get slightly animated during our discussion was in his criticism of the former Mubarak government in Egypt. But given my goal of exposing British negligence in the face of jihadism, my interview with al-Sirri—although he was no sound bite machine—served its purpose. When the interview aired on CBN a few weeks later, I was flooded with e-mails from irate viewers who expressed shock that men like al-Sirri and Saad al-Faqih were living freely in a country that is arguably America's closest ally.[9] I also appeared in a segment on FOX News in which Sean Hannity expressed outrage over what I found in London. He and many others asked, "What's wrong with the Brits?"

★ ★ ★

The answer to Sean's question is this: liberal permissiveness and social engineering have transformed Britain, and especially its capital, into

"Londonistan." During the massive wave of Islamic immigration that has flooded its shores over the past several decades, Britain became the go-to spot for asylum seekers from Muslim countries. British officials essentially welcomed men like al-Faqih and al-Sirri with open arms, and before long, wanted Islamic terrorists from across the Middle East and North Africa were living comfortably in London at British taxpayers' expense. Most simply continued their jihadist activities, confident that politically correct British authorities would not deport them back to places like Egypt and Jordan due to human rights concerns. The Brits' inaction outraged Middle Eastern governments, which were eager to get their hands on these enemies of the state.

"All of this happened under the assumption that if you allowed these people to operate in London, if you allowed them to do whatever they wanted to do, they would not be attacking Britain," terrorism analyst Peter Neumann told me as we sat in his London office. "The government, quite cynically, thought that whatever happened in other countries, whatever these people were plotting in other countries, was of no concern to the British government."

Essentially, Neumann was saying that Great Britain made a deal with the devil. And since the devil isn't known for keeping up his end of a bargain, it's no surprise Britain's unspoken accord with its growing jihadist subgroup did not last; it was irretrievably broken on July 7, 2005, when four British-born, al-Qaeda-linked terrorists murdered fifty-two people in a series of bombings against London's mass transit system, exposing the myopia of Great Britain's open-door policy for foreign jihadists.

"Only then did the policy change," said Neumann. "However, the seeds of the radical Islamists' activity had already been sown."

Indeed. In August 2006, London was the staging ground for a foiled al-Qaeda plot to blow up ten transatlantic airliners bound from Britain to the United States. Coming on the heels of the 2005 mass transit bombings, the '06 plot further convinced British law enforcement and intelligence officials that it was time to shift their focus from the Irish Republican Army to the internationally connected Islamic jihadists in their midst. They may have been too late. In 2008, Britain's then-Home Secretary declared that British intelligence was monitoring some 2,000 potential terrorists, as well as 200 radical Islamic networks and thirty active terrorist plots.[10]

Confronted with such a pervasive threat, British officials have made the occasional nod to "cracking down." They convicted extremist cleric Abu Hamza al-Masri on terrorism charges and deported one of his cohorts, Sheikh Omar Bakri Mohammed, to Lebanon—this only came after both men had spent years openly calling for the overthrow of the British government and the imposition of Islamic sharia law in the UK. Additionally, the aforementioned Abu Qatada currently sits in a London jail, awaiting deportation back to Jordan. So that's three down and literally thousands to go—and perhaps many more.

Britain's Muslim population has exploded over the past thirty years to the point where "Mohammed" is now the most popular name for male babies born in the country.[11] Seemingly every Islamic nation known to man has its own pocket in the British capital, from Turks to Iranians to Somalis to Bangladeshis and beyond. With the increased Muslim numbers have come rising demands that the British government—crippled by a suicidal mixture of political correctness, cultural self-hatred, and multiculturalist ideology—has been all too happy to oblige. Hence the surreal spectacle—captured on videotape in 2009—of thirty London police officers literally running away from a rampaging crowd of Muslim protestors at an anti-Israel rally. Screaming "Allahu Akhbar," the Muslims made verbal threats against the cowering officers while pursuing them for several city blocks.[12] It was a show of force that made abundantly clear who rules London's streets—and it ain't the bobbies.

As that incident showed, Islamists in Great Britain are supremely confident and carry about them an air of assurance that they will one day rule the land of Richard III and Winston Churchill. To that end,

Muslims have established enclaves in cities and towns across Great Britain where they have intentionally segregated themselves from the society at large. These are often no go-zones for police where sharia courts, not British Common Law, are the supreme legal authority.

Somehow, these alarming developments seem to have escaped the attention of most of Britain's political and media elites. More likely, it is willful blindness or outright acceptance of the new, Islamicized "normal." In 2008, the Archbishop of Canterbury—the head of the Church of England and Britain's leading spiritual authority—said that certain aspects of sharia law "seem unavoidable" in the UK.[13] He added that British Muslims could choose to have marital disputes or financial matters settled in a sharia court and declared that Muslims should not be faced with "the stark alternatives of cultural loyalty or state loyalty." In other words, Muslims should receive special considerations and treatment apart from British law. With people like Rowan Williams carrying the mantle for traditional British institutions, it's no wonder many Brits I've spoken to believe their country will be Islamic by the year 2050, or in the very least, will consist of fairly large swaths of self-governed Muslim territories.

Their reasoning is twofold. First, the unchecked flow of Muslim immigrants into Britain, along with their high birthrates, create an unstoppable demographic tidal wave. Many of these immigrants refuse to assimilate or to adjust to the un-Islamic ways of their new "infidel" land; and their intransigence is only encouraged by Britain's unofficial state religion, multiculturalism, which deems Western culture to be no better than any other culture, and typically much worse—even if the other culture includes female genital mutilation and honor killings.

This brings us to the second reason many Brits believe the black flag of Islam will one day replace the Cross of St. George and the Union Jack: the all-out, state-sanctioned assault on Britain's traditional values and Judeo-Christian heritage. Simply put, Christianity is on life support in today's ultra-secular, atheistic Britain, where weekly mosque-goers now outnumber church-goers. While police in London are busy fleeing from

Muslim street punks, an officer in Britain's second-largest city, Birmingham, threatened two Christian evangelists with arrest in 2008 for handing out pamphlets in a predominantly Muslim area, telling them that if they got beaten up by local Muslims, they deserved it.[14]

It's safe to say that Churchill, a fierce critic of Islam and a tireless champion of British values, would be turning in his grave at such news. Drunken hedonism, celebrity worship, militant secularism, and yes, Islam have replaced Christianity as the guiding lights of British civilization— and voices of resistance are few and far between. Two members of the House of Lords, Malcolm Pearson and Baroness Caroline Cox, bravely speak the truth about the Islamic threat, but both are over seventy years old, and there is not a single anti-Islamist voice on the political horizon today in Britain to replace them.

A prime example of the British political class's feckless, pandering approach to Islam is evident in a speech given by David Cameron, then Britain's newly christened prime minister, on Turkish soil in July 2010, just as Turkey's Islamist government was reorienting the country away from the West toward Iran and Syria. With Turkish prime minister Recep Tayyip Erdogan looking on approvingly, Cameron said he was "angry" that Turkey had still not been admitted to the European Union, blaming its exclusion on anti-Muslim bigotry. He went on to blast Israel and suggest that the Israelis—not Hamas—were turning Gaza into a "prison camp."[15]

This was just two months, mind you, after a state-sponsored Turkish organization had organized a flotilla full of left-wing radicals and Islamic terrorists who sailed to the Gaza Strip intending to provoke a confrontation with the Israeli Navy. When radio operators from the Israeli Navy warned one of the ships it was approaching a blockaded area, they were told in reply, "Shut up, go back to Auschwitz," and "We're helping Arabs go against the U.S. Don't forget 9/11, guys."[16] Later, when Israeli commandos boarded the ship after it repeatedly refused to turn around, they were violently attacked by a mob wielding pipes, metal poles, and chairs, with one Israeli being thrown over the side of the ship onto a lower deck.[17] The skirmish resulted in the deaths of nine Turkish jihadis, sparking an international outcry against Israel—yet again—for daring to defend itself. And the British prime minister somehow found this to be the perfect time to side with Islamists—on Muslim soil, no less—and pile on against the only democracy in the Middle East.

Is it any wonder that many indigenous Brits today are uninspired and even ashamed of their identity and their proud history? Lacking cultural confidence and intimidated into silence by a politically correct government that appeases Muslims at every turn, many Brits simply shrug with resignation as masses of Muslim immigrants arrive on their shores bearing religious zeal and an aggressive, clearly defined mission: to make sharia the law of the land.

One notable exception to this discouraging British passivity is the English Defense League, or EDL. I had dinner in London with leaders of the group, which formed in reaction to a March 2009 incident in which a parade honoring British troops returning from the Middle East was disrupted by jeering Muslim radicals who waved signs denouncing the soldiers as "butchers" and "cowards." The EDL is a multi-ethnic collection of average, working-class guys who oppose the Islamization of their neighborhoods and nation. They are staunchly pro-Israel, even waving Israeli flags at their rallies, and openly invite patriotic, non-jihadist Muslims to join their ranks. I think of the EDL as a smaller, British version of the American tea party movement—only instead of high taxes and big government, their focus is on turning back the Islamization of English society.

EDL members are mostly 9-to-5 family men who were largely non-political until they became fed up with the British government's not-so-silent complicity in the spread of Islamic sharia law and Islamism on the home front. They have held several large rallies that the British police seem incapable of protecting from violent counter-protests staged by the usual unholy alliance of radical leftists and Islamists. In a campaign familiar to American tea partiers, the EDL's leftist critics in British government and media circles brand them as "fascists" and "bigots," even as the group publicly welcome Jews (it has an entire Jewish Division),[18] blacks, and any other minorities who favor English legal norms over sharia law.

In meeting with three EDL leaders over dinner, I was struck by their down-to-earth, plainspoken nature. Salt-of-the-earth and working class through and through, these were the sort of guys I grew up with in northeast Philly, only with different accents. They were tough men with old-school common sense, and you could see how they would have little tolerance for today's sissified, pandering British elites. I was also impressed with their knowledge of jihad, sharia, and Islamic geopolitics—they had obviously done their homework on the topic and were not speaking out of blind hatred or ignorance, as their critics suggest. In fact, they were speaking out of personal experience.

The EDLers told me, matter-of-factly, how their town, Luton—about thirty miles north of London—has become a war zone. The town's large, radicalized Pakistani Muslim population is openly hostile to non-Muslims, as Pakistani gangs roam the streets and beat up infidels. These gangs also control the town's drug trade, according to the EDLers, and naïve English girls—some as young as thirteen—have fallen prey to their lavish clothes, smooth talk, and fancy cars. The nightmarish result has been the establishment of sex slave rings in which under-age English girls are routinely violated by Muslim men.[19] Because they're white, female, and non-Muslim, the victims are beneath contempt for their Islamic overlords and are treated as such.

In January 2011, Britain's *Daily Mail* published a shocking exposé on the sex slave rings, focusing on the authorities' reluctance to confront the depraved sex traffickers due to the officials' subservience to multiculturalism:

> Police and social services have been accused of fuelling a culture of silence which has allowed hundreds of young white girls to be exploited by Asian men for sex.
>
> Agencies have identified a long-term pattern of offending by gangs of men, predominantly from the British Pakistani

community, who have befriended and abused hundreds of vulnerable girls aged 11 to 16.

Experts claim the statistics represent a mere fraction of a "tidal wave" of offending in counties across the Midlands and the north of England which has been going on for more than a decade.

A senior officer at West Mercia police has called for an end to the "damaging taboo" connecting on-street grooming with race.

Detective Chief Inspector Alan Edwards said: "These girls are being passed around and used as meat.

"To stop this type of crime you need to start everyone talking about it but everyone's been too scared to address the ethnicity factor.

"No one wants to stand up and say that Pakistani guys in some parts of the country are recruiting young white girls and passing them around their relatives for sex, but we need to stop being worried about the racial complication."[20]

The EDL members told me a growing number of English girls in their town had converted to Islam and begun wearing the burqa-type full body coverings commonly found among Europe's Muslim women. Their husbands are, in many cases, polygamists who use the English girls strictly for child-rearing purposes. The EDLers went back and forth with each other for a few minutes, listing old female classmates and friends from the neighborhood—"good girls" who had been raised in traditional English homes, but were now estranged from their friends and families after converting to Islam and marrying Pakistani Muslims who forced them to cut all ties to their infidel pasts.

Anjem Choudary is no doubt smiling at these developments. If Londonistan has an unofficial symbol, then Choudary, a favorite of the British tabloids who's been called "Great Britain's most hated man," is certainly it. The leader of frequent rallies on London's streets calling for the death of non-Muslims, Choudary delivers his jihadi diatribes in a flawless English accent befitting his middle-class London upbringing.

A former beer-swilling, pot-smoking party boy in his college days at Southampton University (when, according to former classmates, he was known as "Andy" and took a liking to Christian girls), Choudary studied law and even qualified as a solicitor.[21] He now advocates forcefully for a different sort of law to be enforced throughout Great Britain: sharia. At some point after graduation, he began attending a London-area mosque, where he fell under the sway of the now-deported extremist cleric Omar Bakri Mohammed.

Choudary became Bakri Mohammed's right-hand man in leading the notorious Islamist group al-Muhajiroun which, along with its various offshoots like al-Ghurabaa, the Saved Sect, and Islam4UK, has been banned in Great Britain in recent years under the country's counterterrorism laws. With Bakri Mohammed now gone, Choudary has taken the reigns of what is left of al-Muhajiroun. His followers led an infamous 2006 rally in front of the Danish Embassy in London in which up to 300 frothing Islamists protested the publication of cartoons of Islam's prophet Mohammed in a Danish newspaper by waving placards that read, variously: "Butcher those who mock Islam," "Massacre those who insult Islam," "Prepare for the real Holocaust," and "Behead the one who insults the prophet." For good measure, they chanted, "UK you will pay, Islam is on its way," along with the standard guttural shouts of "Allahu Akhbar." London police, true to form, stood by and watched impotently as this jihadist rabble publicly called for the murder of British and Danish civilians. Several of the protestors were later sentenced to prison time for "inciting racial hatred,"[22] which is nice, except that their exhortations to murder had nothing to do with race and everything to do with religion—namely, Islam.

As I waited for him to arrive at the hotel for our interview, I had to wonder what it would take to see Anjem Choudary convicted on similar "hate speech" charges. Some of his greatest hits include calling for the execution of Pope Benedict and helping lead a group, al-Muhajiroun, that posted fliers around London extolling the 9/11 hijackers as "the Magnificent 19." As I was about to discover in our face-to-face meeting, his menacing pronouncements also targeted the British government.

Short, burly, and bespectacled, Choudary arrived along with three bearded friends who were dressed in exaggerated Islamic garb suggesting they had just raided Mullah Omar's closet. After some brief chatter, we got down to business in what would be an expansive, one-hour interview. Choudary has never met a camera he didn't like and was clearly in his element as we started rolling.

"Many people love the idea of jihad, you know?" he told me, as a smile crept across his face. "And they want to engage in it.... There is a huge amount of support [among British Muslims] for people like sheikh Osama bin Laden and Ayman al-Zawahiri."

Choudary himself openly supports bin Laden, referring to him with the honorific title "sheikh," and later in our interview, as "the emir of jihad." As for support for jihad among British Muslims—particularly the young—a steady stream of polls have borne out Choudary's point in the years since 9/11. One poll taken in 2008, for instance, showed that one-third of Muslim students at British universities believe that killing in the name of Islam is justified. [23]

Despite his incendiary rhetoric against the British state, Choudary maintained during our talk that his group is a "non-violent political and ideological movement" that has a "covenant of security" with the British government, meaning they supposedly would not carry out attacks on British soil. Yet several former members have been convicted on terrorism charges. Peter Neumann, the London-based terrorism expert, said Choudary's group serves as a sort of conveyor belt for terrorism whose extreme teachings lead a young Muslim right to the edge of violence— with many choosing to make the short jump into armed jihad.

"A very significant amount of former al-Muhajiroun people were involved in terrorist plots against this country," Neumann told me.

"A number of people have actually gone to Afghanistan, joined the Taliban, and died fighting for the Taliban."

Thus, it came as no surprise that during our interview Choudary refused to condemn the 9/11 attacks or the July 7, 2005 London bombings.

"For the people who carried it out, it was legitimate," he said of the London attacks, which saw fifty-two people slaughtered by four home-grown Islamic terrorists. "If you look at the will of [7/7 bombers] Mohammad Sidique Khan and Shehzad Tanweer, they would be justified. And there are many verses from the Koran and many statements to say that's the Islamic argument. And that is a difficult Islamic argument to refute. And there are many scholars who support that argument as well."

Khan and Tanweer both made their way to Pakistan's tribal regions prior to the bombings, where they likely met with members of al-Qaeda's hierarchy.[24] They were among the some 400,000 Brits of Pakistani origin who travel to their ancestral homeland each year, ostensibly to visit relatives or friends. On the way to grandma's house in Lahore, a growing number of these British citizens take a detour into Pakistan's tribal regions, where they train with al-Qaeda before returning to Britain as well-trained, committed jihadists.[25]

Choudary assured me that he doesn't recommend jihad on British soil for now (after all, the government provides his welfare benefits), but he quickly added that "there are many youth out there who do contact us and do come to our talks and they have other ideas. And we can make sure that those energies are channeled through discussion, dialogue, interaction. But if you take us out of the picture, then you have a very volatile situation."

He delivered these statements in deadpan fashion, gazing directly at me, as he did throughout the interview.

"Some in the British government might consider that a threat," I replied.

"It's not a threat," he countered. "It's a warning. It's a reality check."

The U.S. government, for one, has received the message, and U.S. intelligence sources have told me off the record that Britain's radical

Muslims may be our greatest security threat, due in part to a program that enables them to travel to the United States without a visa. This needs to change, fast. Indeed, no fewer than twenty-eight countries have suffered attacks at the hands of Britain-based jihadists over the past several years, solidifying the country's status as Mecca West for Islamists.[26]

At the end of the day, hurting feelings at 10 Downing Street beats seeing American civilians get blown up. Besides, British officials have no one to blame but themselves for fostering this untenable situation—not that Choudary appreciates their craven, kowtowing behavior.

"I think that the British government is sitting on a tinderbox, you know, full of dynamite," he told me. "And they have the matches in their hand and they're being very flippant. They're not dealing with it properly. It could all blow up in their face and it could be a very vicious situation."

It wasn't hard to read between the lines: if the British government dared arrest Choudary or harass his followers, there would be hell to pay. Despite his clever wording, these were clearly threats against the British state. As he rose to leave, Choudary, perhaps fearing he had spoken too freely, looked me over for a moment.

"I know you'll be passing this tape on to the intelligence services here," he said, heading for the door. "I'll look forward to seeing your story when it airs."

I never showed the tape of our interview to anyone before it aired on CBN. But I'll wager I could have showed it to the entire British Parliament, the directors of the BBC, and the Queen herself, and it still wouldn't have affected Choudary's freedom one iota.

★　★　★

Great Britain, as we've come to know it, is on life support. The heady days of the "stiff upper lip," when the Brits carried the banner for advancing Judeo-Christian, Western civilization to the ends of the earth, have passed away, never to return. Despite his woeful record of groveling to the Islamic world, Prime Minister Cameron made headlines in early 2011 for proclaiming British multiculturalism a failure. While he perhaps deserves some kudos for stating the obvious, his declaration—even if, improbably, it led to meaningful action—comes too late. What's left of Britain today is a spiritually dark place that's on course for pseudo-Third World social unrest and widespread religious and ethnic strife in the not-so-distant future. An overwhelming chunk of this social and cultural decay has been driven by Islam's rapid, aggressive ascent in the country over the past four decades.

For the American observer of the decline and fall of the British state, there are lessons to be learned to ensure the United States does not meet a similar fate. Unfortunately, those lessons are being ignored by the U.S. government, and the Brits' mistakes are being repeated here. Let us count the ways:

- A steady increase in Muslim immigration and refugee resettlement, along with the inevitable mosque-building campaigns and calls for special preferences and sharia compliance.
- The establishment of self-isolating, insular Islamic enclaves—Dearbornistan, anyone?
- Government promotion of increasingly vocal and influential Islamist organizations like CAIR and ISNA.
- Islam's expansion out of the major cities and into the heartland and small towns.
- Government policies that favor Muslim states and castigate Israel.
- Unrelenting political correctness and emerging speech codes—driven by political and media elites—regarding all things Islam.
- The potential for hardened Islamic terrorists to be released onto U.S. streets if the Obama administration cannot achieve its plans to hold civilian trials for foreign jihadists

and to close Guantanamo Bay prison. Judging by the
Obamis' track record, you can bet it won't.

- A loss of Judeo-Christian identity. This is encouraged by
  President Obama, who never misses a chance to remind
  Americans that we do not live in a Judeo-Christian
  nation—statistics and history be damned.

- A descent into cultural hedonism and depravity, and the
  systematic trashing of America's traditions, heroes, and
  history. No news flash here. Flip on the TV, pick up a
  newspaper, or better yet, flip through your child's public-
  school history textbook.

All of the above also unfolded in Great Britain. Now Anjem Choudary
and others like him eagerly await the day when they will preside as
judge, jury, and executioner in Islamic courts on British soil.

★ ★ ★

The terrorist had called me a taxi, which now sat idle outside Saad
al-Faqih's house waiting to zip me to the other side of London and my
interview with Anjem Choudary. But as al-Faqih led me to the door, I
had one more question to ask: where was this civilizational conflict
between the West and the Muslim world heading over the next few years?

Without hesitation, he gave me an unnerving answer: "No matter
what Muslim leaders do, there will be more friction with the West—
regardless of al-Qaeda. There will be more confrontation between the
West and Muslims, with attacks even bigger than in 2001."

Attacks bigger than 9/11—and this was straight from the mouth of
a man who reportedly has direct links to al-Qaeda's hierarchy.

CHAPTER SEVEN

EMBOLDENING IRAN: HELLO, MAHDI

The president of the United States shook the terrorist's hand.

Cameras flashed. Onlookers gasped. Security contingents for both sides pressed in tightly, seemingly as shocked as everyone else standing in the lobby of the United Nations building that U.S. president Barack Obama and Iranian president Mahmoud Ahmadinejad were clasping hands. Although both men had been invited to address the UN General Assembly only two hours apart, no one expected they would actually come face to face. Ever since Ahmadinejad had assumed power in 2005, handlers for both George W. Bush and Barack Obama had taken great pains during the General Assembly to avoid any random meetings between the leader of the free world and the Holocaust-denying public face of the world's most dangerous rogue regime.

No U.S. president had spoken in person with an Iranian leader since Ayatollah Khomeini's Islamic Revolution deposed the Shah in 1979. And the effects of Iran's recent, successful nuclear test—an act that completely blindsided U.S. intelligence agencies, which predicted the Iranians would not have such a capability until 2015 at least—were still reverberating throughout the world. So was Ahmadinejad's pronouncement that Iran's newfound status as a nuclear power meant that the destruction of Israel and America, and the return of the Shiite Twelfth Imam, or Mahdi, would occur "in the next eighteen months." Each day, large rallies in Tehran featured speakers trumpeting that Allah had granted the forces of Islam a mighty victory over the West, with Supreme Leader Khamenei publicly giving his blessing to the Iranian bomb in order to dispel any doubt as to whether nuclear weapons were "Islamically correct." Even secular Iranians who detested the regime were caught up in the spectacle, seeing Iran's membership in the exclusive nuclear club as a source of pride—finally, the great Persian nation that ruled much of the known world under Cyrus and Xerxes had reassumed its rightful position as a global force.

The news had the opposite effect in Washington, D.C. and European capitals, where panicked leaders had assumed they had at least two or three more years of diplomatic maneuvering to try and dissuade the mad mullahs from acquiring the bomb. After all, the "Stuxnet" computer worm that had attacked Iran's nuclear installations in 2010—and which was likely a joint cyber-creation of the United States and Israel—had, by many accounts, set back Iran's drive for nuclear weapons considerably. And U.S.-led economic sanctions were biting the average Iranian enough that some observers expected the eruption of another bout of massive civil unrest against the regime. It seemed everything was going the West's way, without a shot being fired. Then came the nuclear test, and the stunning revelation that Iran had weathered the Stuxnet-and-sanctions storm by plugging away at two secret nuclear installations, one carved into the side of a mountain in the deserts of central Iran and the other buried deep beneath the ground in a fortified bunker near the country's eastern border. The end result was that the Iranians, who are believed to have created the game of chess over 2,000 years ago, had outwitted the West and emerged victorious in the two sides' long-running nuclear chess match.

Now all of Israel was in an uproar, with talk of an impending second Holocaust saturating the Knesset and the airwaves. Indeed, Hezbollah,

Hamas, and Syria, emboldened by their Iranian patron's nuclear trump card, rattled their sabers toward Israel and boasted of the imminent demise of the "Zionist cancer." Accordingly, each day brought an increased number of rockets launched out of Gaza and southern Lebanon targeting Israeli towns and cities.

In Sunni Arab countries like Egypt, Saudi Arabia, and Jordan, newly installed revolutionary governments and the old monarchies alike were offering conciliatory words to the Iranian regime in public, but behind the scenes they were in a state of complete chaos, petrified at the nuclear-armed, Shia hegemon in their midst and working feverishly to acquire their own nuclear deterrents. Although Iran's benefactors in China and Russia urged restraint and declared their confidence that Iran would wield its nuclear arsenal "responsibly," rumors were circulating that the United States, Europe, and Israel were planning a joint operation to neutralize Iran's nuclear weapons stockpile, estimated to consist at that point of only three or four bombs.

However, anonymous sources within the Obama administration had leaked information to the *New York Times* and *Washington Post* that seemed to suggest otherwise. The message relayed by these insiders was that the administration was confident it could contain a nuclear Iran. "We'll provide a nuclear umbrella for the Sunnis and for Israel like we did for Europe for half a century with the Soviets," one administration official told the *Times*. "Don't be fooled by the Iranians' bluster. At the end of the day, they're rational actors who won't jeopardize their regime by using a nuclear weapon. It's just an insurance policy for them, not a means to jump-start some sort of Islamic Apocalypse, like voices on the right would have us believe. That kind of paranoia is not helpful as we try to engage the Iranians and learn their intentions here."

Despite the comforting leaks emanating from White House officials and their reassurances on the Sunday morning talk shows, the American public was fixated on the Iranian threat with an intensity unseen since the Iranian hostage crisis thirty years earlier. News clips aired daily of

Ahmadinejad promising "the coming end of the American aggressor" before mass rallies in Tehran. In one event, he was joined by his close ally, the Venezuelan despot Hugo Chavez, who was rumored to be working on a nuclear program of his own in America's backyard, with Russian, Iranian, and North Korean help.

Meanwhile, commentators duked it out nightly on cable news shows over what should be done about nuclear Iran, with prominent voices on the Left urging a summit between Obama and Khameini, and denouncing Americans' outcry against Iranian nukes as "anti-Muslim bigotry." American Islamist groups like CAIR took that memo and ran with it, appearing *ad nauseum* on cable news and in the mainstream press to complain of the naked "Islamophobia" being displayed toward an Iranian regime "that has not attacked anyone." Their common refrain: "Why is Israel allowed to have nuclear weapons and Iran is not? Israel has attacked its neighbors. Iran has not. Who is the bigger threat?"

In short, the world seemed on the brink of war, and the American people—a majority of whom, polls showed, favored a preemptive strike against Iran—were demanding that Washington show some leadership and take a strong public stand against the Iranian regime. So, too, were the governments of Europe and Israel.

Yet there stood President Obama at the UN, sharing a cordial moment with Mahmoud Ahmadinejad in front of the entire world. The Iranian tyrant smiled as he spoke a few words to the much taller Obama, who nodded as he leaned in to listen. Obama then stepped back and gave Ahmadinejad a few words in return, followed by a pat on the shoulder, just as he had done with Hugo Chavez during a similar encounter in 2009. And then it was over. Both sides went their own way, closely shielded by their security teams, as cameras continued to flash and reporters yelled out questions in vain.

The encounter lasted all of thirty seconds, but its aftershocks reverberated throughout the world, with Israel and the Sunni Arab states particularly disheartened. It was, in their eyes, and in the eyes of the president's conservative critics stateside, a show of unforgiveable appease-ment and weakness in the face of a bullying, genocidal dictatorship.

Some suggested the brief meeting wasn't a coincidence at all, and that Obama had planned to "accidentally" bump into Ahmadinejad in order to cool tensions and extend yet another olive branch to the Iranian regime. If that was indeed the strategy, it failed miserably. Just minutes after Ahmadinejad's brief chat with Obama, he took to the UN stage and delivered a blistering tirade against the United States and Israel that frequently invoked Islamic apocalyptic prophecies. He also offered to share nuclear technology and provide an "Islamic nuclear umbrella" to any Muslim nation that was interested.

Although White House spokesmen attempted to frame "The Shake," as it became known, as a thawing out moment of Reagan/Gorbachev proportions, polls showed that 80 percent of Americans strongly disap-proved of it. As for Ahmadinejad, he and Iran's Supreme Leader were maximizing the propaganda value of the encounter, boasting that the head of the world's most powerful nation had come crawling before the might of a nuclear Iran. "Now that we have the world's ultimate weapon," Ahmadinejad proclaimed, "the Americans are our dogs, and we are their master. Islam, too, is their master, and it will soon be master of the whole world."

★ ★ ★

The scenario I've just outlined is fictional—for now. Come 2012 or 2013, it may prove quite prescient. If so, it would signal that the global struggle against Islamic jihadists is lost—period. If Iran, the world's lead-ing state sponsor of Islamic terrorism, acquires the deadliest weapons known to mankind, the whole game changes. Think about it—the Ira-nian regime is the chief benefactor of the terrorist groups Hezbollah, Hamas, and Palestinian Islamic Jihad. It funds the Taliban in Afghanistan and Shiite militias in Iraq and Yemen. In addition, Syria, and increasingly Sudan, are virtually Iranian client states. How will all these well-armed jihadist (or in Syria's case, fascist) entities behave once they are covered by an Iranian nuclear umbrella?

Take Hezbollah, for instance—an Iranian-created paramilitary force that has global reach, including a presence on U.S. soil, as we'll see shortly. Suppose, God forbid, a group of Hezbollah operatives—at Iran's behest— blow up a few select buildings in New York City. The explosives used in the attack are later traced back to Iran. Does the United States hesitate to strike back for fear of an Iranian nuclear response? It's true that Iran does not yet possess an ICBM capability, as far as we know, that would enable it to reach the United States with a nuclear-tipped weapon of mass destruction. But U.S. officials estimate Iran will indeed have ICBMs by 2015,[1] and in the meantime, Russia and China are no doubt glad to share such technology with their Iranian ally to help it get there even sooner.

U.S. officials are also well aware Iran has conducted missile tests in the Caspian Sea that mirror the technique used in an electromagnetic pulse, or EMP, attack. In such a scenario, a nuclear weapon would be fired into the atmosphere and detonated above a country like the United States. The ensuing blast would give off powerful electromagnetic pulses that would fry America's entire electrical grid, sending the world's most powerful and technologically advanced nation back to the 1800s in one fell swoop. Congressional hearings have warned about the threat posed by an EMP attack, but little has been done to harden the nation's infrastructure to guard against such a catastrophe. It's not difficult to imagine an unmarked Iranian ship positioning itself a few hundred miles off America's Atlantic coast and firing a nuclear-tipped missile from its platform and into the atmosphere above New York City or Washington, D.C. The ship would then be immediately destroyed, and the Iranian jihadists aboard would "martyr" themselves, without a trace left behind—meaning plausible deniability.

Is the Obama administration even discussing such a doomsday possibility in its national security briefings and meetings? EMP may sound like science fiction, but it is, in fact, a very real threat, as any credible national security expert will attest. As discussions and debate over what to do about Iran's nuclear weapons program intensify, shouldn't Americans be informed about the whole host of dangers, like EMP, that a nuclear-armed Iran would pose?

Rest assured, Israelis are having this conversation on a daily basis. Could Israel still retaliate against Hamas and Hezbollah missile attacks if Iran threatened to intervene with nuclear weapons to defend its proxies? Or perhaps Iran would simply share its nuclear arsenal with said terror groups and have them do the dirty work. Israel's Ambassador to the United States, Michael Oren, told me during an interview in May 2010 that it is "a working assumption of the state of Israel" that Iran may do just that.

Here's another question: would Iran be willing to share its nukes with al-Qaeda? Why not? Al-Qaeda has long been hungry to acquire nuclear weapons, and as the two sides have shown in the past, they can easily overcome the Sunni-Shia divide and work together toward their common goal of eliminating America and Israel from the map. When it comes to jihadi cooperation against Christians and Jews, the old adage "the enemy of my enemy is my friend" is the order of the day.

★ ★ ★

As for that hypothetical handshake between Obama and Ahmadinejad, consider our president's list of photo-ops with repressive, anti-American dictators since assuming office in January 2009:

• During the 2009 G8 Summit in Italy, Obama became the first U.S. president to shake hands and exchange pleasantries with Libyan dictator Moammar Ghaddafi.[2] Ghaddafi, who was once the target of airstrikes during the Reagan administration, was responsible for the 1988 bombing of Pan Am Flight 103, which killed 270 people, including 190 Americans. He also orchestrated the 1986 bombing of a Berlin discotheque that killed an American soldier and wounded 63 more. Having presided over the 1996 massacre of 1,200 Libyan prisoners who had protested their living conditions, Ghaddafi is, at the time of this writing, occupying himself slaughtering his own people who have risen in revolt against his 40-plus-year tyranny.

• At the 2009 Summit of the Americas in Trinidad, Obama engaged in a grip-and-grin with Venezuela's socialist demagogue, Hugo Chavez. For a guy who has systematically destroyed Venezuelan democracy and who once called America "the most savage, cruel, and murderous empire that has existed in the history of the world,"[3] Chavez was treated awfully warmly when he ran into Obama. Obama approached Chavez—not the other way around—shook his hand, was photographed sharing a laugh, and later, engaged in private conversation with the staunch Iranian ally.[4] He also accepted a "gift" from Chavez in the form of a notoriously anti-American book, an act Obama later called "a nice gesture."

Obama glibly dismissed criticism of his meeting with Chavez, remarking, "It's unlikely that as a consequence of me shaking hands or having a polite conversation with Mr. Chavez that we are endangering the strategic interests of the United States."[5] As we'll see shortly, that assumption is dangerously wrong.

• Obama bowed not only to the King of Saudi Arabia, but also broke out a weird, half-bow in April 2010 for Chinese dictator Hu Jintao as they met at a Nuclear Security Summit in Washington.[6] I'd also mention Obama's full-on, he-must-have-dropped-a-contact-lens bow to the Emperor of Japan in November 2009, but hey, Japan is only a former enemy, not a current one.[7]

"C'mon Stakelbeck," you might say, "Chavez is just a clown. As for Ghaddafi, he's washed up, and it was the Bush administration, not Obama, that normalized relations with him. Oh, and the bows were just signs of inexperience early on. Ahmadinejad is a whole different story. There's not a snowball's chance that Obama would be caught dead in the same room with that Holocaust-denying madman, let alone shake his hand."

My reply? How soon you forget. As far back as July 2007, during the Democratic primaries, then-Senator Obama declared that, if elected president, he would indeed meet with Ahmadinejad—without precondi-tions. He did not back down from that stance when pressed in the ensu-ing months—convinced, no doubt, that by the sheer force of his own dazzling charisma, he could talk the Iranians out of their genocidal pretentions.[8]

Eventually it became apparent that Obama was going to win the Democratic nomination, and the mainstream press decided it would no longer be prudent to ask their man difficult questions about pesky dis-tractions like national security. So the president-to-be was no longer pressed about a potential tête-à-tête with Ahmadinejad. Turns out it wasn't necessary. The Obama administration's repeated, cringe-worthy attempts to engage in dialogue with the world's leading state sponsor of terrorism have told us all we need to know.

• In March 2009, on the occasion of Iran's annual New Year's celebration known as Nowruz, Obama sent a video greeting called "A New Year, A New Beginning" to the "people and leaders of the Islamic Republic of Iran."[9] By referring to Iran as an Islamic Republic, which he did twice during his stunningly naïve, 600-word ode to engagement, Obama sent a clear signal that the United States, under his watch, was fully prepared to co-exist with the current regime. Any threat of regime change, any promotion of Iranian democracy, was now officially off the table. In other words, "Rest easy, mullahs—continue to develop nuclear weapons, sponsor terrorism, menace Israel, jail non-Muslims, and crack the skulls of democratic activists. We will not stand in your way."

After some years of nervousness during the presidency of George W. Bush, when regime change was an option at least being considered in Washington, the Iranian terror masters viewed Obama's use of the term "Islamic Republic" as a sign they were now safe. America, under the Obama administration, respected the Iranian regime and would accept Ahmadinejad and the mullahs as the legitimate government of Iran. A new beginning, indeed—at least for the United States. Following Obama's deferential video address, Iran's Supreme Leader, Ayatollah Ali

Khamenei, publicly rejected The Great Healer's plea for dialogue, declaring he'd seen no evidence of a positive change in U.S. policy toward Iran.[10] Undaunted, Obama once again sent Nowruz greetings to the "Islamic Republic of Iran" in March 2010, reminding the regime that his "offer of comprehensive diplomatic contacts and dialogue stands." And once again, he ended up with egg on his face when his outreach efforts were denounced by Khamenei, who accused the United States of plotting to attack Iran.[11]

• In June 2009, as mass protests raged in cities across Iran following the fraudulent reelection of Mahmoud Ahmadinejad to the Iranian presidency, it seemed that the Islamic regime's 30-year reign of terror may be coming to an end. The protests, which became known as the Green Revolution, saw millions of Iranians take to the streets over a period of several weeks in a show of civil unrest the likes of which had not been seen in Iran since the 1979 Islamic Revolution. Many demanded a recount that would see opposition candidate Mir-Hossein Mousavi, who was widely viewed as the real winner in the tainted election, unseat Ahmadinejad as president.

The mullahs reacted to the protests in typically brutal fashion, sending their plainclothes *Basij* goon squads to beat, arrest, and murder protestors in horrifying scenes that were broadcast throughout the world. The Iranian people were literally dying in the streets for a chance at democracy. This was not the Egyptian uprising of 2011, when the most likely candidate to replace the strongman Hosni Mubarak was a much worse alternative, the Muslim Brotherhood. In the case of Iran, *nothing* could be worse than the mullahs.

As events unfolded and the Iranian regime's atrocities grew worse, I received daily reports from Iranian dissidents and pro-democracy activists in Tehran. At some point during the course of every conversation, my Iranian contacts all asked the same question, in a tone of utter desperation: "Where is Obama?" They were expecting the so-called leader of the free world to make a strong and unequivocal public statement in support of the protestors and to condemn the Iranian regime for its bloody crackdown. In essence, what they wanted—and fully anticipated—from a sitting American president as they stood up to tyranny was something along the lines of "Mr. Gorbachev, tear down this wall," or "Ich bin ein Berliner." Instead, from President Obama, they got this:

> It's not productive, given the history of U.S.-Iranian relations, to be seen as meddling ... in Iranian elections. ... [W]hen I see violence directed at peaceful protesters, when I see peaceful dissent being suppressed ... it is of concern to me and it is of concern to the American people. That is not how governments should interact with their people, and it is my hope the Iranian people will make the right steps in order for them to be able to express their voices.[12]

The world's most dangerous regime, an avowed enemy of the United States, was teetering on the brink of collapse—and we didn't want to *meddle*? Mind you, no one was expecting American boots on the ground in Tehran. There are many ways a U.S. administration can back a courageous, fledgling democracy movement, both publicly and behind the scenes: think of Ronald Reagan's support for Lech Walesa's Solidarity movement in Communist Poland during the 1980s. That was the kind of "meddling" that won the Cold War.

A few emphatic statements by Obama in support of the Iranian people early on in the protests, an influx of funds to Iranian pro-democracy leaders on the ground, stepped up activities by U.S. agents inside the country: all of these could have possibly helped tip the scales decisively against the regime—or perhaps they wouldn't have. You can never know in such situations unless you act boldly, like a true leader should, and *give it a try*. What about a joint statement released by Obama along with the leaders of Germany, Great Britain, and France presenting a united front in support of the Iranian people? Something. *Anything*.

On June 18, 2009, some 1 million Iranians took to the streets of Tehran to protest the Islamic regime.[13] In a brutally repressive country with one of the most fearsome intelligence apparatuses in the world, it was an earth-shattering moment. But we didn't want to meddle, and so a potentially historic opportunity for a free Iran was lost. The Iranian regime eventually restored order, tightened its grip, and returned to its familiar pattern of developing nuclear weapons and threatening Israel and the West.

Compare Obama's deafening silence during the Iranian uprising to his loud praise for the Egyptian revolution in February 2011, in which a staunch opponent of Islamic jihadism, Hosni Mubarak, was forced to resign as Egyptian president. It was universally acknowledged at the time that the group with the most to gain from Mubarak's ouster was the powerful, well-organized Egyptian Muslim Brotherhood. Yet Obama helped push Mubarak—a longtime U.S. ally, albeit an unsavory one—out the door anyway, setting up a situation where Egypt, the most populous and influential Arab nation, may very well fall into the Brotherhood's radical hands in the not-too-distant future. In short, the Obama administration had no qualms about "meddling" in the affairs of Egypt, bolstering Islamists in the process. But the Obamis just couldn't bring themselves to do the same with an arch-enemy like Iran.

Then-White House spokesman Robert Gibbs added insult to injury shortly after the Iranian protests died down by referring to Ahmadinejad as "the elected leader of Iran."[14] Gibbs later tried to backtrack, but his comment was logical enough in light of his boss's reference to Iran as an "Islamic Republic." A few years ago, a statue of Ronald Reagan was erected in Warsaw to honor his unyielding support for Poland in its fight against Communism. It's safe to say that when Iran's regime finally does fall, busts of Barack Obama won't be coming to Tehran.

• In December 2009, at a security conference in Bahrain, Secretary of State Hillary Clinton was snubbed not once, but twice, when she attempted to speak to Iran's foreign minister, Manouchehr Mottaki. Clinton apparently chased after Motakki both inside and outside a gala dinner held during the conference in a futile attempt to get him to acknowledge her. That's right: an American secretary of state pursued an official from Iran, an illegitimate, terrorist regime, and was rebuffed. Twice. In front of other world leaders and diplomats. Apparently, the "new beginning" in U.S.-Iranian relations envisioned by the Obama administration includes lots of groveling and public embarrassment for U.S. officials. Clinton's Mottaki debacle was later recounted in *Foreign Policy* magazine:

> Clinton's first attempt came just as the dinner ended. All the leaders sitting at the head table were shaking each other's hands. Mottaki was shaking hands with Jordan's King Abdullah II when Clinton called out to him.
>
> "As I was leaving and they were telling me, 'Hurry up, you have to get to the plane,' I got up to leave and he was sitting several seats down from me and he was shaking people's hands, and he saw me and he stopped and began to turn away," Clinton told reporters on the plane ride home.
>
> "And I said, 'Hello, minister!' And he just turned away," said Clinton, adding that Mottaki seemed to mutter something in Farsi but was clearly trying to avoid her.
>
> ...The *next* attempt by Clinton came outside the conference space, in the driveway while both leaders were waiting for their motorcades to pull up. Again, Clinton called out to Mottaki with a greeting and again, Mottaki refused to respond.[15]

If Clinton's experience was any indicator, an encounter between Obama and Ahmadinejad at the UN may not consist of a handshake, but rather the president of the United States playing a game of pin-the-tail-on-the-tyrant.

• Although Iran is directly assisting in the murder of U.S. troops in Afghanistan (not to mention Iraq), President Obama told a gathering of journalists in August 2010 that the Iranians "could be a constructive partner" in creating a stable Afghan nation, and as such, should be involved in any regional talks on the matter. He added that the United States and Iran have a "mutual interest" in fighting the Taliban.[16] As noted by Stephen Hayes and Thomas Joscelyn at the *Weekly Standard*, on the very same day that Obama argued for an Iranian role in Afghanistan's future, "in the Farah province, which shares a border with Iran, Afghan and Coalition forces killed two Taliban facilitators of foreign fighters—each carrying automatic weapons and large amounts of Iranian money. Colonel Rafael Torres, a Coalition spokesman, noted that ongoing external support for the Taliban 'only brings instability and peril to the Afghan people.'"[17]

A hint about which "external" force Colonel Torres was referring to: it starts with an "I" and ends with an "N." As Hayes and Joscelyn described in their piece, the incident in Farah province provided just a small glimpse of what Iran is up to in Afghanistan—not opposing the Taliban, as Obama suggested, but directly assisting them:

> Documents released as part of the Wikileaks dump show that U.S. commanders receive regular reports of collusion between the Iranians, al Qaeda, the Taliban, and the Hezb-e-Islami Gulbuddin (HIG) Islamist group. The Iranians arm, train, shelter, and fund the jihadists.
>
> A February 7, 2005, threat report describes how the "Iranian Intelligence agencies brought 10 million Afghanis (approximately $212,800)" into Afghanistan to fund jihadists. A February 18, 2005, report says that a group of Taliban leaders living in Iran are orchestrating attacks against Coalition forces: "The Iranian government has offered each member of the group 100,000 Rupees ($1,740) for any [Afghan] soldier killed and 200,000 Rupees ($3,481) for any [government] official." A June 3, 2006, threat report says that two Iranian agents "are helping HIG and [Taliban] members in

carrying out terrorist attacks against the AFG governmental authorities and the [coalition force] members, especially against the American forces."

...A September 2008 threat report says that a group of Arabs tied to one of Osama bin Laden's deputies was planning "to carry out suicide attacks against U.S. and Italian troops" or any foreign personnel in the area. The suicide bomber cell received assistance from "four Iranians" who work for Iran's intelligence service and "are supporting [the cell]...through intelligence" and "coordinating the activities."[18]

President Obama has to be fully aware of such activities. He no doubt receives briefings and intelligence reports on Afghanistan on a daily basis. So why would he willfully cover up Iran's jihad against U.S. troops in Afghanistan and suggest that the Iranians could actually be a force for good there? Worse, he fed this misinformation to journalists, who then turned around and fed it to the American people.

The result is a continued misunderstanding among much of the American populace about the severe and multifaceted nature of the Iranian threat. For the Obamis, when it comes to Iran, it's *engagement uber alles.* Therefore, the deception over Iran's role in Afghanistan is worth it, since it glosses over the mullahs' skullduggery and doesn't ruffle any feathers in Tehran. In the Obama administration's eyes, this increases the chances of an ever-elusive "grand bargain" between the United States and Iran that would see the Iranians give up their nuclear weapons program and support for terrorism in exchange for normalized relations with the United States—as if that's something the ayatollahs even want. Hence, the spectacle of an Iranian delegation being invited by the Obama administration to take part in a NATO conference on the future of Afghanistan in October 2010—just two weeks after Afghan officials intercepted a large shipment of Iranian weapons meant for the Taliban.[19]

We can guess what our troops in the field in Afghanistan and Iraq, who are being killed by Iranian-supplied arms, think about this brilliant outreach strategy hatched inside the Washington beltway. One person who isn't complaining about a stepped-up Iranian role in his country, however, is Afghan president Hamid Karzai. He brazenly admitted in October 2010 that his office has received "bags of money" from the Iranian regime.[20] Once again, who says Sunni and Shia can't work together?

★ ★ ★

The Obama administration's quixotic quest to romance Iran's regime follows three decades of Iranian terrorism directed at U.S. interests. The mullahs' jihad against America began in earnest in November 1979, shortly after the Ayatollah Khomeini came to power, when Islamic revolutionaries seized the U.S. Embassy in Tehran and took fifty-two American citizens hostage. The hostages were released 444 days later, only after the United States, thanks to an overmatched Jimmy Carter, was made to look impotent before the eyes of the world.

A failed American rescue mission to free the hostages in the spring of 1980 resulted in the destruction of two aircraft and the deaths of eight U.S. servicemen in the Iranian desert. The incident only added to the mullahs' fanatical belief that Allah was on their side, with Khomeini later crediting divine intervention for the doomed American effort. To drive the point home, he had the dead soldiers' bodies paraded through the streets of Tehran.

Whether desecrating the corpses of American servicemen or humiliating U.S. hostages before the cameras, the Iranian regime's scornful view of the country it regards as *The Great Satan* was made abundantly clear from the outset of the Islamic Republic. The regime felt, as Khomeini was fond of saying, that *America can't do a damn thing* to stop the Allah-ordained advance of Iran's Islamic Revolution across the Middle East and beyond.

Carter's fecklessness during the hostage crisis only emboldened the Khomeinists to strike America again. In 1983, Iran supported and directed the Hezbollah truck bombing of the U.S. Marine barracks in

Beirut, where U.S. forces formed part of a multinational peacekeeping mission. Two hundred forty-one U.S servicemen were killed in what was the deadliest terrorist attack against Americans until 9/11. Rather than strike back against Iran, Syria, and Hezbollah—all of which, NSA transcripts later revealed, had a hand in the bombing[21]—President Reagan opted to withdraw from Lebanon.

It was a fateful decision, as Osama bin Laden witnessed the hasty American retreat, the first of many over the course of the '80s and '90s, and concluded that the United States was a paper tiger. Iran's mullahs also took note of how they literally got away with murder against American citizens—not once, but twice. Indeed, just seven months before the Beirut barracks bombing, Hezbollah operatives—also at the direction of Iran and Syria—had carried out a suicide bombing against the U.S. Embassy in Beirut that killed sixty-three people, including seventeen Americans.[22] It was theretofore the deadliest attack against a U.S. diplomatic mission, but again President Reagan, who showed such boldness in confronting Soviet Communism and Libyan terrorism, refrained from ordering a retaliatory response against Iran, Syria, or Hezbollah. And so the Iranian reign of terror continued, usually directed through its proxy, Hezbollah.

The infamous terrorist behind much of the Iranian/Hezbollah-enacted carnage was Imad Mugniyeh, a senior Hezbollah commander who stayed in Iran frequently and worked closely with the Iranian Revolutionary Guards Corps. Mugniyeh was killed by a car bomb in Damascus in 2008 in an act that Hezbollah has blamed on Israel. His demise followed three decades of terrorist mayhem against U.S. interests that saw him mastermind the Marine barracks and Embassy bombings in 1983, as well as the taking of Western hostages in Lebanon throughout the 1980s, under orders from Iran. Some of the hostages, including the CIA's then-Beirut station chief William Buckley, were tortured and killed. The U.S indicted Mugniyeh for his part in the 1985 hijacking of TWA Flight 847, during which one of the passengers, U.S. Navy diver Robert Stethem, was brutally murdered. Mugniyeh is also suspected of having had a role in the

1996 bombing of the Khobar Towers apartment complex in Riyadh, Saudi Arabia, which killed nineteen U.S. servicemen.[23]

Mugniyeh took his marching orders from the office of Iran's Supreme Leader and answered directly to the chief of the Iranian Revolutionary Guards' al-Qods Force.[24] In other words, Mugniyeh carried out his 25-year jihad against America with full Iranian direction and support. Considering that Iran, as we've seen in this chapter, has been waging war against the United States in numerous ways since 1979, this should come as no great shock. Nor should have the 9/11 Commission's call in 2004 for further investigation into whether Iran had any role in the attacks of September 11, 2001. The fact that up to ten of the 9/11 hijackers passed through Iran in late 2000 without having their passports stamped rightfully caught the commission's attention.[25]

Mugniyeh's targets in the Western Hemisphere weren't limited to the United States. The not-so-dearly-departed terrorist architect also engineered the 1992 Hezbollah bombing of the Israeli Embassy in Argentina, which killed twenty-nine people, and the group's 1994 bombing of a Jewish community center in Buenos Aires, which killed another eighty-five. Hezbollah was able to carry out these attacks—with Iran's backing, of course—in part because it boasts a considerable network in Latin America, particularly in the tri-border region of Argentina, Brazil, and Paraguay.

For the United States, that means Hezbollah members are literally the terrorists next door—and according to Joseph Myers, a former U.S. Army lieutenant colonel and counterinsurgency expert, even closer. I sat down with Myers in January 2011, shortly after his retirement from active duty, which included lengthy stints in Latin America and Afghanistan, to discuss the Hezbollah threat in the West. Myers, who specialized in tackling armed insurgencies during his distinguished 30-year military career, told me he views Hezbollah as an even bigger threat to America than al-Qaeda:

> While our national security agencies focus mainly on Al Qaeda,
> I believe that Hezbollah is the most potent and powerful ter-

rorist insurgent threat in the world today, in terms of a potential threat to America. They are a terrorist organization that,
one, has global reach. Two, they're state supported by Iran and
they have state intelligence services that support them. That
gives them the capabilities—the unique capabilities—that Al
Qaeda might not necessarily have. ... We know that they have
conducted attacks against American interests and that they
routinely surveil American interests around the world.

Myers went on to say that Latin America has emerged as a Hezbollah
stronghold—and that the group has cells in the United States as well:

We know that we have a Hezbollah threat in Latin America:
it's there. It's latent. ... Hezbollah is located in the tri-border
region, they're located on Margarita Island, off the coast of
Venezuela, they're located in Panama ... they're really all over
the place. ... Hezbollah uses Latin America and the Western
Hemisphere predominantly for fundraising purposes. But it's
the latent military capability, the latent military threat that
they represent in the United States, that concerns me. Because
that is a card they could play if the United States ever decided
to engage in any kind of military action or subversive action
against the Iranian military program. To the point where the
Iranians could use their surrogates in Hezbollah to attack
American interests in America. They could activate cells and
operatives right here.

Perhaps the most active hotbed of Iranian and Hezbollah activity in the
Western Hemisphere is Venezuela. Over the past six years, Venezuelan
tyrant Hugo Chavez and Mahmoud Ahmadinejad have regularly traded
public displays of affection, mugging and hugging for the cameras on
numerous state visits to one another's capitals. But cooperation between
Iran and Venezuela goes far deeper than the bro-mance between their

dictators. Prior to 2005, the amount of trade between Iran and Venezuela was zero. Nada. Nothing. Since then, the two countries have done over $40 billion in trade, and Iran has established a broad network of businesses and entities throughout Venezuela and the surrounding regions.

Why the sudden—and massive—Iranian investment in Chavez's socialist paradise? The answer seems obvious: Iran is putting itself in better position to attack the United States. Witness the revelation in November 2010 by the German daily *Die Welt* that Iran is planning to place medium-range missiles on Venezuelan soil. According to the article, Venezuela has agreed to the establishment of a jointly operated military base, manned in part by Iran's Revolutionary Guards, which would house Iranian Shahab-3 and Scud missiles.[26] Take a wild guess where those missiles would be aimed. It's not an exaggeration to say we could be seeing the beginning stages of a modern-day Cuban Missile Crisis taking shape in Venezuela—indeed, just imagine if those Iranian Scuds become nuclear-tipped.

Roger Noriega, a top State Department official under the George W. Bush administration and former U.S. ambassador to the Organization of American States, is a foremost authority on the Tehran/Caracas Axis with impeccable on-the-ground sources inside Venezuela. He told me during a taping of my CBN show, *Stakelbeck on Terror*, in late 2010 that he believes Iran is now helping Hugo Chavez develop a nuclear weapons program of his own. In addition, Noriega supplied exclusive aerial photos that showed the location of a Venezuelan "tractor factory" that produces weapons, not tractors, and is manned by Iranian guards. He also presented evidence that Iran is mining for uranium in Venezuela's Roraima Basin for use in its nuclear weapons program, in clear violation of UN sanctions. For good measure, Noriega provided never-before-seen photos of Venezuelan officials meeting with Hezbollah leaders in Beirut.

The extent of the relationship between Chavez and the mullahs, as laid out by Noriega, was shocking. Yet this gathering anti-American storm in our own backyard has been virtually ignored by the Obama administration as it doggedly pursues diplomacy with the likes of Chavez and the

Iranian regime. Similar moves by the Iranians to solidify ties with Chavez allies Bolivia and Nicaragua have likewise been overlooked. As a result, it looks like we can bid *adieu* to a long-running U.S. policy first laid out in the Monroe Doctrine of 1823: that America would let no hostile foreign power establish a beachhead in the Western Hemisphere.

★ ★ ★

The Iranian regime is indisputably committed to the destruction of the United States and Israel. It has made its intentions in that regard abundantly clear for thirty-two years, through both words and deeds. Why, then, would the Obama administration persist in attempting to woo the mullahs, for whom anti-Americanism forms the bedrock of their regime? The short answer is that the U.S. government is plagued by the same blind spot in its dealings with messianic, Shia Iran that it has shown in its approach to Sunni jihadist groups from al-Qaeda to the Muslim Brotherhood: a complete misunderstanding of the ideology that drives the enemy.

In chapter one I introduced you to "Reza Kahlili," who worked as an undercover agent for America inside the Iranian regime. Kahlili told me the Iranians are driven by an apocalyptic ideology that pines for the return of the mythical Shiite "twelfth imam," also known as the Mahdi. According to legend, the twelfth imam disappeared when he was a young boy, purposely hidden by Allah sometime in the late ninth century. Many Shia, including Ahmadinejad, believe this Islamic messiah figure is currently hiding at the bottom of a well in the Iranian city of Jamkaran, awaiting the end of days. It's then that he will supposedly reemerge, accompanied, ironically enough, by Jesus Christ, to lead Muslims to victory over the hated Christians and Jews and subjugate the world to Islam.

To review, a little boy who has been hiding at the bottom of a well in Iran for ten centuries will appear one day soon, Jesus in tow, to establish global Islamic rule. Although this scenario sounds like sheer madness, Kahlili, who became intimately familiar with the regime's end times propaganda through his espionage activities inside the Revolutionary

Guards, told me that "Twelver" ideology is an animating force behind Iran's policymaking:

> I was there so I know the ideology. This is a messianic regime. They go from the centuries old hadiths, which has predicted this day. This day for them, is the ultimate day in Islam. It's the day of justice in their view. And in that day, 1/3 of the world population has to die due to nuclear wars, another 1/3 due to hunger and chaos and havoc. And then Imam Mahdi the Shiites' 12th imam will reappear, kill the rest of the infidels and raise the flag of Islam in all corners of the world. ... They deeply believe this. Government organizations are analyzing current events and comparing them to hadiths. ... Everything is in place. And the only part missing is for them to become a nuclear powered state. Then they are going to attack Israel, they are going to attack oil fields in the Persian Gulf and European capitals. Millions are going to die, there's going to be a total breakdown in the global economy. There's going to be havoc, lawlessness and hunger. We are going to witness the most destruction humanity has witnessed and the biggest depression they have experienced. And this is exactly what they are after.

How seriously does the Iranian regime take its "Twelver" dogma? Each year, before he begins his rambling address to the UN General Assembly in New York, Ahmadinejad publicly calls for the swift return of the Mahdi. Both he and Iranian supreme leader Ali Khamenei have gone on record as saying they believe the Mahdi's reappearance will happen very soon, amid a time of great global chaos. Despite these pronouncements, not once when discussing the Iranian nuclear threat have President Obama or his predecessor, George W. Bush, referenced the apocalyptic belief system of Iran's leadership. Yet it's fair to say that a regime that believes its messiah will return only when the world is gripped by violent upheaval would seek to create just that sort of condition by, say, attacking America or Israel with nuclear weapons—particularly when martyrdom, or dying for the sake of Allah, is elevated above all. Here's more on that, from Kahlili:

> The sermons were every day. And the ideology of martyrdom and ending up in heaven next to Imam Ali and prophet Mohammed was the main focus of the clerics. Khomeini preached the ultimate sacrifice.... You have to die for the glorification of Allah: this is the ultimate prize for a Muslim.... The reason for the failure of every American administration [in dealing with Iran] is that they do not understand the ideology.

The Iranian regime showed just how willing it is to sacrifice its citizens during the Iran-Iraq War in the 1980s, when it sent thousands of brainwashed teenagers and young boys to clear minefields while wearing plastic "keys to paradise" around their necks. The wide-eyed recruits were assured they would receive eternal rewards in heaven.

The fatalistic mindset of the Iranian regime ensures that we could throw the Cold War doctrine of Mutually Assured Destruction, or MAD, out the window if Iran acquires nuclear weapons. The atheistic Soviets were living for this world; the Iranians are living for the next. As a result, the Iranian regime has no qualms about sacrificing millions of Iranians for—in their view—the greater good of wiping Israel off the map. This means that nuking Tel Aviv is worth weathering what would surely be a devastating Israeli retaliation against Iranian cities. Iran's leaders believe their 70-million-strong population can survive such an exchange, but that tiny Israel's population cannot. As former Iranian president Hashemi Rafsanjani put it back in 2001:

> If a day comes when the world of Islam is duly equipped with the arms Israel has in its possession, the strategy of colonialism would face a stalemate because application of an atomic

bomb would not leave anything in Israel but the same thing would just produce damages in the Muslim world.[27]

Obama administration officials hear such threats against Israel and America and conclude that the Iranians are just blowing smoke, that no one can be *that* crazy. "The Iranians are like anyone—they have a price," they say. "We can negotiate with them. At the end of the day, they're reasonable people and they want to remain in power. They would never be so foolish as to actually use a nuclear weapon. And all that talk about the Mahdi and wiping Israel off the map is just gibberish for domestic consumption."

Indeed, it seems the Obama White House has resigned itself to the fact that Iran will acquire nuclear weapons. As far back as July 2009, Secretary of State Hillary Clinton said that the United States would protect its allies in the Middle East with a nuclear defense umbrella that would dissuade Iran from using its own nukes.[28] Iran didn't even have the bomb, and already a top Obama administration official was referring to a day when it would, as if it were inevitable. *Containment* is a term that is back in vogue in Washington.

The message from Jerusalem, however, is quite different. Based on my conversations with Israeli officials, both on and off the record, since 2005, I believe Israel will use every means at its disposal, including a military strike, to prevent the existential threat posed by a nuclear-armed Iran. This means Israel will have to do America's dirty work and deal as best it can not only with the likely retaliatory onslaught by Iran, Syria, Hezbollah, and Hamas, but also with the thunderous condemnation of most of the world, possibly including the Obama administration. Welcome to the not-so-brave new world of American "soft power," where allies are abandoned and terrorists are emboldened.

CHAPTER EIGHT

IT'S THE IDEOLOGY, STUPID

Duning the summer of 2000, Noman Benotman stood face-to-face with Osama bin Laden in Afghanistan, listening as the al-Qaeda kingpin described, in detail, his plans for an upcoming major operation against the United States that would later be known simply as "9/11."

Benotman, a former top commander of an Islamic terrorist organization called the Libyan Islamic Fighting Group (LIFG), was one of 200 global jihadist leaders summoned to Afghanistan by bin Laden one year before 9/11 for a meeting to discuss strategy.

Benotman's participation in that fateful terrorist summit was no coincidence; he was held in high regard by al-Qaeda's hierarchy as a veteran *mujahid*, or holy warrior, and trusted confidante.

Now, nearly a decade later, I was standing face-to-face with Benotman in a London hotel room.

Benotman, who says he left the jihadist world behind shortly after 9/11, had agreed to meet with me to discuss, among other things, his former close associations with both bin Laden and al-Qaeda's second-in-command, Ayman al-Zawahiri. Throughout my hour-long interview with

Benotman, he recounted face-to-face meetings with bin Laden and Zawahiri in which the two al-Qaeda leaders gleefully discussed murdering American civilians with a bloodlust that seemed insatiable.

According to Benotman, his warnings to Zawahiri that a major operation on U.S. soil would provoke an overwhelming American response were greeted with laughter and quickly dismissed. Today, ten years after the 9/11 attacks sparked an American "War on Terror" that has seen al-Qaeda's leadership severely weakened and the group's operatives pursued to the ends of the earth, Zawahiri's flippant response to Benotman's concerns sounds unbelievable. How could al-Qaeda have been so confident that the most powerful nation in the world would take 9/11 lying down?

Simple: Benotman told me that, based on their study of recent history, both Zawahiri and bin Laden firmly believed America was a "paper tiger" that would respond weakly when attacked. Indeed, the roll call of U.S. fecklessness in the face of Islamic terror up until 9/11 was shameful and well documented: from the Iranian hostage crisis to the Beirut Marine barracks massacre; from the 1993 World Trade Center bombing to Black Hawk Down in Somalia; and from the Khobar Towers attack to the African embassy bombings and the attack on the USS *Cole* destroyer in Yemen, in which seventeen U.S. sailors were killed by an al-Qaeda suicide bomber.

In each case, the U.S. response was either to cut and run, issue a "strong" condemnation, or simply not to respond at all. The lone, pitiful exception was the Clinton administration's response to the 1998 African embassy bombings, which consisted of lobbing a few cruise missiles into Afghanistan and into an empty pharmaceutical factory in Sudan. During Clinton's presidency we witnessed no fewer than five major Islamic terrorist attacks against U.S. interests, each of them gradually escalating in their ferocity and boldness. Yet the most Clinton could muster in the face of this growing terror onslaught by al-Qaeda and its surrogates were those cruise missiles to nowhere. Is it any wonder, then, that by the summer of 2000, bin Laden and the boys were confident that the United States would take 9/11 on the chin?

Yet that attack would finally propel our political class into action, with the 9/11 Commission exposing the defective institutional mindset that caused American leaders to ignore the Islamic terrorist threat for so long. And what did the commission identify as the root cause of the 9/11 attacks? Notably, they didn't cite the supposed reasons so often trumpeted by the liberal political establishment and media elites, such as poverty, mental illness, or lack of education. Nor did they blame the Israeli-Palestinian conflict, that other trusty crutch of the Left's arguments on national security.

No, what motivated the 9/11 attackers, according to the bipartisan 9/11 Commission, was a seductive jihadist ideology rooted in Islamic law that had been lying dormant during the decline of the Ottoman Empire, but had been revived and renewed in the twentieth century.

My numerous interviews with current and former Islamic terrorists and radicals over the years have repeatedly confirmed this point. Ideology is the lubricant that makes the international Islamic terrorist machine operate.

During our interview, Noman Benotman stated that jihadist ideology did not represent some new, distorted interpretation of Islam, as Obama administration officials have steadily maintained. Benotman argued it was rooted in the Koran itself:

If any Muslim appears and says ok, there is no jihad in Islam whatsoever, please believe me, he is a liar. A pure liar. People, they need to face it because it is a serious issue. Jihad, it's part of Islam because it is something that's in the Koran. There are more than 40 verses, I think, in the Koran that mention jihad. Not just one or three or ten. From a Muslim perspective, the Koran is not a book written for someone or a constitution. It's the words of God.

When it comes to jihadist ideology and what motivates terrorists, who are you going to believe: a former Islamic terrorist like Noman Benotman who has rubbed shoulders with al-Qaeda's leadership, or those two noted Islamic scholars, Eric Holder and Janet Napolitano? Call me crazy, but for a realistic assessment of the jihad threat, my money is on Benotman.

Nevertheless, since the 9/11 Commission published its report in 2004, the U.S. government has steadily removed from its national security strategy documents and terrorism assessments any reference to Islamic ideology, jihadist teachings, or Koranic injunctions to subdue the earth. Federal agencies charged with protecting the American public have issued guidelines forbidding their employees from making any mention of Islam, the Koran, or jihad.

In short, the people tasked with preserving our national security have stopped listening to what our jihadist enemies are saying about why they hate us and why attacks against Americans are justified. Instead, American officials, crippled by political correctness, have chosen simply to ignore the fact that Islamic terrorism does not just occur out of thin air, but is driven by a rigid, longstanding, and Koranically inspired ideological system. They ignore what guys like Noman Benotman have to say, to America's great detriment—because it was evident from my lengthy conversation with Benotman just how alluring that jihadi ideology truly is. While the former terror commander has left the battlefield behind and publicly broken with his former al-Qaeda comrades, he still clings to some of the ideological tenets, like "defensive jihad," that drove him into bin Laden's world in the first place.

My interview with the UK's most notorious Islamist mouthpiece, Anjem Choudary, whom we met in chapter six, demonstrates the folly of ignoring what our enemy says. Choudary has led several pro-jihad groups in the UK that have been banned by the British government. But he is no marginal figure in the British Muslim community—he and his organization have a wide following, particularly among students and young professionals. And he makes no apologies for why he believes attacks against the West are justified.

Choudary's life, like that of most of the terrorists discussed in this book, contradicts the liberals' "poverty-breeds-terrorism" meme. He was raised in England and has hardly led an impoverished life, as evidenced by his law degree from a leading British university. And he bluntly attributes his beliefs to a single source: the Koran. "You can't say that Islam is a religion of peace," Choudary told me, contravening another left-wing shibboleth. "Because Islam does not mean peace. Islam means submission. So the Muslim is one who submits. There is a place for violence in Islam. There is a place for jihad in Islam."

So we've noticed—at least some of us.

Choudary seeks to bring about a unified Islamic super-state, or caliphate, with one all-powerful leader, or caliph, at its helm. Once this caliphate is established, Muslims will turn their attention to violently subjugating the non-Muslim world. From China to America, Choudary told me, "We believe that one day the entire world will be governed by the sharia." This is the endgame for Choudary and his group, just like it is for virtually every Islamist organization, from al-Qaeda to the Muslim Brotherhood. Choudary elaborates on the methods of global conquest:

> The other thing about the Islamic state is that it has no boundaries or borders. One of the names of the Islamic state is called the ever-expanding kingdom. Meaning you will continue to conquer and remove the obstacles in the way of implementing the sharia outside of its frontiers. So wherever it is established, you will continue to have a foreign policy of having treaties or having jihad, meaning to conquer.

And where might Choudary get that idea? How about Sura 8, verse 39 of the Koran, which says, "And fight with them until there is no more persecution and religion should be only for Allah."

At the end of the day, Choudary told me, Islam itself is "not just a spiritual belief. It is, in fact an ideology which you believe in and you struggle for and you are willing to even die for, because you believe in that: that is your whole life."

In other words, it's the ideology, stupid.

★ ★ ★

The Obama administration and the mainstream media still keep their heads in the sand about jihadist ideology, even as empirical research confirms its centrality to Islamic terrorism. An article published in *The Economist* magazine in December 2010 reviewed recent academic studies on homegrown terrorism and found that economic or educational factors are rarely related to the radicalization process.[1]

These studies simply corroborate what is apparent from even a cursory study of the topic. We only need to remember that Osama bin Laden is the son of a billionaire and that his deputy, Ayman al-Zawahiri, is a trained medical doctor who comes from one of the most prestigious families in Egypt. Or that would-be Times Square bomber Faisal Shahzad, who attended university in the United States and obtained an MBA, had a well-paying job in the financial sector and lived in an upscale Connecticut community. What drove him to attempt to kill hundreds of American citizens? The 800-pound gorilla in the room that everyone wants to ignore: ideology. Indeed, the examples of well-educated, middle-class Islamic terrorists are plentiful, from Hamas leaders to the 9/11 hijackers to Underwear Bomber Umar Farouk Abdulmutallab and beyond.

Yet to make any mention of the Islamic doctrine of jihad, the Koranic injunctions to wage war against the infidels until they are subdued, or the nearly universal Jew-hatred that is preached from Islamic pulpits all over the world results in cries of "Bigot!" and "Islamophobe!"

The sad truth is that the "extremist" element of "radical" Islam is anything but extreme or radical to a true believer. The ideology that drives jihadist movements around the world is found in the Koran and in the traditions and history of Islam, and is preached daily in mosques and madrassahs all over the world. Far from being "isolated," this is the *mainstream* interpretation of Islamic scripture. For instance, a fatwa was issued in early 2011 by Dr. Imad Mustafa of Egypt's al-Azhar University, the oldest and most respected Islamic institution in the world, endorsing al-Qaeda's doctrine of "offensive jihad."[2] According to Mustafa, Muslims may wage war against non-Muslims whenever Muslims are prohibited from exercising any element of Islamic law, including polygamy, wife-beating, child marriage, or apostate killings—meaning virtually anywhere in the West.

Was the Muslim world outraged by Mustafa's fatwa? Better yet, did Muslim-American groups uniformly condemn Mustafa? The answer, on both counts, is: of course not. And how dare you even ask? *Islamophobe.*

And there is hardly any condemnation from Muslims anywhere of the widespread anti-Semitism peddled throughout the Middle East and in many Islamic communities in the West. A widely celebrated purveyor of Islamic Jew hatred is Yusuf al-Qaradawi, one of the world's most well-known Islamic scholars. The jihadist equivalent of a televangelist, al-Qaradawi broadcasts a weekly program on al-Jazeera, *Shariah and Life*, which is the network's most watched show. Virtually any week you can see al-Qaradawi railing against the "treacherous Jews" or invoking any number of anti-Semitic blood libels. Qaradawi, a spiritual leader of the terrorist group Hamas and of the Egyptian Muslim Brotherhood, was also the first prominent Sunni cleric to endorse suicide bombings, an edict that was followed by a wave of terror attacks against Israeli civilians in buses, pizzerias, university campuses, discos, and elsewhere.

It's crucial to understand that Qaradawi is not some marginal figure—he is one of the world's most well-respected Islamic scholars and controls one of the most popular Islamic websites, Islamonline.net. Shortly after returning from exile to his native Egypt following the overthrow of Mubarak, a massive crowd of between one and two million people turned out in Tahrir Square to hear him lead Friday prayers. During his sermon, he beseeched Allah to allow for the conquest of Jerusalem's al-Aqsa mosque[3]—a thinly veiled call for the destruction of

Israel. Riled up by his words, more than a million Egyptians chanted in unison, "To Jerusalem we are heading, martyrs in the million."[4]

Having been back in Egypt only a few days, Qaradawi enticed more than a million people to vow to sacrifice their lives in a war to wipe out Israel—that's some power. And where did Qaradawi receive his Islamic education? Al-Azhar University, the same school where Imad Mustafa, who issued the recent "offensive jihad" fatwa, now teaches.

In March 2008 Dutch parliamentarian Geert Wilders released a short internet film, *Fitna*, that sparked protests by Muslim groups worldwide. Wilders was subject to scores of death threats, and today he requires 24/7 protection by bodyguards. The movie was originally scheduled to be released on YouTube, but the online giant refused to post it after threats were made against the company and its employees. And what exactly did Muslims find so incendiary about *Fitna*? The film interspersed Koranic verses with video clips of Islamic clerics citing those verses to promote violence, Jew-hatred, and Islamic supremacism. All Wilders did was turn a mirror on the Muslim world to expose the ideology that has taken hold of Islamic communities, including in the West. As a result of such truth telling, Wilders is now on trial for criminal "hate speech," an Orwellian charge that has been cheered on by leftist Dutch politicians and their media sycophants.

While the problem of violent Islamic ideology is deeply entrenched in the Middle East and Europe, Islamists in the United States are working hard to catch up. In 2006, I broadcast a CBN report on a visit I made to Dearborn, Michigan, a city outside Detroit that boasts America's largest Arab-Muslim community. While I was there I sat down with Imam Mohammed Ali Elahi, a prominent Iranian cleric in Dearborn's Shia community and leader of the Islamic House of Wisdom, one of the largest mosques in America (and formerly home to a Christian church). Elahi began our interview with the standard odes to interfaith cooperation and tolerance, and made sure to condemn the 9/11 attacks. But when I asked about the terrorist group Hezbollah, the conversation dramatically changed. Gone were the paeans to moderation and interfaith harmony, and in came the defense of Hezbollah and justifications for their acts of terrorism against Jews. And while Elahi condemned the 9/11 attacks, he couldn't bring himself to admit that al-Qaeda was behind the carnage, suggesting instead the Israeli Mossad may have been involved.

In my report, I featured photos of Elahi taken from the Islamic House of Wisdom's website that showed him with Iran's jihadist godfather, Ayatollah Khomeini, and other leaders of the Iranian regime. (As of this writing, the website features a video of Elahi's February 11, 2011 homily titled "Imam Khomeini: More than a Political Leader"—an entire sermon dedicated to Elahi's praise for the late Iranian terrorist supremo.)[5] I also highlighted a picture of Elahi talking to Hezbollah's late spiritual leader, Sheikh Fadlallah, whose death in July 2010 occasioned a large gathering in the Islamic House of Wisdom to mourn his passing. Yet none of Elahi's associations with Iranian leaders and Hezbollah ideologues have prevented local politicians or the FBI's Detroit Field Office from courting him as an "interfaith" leader. In fact, when I met in late 2005 with then-Special Agent in Charge of the FBI's Detroit field office, Daniel Roberts, he asked me to pass on his personal greetings to Elahi after I informed him I'd be meeting with the longtime shill for the ayatollahs.

Remember that Elahi's Islamic House of Wisdom is one of the largest Islamic centers in America. It's also just one example of how deeply jihadist ideology has made inroads in the American Muslim community.

In chapter one I discussed the 2005 Freedom House report that detailed the Saudi-financed hate literature found in U.S. mosques. Promoting hatred of Christians and Jews, bizarre conspiracy theories, the subjugation of women, and anti-American screeds, the materials advocated the precise jihadist ideology that our political class insists is only followed by a few isolated cranks who misunderstand their own religion. But the literature was collected from some of America's largest and most respected Islamic houses of worship across a wide range of cities, including New York City, Washington, D.C., Chicago, Dallas, Houston, San Diego, and Oakland. Some of the worst propaganda was found at the Islamic Center of Washington, D.C., which is located about a mile from the White House and was visited by President Bush just three days after the 9/11 attacks. That means the kind of jihadist promulgations that inspired the 9/11 terrorists were being distributed right under the noses of White House officials and the media pool covering the event.

The centrality of jihadism in America's Islamic communities is borne out in the disturbing saga of Jamal Miftah. A Pakistani-born Muslim, Miftah came to the United States with his family in 2003 to escape the jihadist violence plaguing his home country. But when he sent a letter to the editor of his local Oklahoma newspaper, the *Tulsa World*, in October 2006 condemning al-Qaeda and calling on Muslims to denounce terrorism, he was shocked at the response from the leaders and members of his mosque, the Islamic Society of Tulsa. Shortly after his letter was published, he arrived at the mosque and was surrounded by an angry crowd of worshippers who called him an anti-Muslim traitor. The confrontation was so unnerving that Miftah later filed a police report.

Miftah, whom I interviewed in his Tulsa home in 2007, was told by mosque leaders that he had betrayed the Muslim community by speaking negatively about it in front of infidels. He was accused of slandering Islam, expelled from the mosque, and told he could only return when he publicly apologized and retracted his letter. During our interview, he was in fear for his life. He told me that under Islamic law, anyone who slanders Islam can be killed. Is it any wonder there has never been a widespread reform within Islam when anyone who questions 1,400 years of Islamic law and tradition is threatened with death? And remember that Jamal Miftah was not in Saudi Arabia or Pakistan, but in America's heartland in Tulsa, Oklahoma.

★   ★   ★

To gain a better grasp of what motivates Muslims to embrace jihadist ideology, I sat down with a former terrorist operative named Tawik Hamid. As part of Egyptian Islamic Jihad, the same group that assassinated Egyptian president Anwar Sadat, Hamid was in contact with al-Qaeda's second-in-command, Ayman al-Zawahiri. Today, Hamid speaks out forcefully against jihadist ideology. He has written about what transpired in his life as he adopted the jihadi mindset and was conditioned by adherents of Islam's Salafi sect to accept violence:

I passed through three psychological stages to reach this level of comfort with death: hatred of non-Muslims or dissenting Muslims; suppression of my conscience; and acceptance of violence in the service of Allah. Salafi religious indoctrination played a major role in this process. Salafists promoted our hatred for non-Muslims by emphasizing the Quranic verse that read, *"Thou wilt not find any people who believe in Allah and the Last Day loving those who resist (i.e., do not follow) Allah and His Messenger."* (Quran 58:22)

Salafi writings also helped me to suppress my conscience by holding that many activities I had considered to be immoral were, instead, *halal*—that is, allowed by Allah and the Prophet.

…Once I was able to suppress my conscience, I was open to accepting violence without guilt—the third psychological stage. One Salafi method of generating this crucial attitude is to encourage violence against women, a first step in developing a brutal mentality. A mind that accepts violence against women is much more likely to be comfortable murdering hated infidels and responding to the verse that reads: *"O Prophet, strive hard (fight) against the unbelievers and the Hypocrites, and be harsh with them. Their abode is Hell, an evil refuge indeed"* (Quran 9:73). It is clear that the three psychological stages in Salafism that I have described are deeply interconnected.[6]

This radicalization process and its connection to jihadist ideology were analyzed in a report published by the New York Police Department's Intelligence Division in 2007. Reviewing much of the analysis of homegrown terror plots in the United States, the authors of

"Radicalization in the West: The Homegrown Threat" identified a four-step process that leads an individual or group to accept jihadist ideology and to act on it:

- Pre-radicalization: The subject is searching for something else in their life and comes into contact with radicalization agents.
- Identification: The individual begins to adopt various changes of dress, mannerisms and lifestyle in accordance with adopting a new set of beliefs.
- Indoctrination: Now involved with a new set of associates, they are subjected to intense ideological training that reinforces jihadist narratives and justifications for violence.
- Jihadization: The individual agrees that violence is necessary for the "defense" of Islam, and is recruited to engage in violent acts.[7]

The report's authors stress that this process can happen over long periods of time, or can occur rather quickly. But there is one essential element that motivates the radicalized individual to justify violence and eventually act on it:

> What motivates young men and women, born or living in the West, to carry out "autonomous jihad" via acts of terrorism against their host countries? The answer is ideology. Ideology is the bedrock and catalyst for radicalization. It defines the conflict, guides movements, identifies the issues, drives recruitment, and is the basis for action. In many cases, ideology also determines target selection and informs what will be done and how it will be carried out.[8]

Once a terrorist group draws in a recruit through appeals to "jihadi cool" or other methods, it is the ideology and indoctrination process that transforms him or her into a terrorist. The sense of community that is forged during this process is aided by what the NYPD report termed as "radicalization incubators":

> Critically important to the process of radicalization are the different venues that provide the extremist fodder or fuel for radicalizing—venues, to which we refer to (sic) as "radicalization incubators." The incubators serve as radicalizing agents for those who have chosen to pursue radicalization. They become their pit stops, "hangouts," and meeting places. Generally, these locations, which together comprise the radical subculture of a community, are rife with extremist rhetoric. Though the locations can be mosques, more likely incubators include cafes, cab driver hangouts, flophouses, prisons, student associations, non-governmental organizations, hookah bars, butcher shops, and book stores. While it is difficult to predict who will radicalize, these nodes are likely places where like-minded individuals will congregate as they move through the radicalization process.[9]

What about places like the Halalco supermarket and Islamic bookstore in Falls Church, Virginia, which we discussed in chapter five? This is the largest Islamic supermarket in the Washington, D.C. area, located only a mile away from the notorious Dar al-Hijrah mosque that has produced a long string of terrorists. Not only was wanted al-Qaeda cleric Anwar al-Awlaki the former imam at the mosque, but it was also the spiritual home to at least two of the 9/11 hijackers. And a former youth leader at the mosque, Ahmed Omar Abu Ali, is currently serving a life sentence in federal prison for his role in an al-Qaeda plot that aimed to assassinate President George W. Bush. Dar al-Hijrah was also the spiritual home of the Fort Hood terrorist, Army Major Nidal Hasan. How many members of the mosque have gone to Halalco to hang out, or pick up a copy of some jihadist author's books, or purchase a set of Anwar al-Awlaki sermons or *The Protocols of the Elders of Zion*?

Another radicalization incubator identified by the NYPD report is the Muslim Student Association (MSA), an organization located on hundreds of college campuses across the country. According to the NYPD, jihadists have used this group as a forum for recruiting and indoctrinating like-minded individuals. Remember the five D.C.-area men who were captured in Pakistan in December 2009 attempting to join the Taliban? One of them, Ramy Zamzam, was the MSA regional president for the Washington, D.C. area. Zamzam was just one in a long line of MSA leaders who have been arrested and convicted on terrorism charges.

Another MSA leader, Tarek Mehanna, is currently awaiting trial in Boston on charges of plotting domestic terror attacks. Mehanna was an MSA bigwig at the Massachusetts College of Pharmacy and Health Science, where he attended dental school. He was also a prolific, pro-al-Qaeda blogger who regularly praised jihadist authors and rallied others to the cause of convicted terrorists. Furthermore, Mehanna was an associate of Daniel Maldonado, who is currently serving a 20-year prison sentence for traveling to Somalia to join the al-Shabaab terrorist organization. Finally, Mehanna was a devoted fan of several jihadist ideologues, including two prominent Muslim Brotherhood figures: Abdullah Azzam, who mentored Osama bin Laden and who helped lay the foundations for what became al-Qaeda; and Sayyid Qutb, the "godfather" of modern jihadist ideology who was executed by Egyptian authorities in 1966 for plotting the overthrow of Egypt's government and the installation of a sharia-compliant Islamic state.[10]

Are you confident that the FBI or your local police know what's going on inside the local MSA in your community? How about in Columbus, Ohio, where I reported in 2007 on the largest known al-Qaeda cell discovered operating in the United States? As many as a dozen men were involved, but amazingly, only three people were ever charged in the case. One of the leaders of the cell, Christopher Paul, was born and raised in

Worthington, Ohio, converted to Islam, and eventually traveled to Afghanistan, where he fought with the Taliban in the early 1990s. When Paul returned to the United States, he began forming his own cell and was hired by the Masjid Omar Ibn El Khattab mosque to teach martial arts. Paul even conducted jihadist training in a nearby state park.

One prominent figure at the El Khattab mosque during Paul's tenure there was a Muslim cleric named Salah Sultan. At the same time Sultan was being hailed as a moderate Muslim leader by the local *Columbus Dispatch* newspaper, he was spouting jihadist propaganda on TV programs throughout the Middle East, claiming in one spot on Saudi TV that the U.S. government was behind the 9/11 attacks. He later appeared on Egyptian television and invoked a notorious Islamic hadith asserting that the Day of Judgment won't come until Muslims kill all the Jews. For good measure, Sultan—who now lives in Bahrain—threatened that the United States was set for destruction and invoked *The Protocols of the Elders of Zion* to support his belief that the world is controlled by a global Jewish conspiracy. With Islamist firebrands like Sultan holding court, is it any wonder an al-Qaeda cell thrived at a mosque in middle America?

★ ★ ★

Predictably, the U.S. government's head-in-the-sand approach to jihadist ideology has not been productive in combating homegrown Islamic terrorism, as demonstrated starkly in the failure to act on any of the warning signs shown by Nidal Hasan before he massacred thirteen U.S. soldiers at Fort Hood. The senators who led the investigation into the attack wrote, "The first thing the Defense Department must do now is explicitly identify the threat posed by violent Islamist extremism, rather than cloaking it with vague terms such as 'violent extremism' or 'workplace violence.' Then our military must train service members on the signs and stages of violent Islamist radicalization so it can be reported and dealt with quickly and directly."[11]

In other words, stop ignoring the ideology.

This willful blindness is a problem throughout our entire national security apparatus, resulting in a long line of baffling statements made by our government's top counterterrorism officials. Take for example a 2010 speech at Stanford University in which the Chairman of the Joint Chiefs of Staff, Admiral Mike Mullen, claimed Islamic terrorism was not going to be defeated by identifying and combating a violent ideology, like we did against Nazism, but through education programs:

> "Attacking the humiliation, the hopelessness, the illiteracy and abject poverty which lie at the core of the attraction to extremist thought will do more to turn the tide against terrorism than anything else," the chairman said. "We can continue to hunt and kill their leaders, and we will. But when a person learns to read, he enters a gateway toward independent education and thought. He becomes more capable, more employable, and enjoys a sense of purpose in his life. He will understand the Quran for what it is and not merely what his mullah tells him it is, who is equally uneducated."[12]

As explained above, most al-Qaeda leaders are highly educated and come from privileged backgrounds. Would an educational program have turned Osama bin Laden, a trained engineer and the son of a billionaire, into a peaceful philanthropist? Let's not forget that bin Laden was indoctrinated while he was studying at the University of Jeddah under the instruction of top Palestinian Muslim Brotherhood figure Abdullah Azzam. And when bin Laden fled from Saudi Arabia, he took refuge in Sudan under the protection of another top Muslim Brotherhood leader, Hassan al-Turabi, who has been called "the Pope of Terrorism" and who holds advanced law degrees from the University of London and the University of Sorbonne in France.[13] No doubt we'll soon hear that the State Department has started a rehabilitation program for jihadist leaders to earn their Ph.D.s.

We saw another risible example of the Obama administration's "see no evil" approach to Islamic ideology when Director of National Intelligence James Clapper testified before Congress in February 2011 that the Muslim Brotherhood was a "largely secular" organization. Again, this is the "*Muslim* Brotherhood," which should have been his first clue. Clapper uttered this inexplicable falsehood as the Egyptian revolution unfolded and the U.S. government confronted the possibility that the Brotherhood could ultimately gain power in the country with the largest army in the Arab world.[14]

But perhaps the most stunning display of naïveté concerning the jihadist threat came in a speech by President Obama's top national security and counterterrorism advisor, John Brennan, that was hosted by two Islamic groups at New York University. The debacle began when Brennan was introduced by Dr. Ingrid Mattson, then-president of the Islamic Society of North America—a Muslim Brotherhood front group named by the Justice Department as an unindicted co-conspirator in the Holy Land Foundation terrorism funding case. But that designation didn't stop Brennan from effusively praising Mattson and her tainted organization, extolling her "leadership as an academic whose research continues the rich tradition of Islamic scholarship, and as president of the Islamic Society of North America, where you have been a voice for the tolerance and diversity that defines Islam."[15]

Sounding like a Saudi ambassador, Brennan launched into a paean to Islam, expressing his "respect for a faith that has shaped my own worldview," referencing his personal experience traveling the world and learning about "the goodness and beauty of Islam," and speaking about a long-ago trip to Indonesia in which he "came to see Islam not how it is often misrepresented, but for what it is, how it is practiced everyday by well over a billion Muslims worldwide—a faith of peace and tolerance and great diversity." Brennan also waxed poetic about Middle Easterners who taught him that all of us, everywhere in the world, aspire "to practice our faith freely"—apparently the widespread persecution of

Christians throughout the Middle East, and the sharia-inspired laws that punish conversion from Islam with penalties up to and including death, failed to make much of an impression on him.

Although he found no fault on the part of the Muslims, Brennan gave credence to a long list of Islamic grievances against America. Denouncing the supposed "ugly rise in scapegoating and fearmongering" against Muslims in America, he bemoaned that U.S. Muslim communities "have also been targeted from the other side by inexcusable ignorance and prejudice here in the United States, Europe, and elsewhere." He then condemned his own government for a litany of supposed past transgressions against Muslims, including violations of the Patriot Act, profiling, excessive surveillance, no-fly lists, and scrutiny of Islamic charities.

Throughout his speech, Brennan fully adopted the Islamic worldview and the accompanying terminology, referring to Israel as "Palestine," calling Jerusalem by its revanchist Arabic name "al-Quds," speaking about the "sacred obligation of zakat [charity]," and praising the Saudi regime's custodianship over "the two holy mosques at Mecca and Medina." For good measure, he sprinkled into his speech extended Arabic-language remarks and a recitation from the Koran.

Amidst all the fawning over Islam's beauty and tolerance, Brennan indicated where the impetus for the government's refusal to address jihadist ideology ultimately lies: "President Obama declared in his address in Cairo that he considers it part of his responsibility as president to fight against negative stereotypes of Islam. This is not only a matter of civil rights. It's a matter of our national security and it's a matter of our morality as a nation." Brennan reiterated the point while yet again condemning anti-Muslim bigotry, declaring, "Ignorance is a threat to our national security. Prejudice is a threat to our national security. Discrimination is a threat to our national security."

And there you have it. President Obama believes "fighting negative stereotypes of Islam" is a national security matter of the highest order. Noticing that nearly all terrorists are Muslims, and that they justify their atrocities by citing Islamic scripture, and that this interpretation is promoted widely in Islamic communities throughout the world—why, that would cast Islam in a negative light and promote negative stereotypes. Those dots just cannot be connected—thus we're left with the continued insistence that every new jihadist attack and every foiled Muslim terrorist plot is just a random, isolated event occurring without any larger context.

In other words, the reason why the military, the Justice Department, the Defense Department, the Department of Homeland Security, and every other branch of government are willfully blind to jihadist ideology is because that attitude is enforced from the very top. The directive to placate Muslims even extends to NASA, where the agency's chief, Charles Bolden, boasted to the pro-jihad TV network al-Jazeera that NASA's "foremost" mission, as charged by Obama personally, is to "reach out to the Muslim world and engage much more with dominantly Muslim nations to help them feel good about their historic contribution to science...and math and engineering."[16] You read that correctly: according to NASA's director, the space exploration agency's main priority is to make Muslims "feel good" about themselves.

As for John Brennan, his national security prescriptions—such as reaching out to "moderates" he has apparently located in the Hezbollah terrorist organization[17]—are right in line with Obama's pro-Islam policy. And nothing exemplifies this policy more than Brennan's refusal to acknowledge jihadist ideology. Incredibly, he has argued that we should not even refer to Islamic terrorists as "jihadists" because jihad is actually a peaceful, "legitimate tenet of Islam"[18]—a false assertion that was debunked by Islam expert Andrew Bostom, who noted that thirty-six of the forty uses of the word "jihad" in the Koran refer to warfare and fighting.[19]

Obama himself presented his view on the topic during a November 2010 visit to a college in Mumbai, India. During a townhall-style discussion with an audience of Indian students, a woman asked Obama to explain his opinion on jihad. Considering the city where these students lived was subject to a horrific jihadist massacre just two years earlier, the student had a justifiable interest in discovering what the leader of the free world thinks about the ideology that had spawned such violence. Obama answered her question with a Brennan-style tribute to the glory of Islam, combined with the usual multiculturalist platitudes:

> The phrase "jihad" has a lot of meaning within Islam and is subject to a lot of different interpretations, but I will say that, first, Islam is one of the world's great religions. And more than a billion people who practice Islam, the overwhelming majority view their obligations to their religion as ones that reaffirm peace and justice and fairness and tolerance. I think all of us recognize that this great religion, in the hands of a few extremists, has been distorted by violence towards innocent people that is never justified. So I think one of the challenges that we face is how to isolate those who have these distorted notions of religious war, and reaffirm those who see faiths of all sorts, whether you are a Hindu or a Muslim or a Christian or a Jew or any other religion, or you don't practice a religion, that we can all treat each other with respect and mutual dignity, and that some of the universal principles that Gandhi referred to, that those are what we're living up to, as we live in a nation or nations that have very diverse religious beliefs.[20]

One wonders whether Obama's panegyrics about Islam's inherent "peace" and "tolerance" were warmly received in a city in which 164 people had recently been murdered and 300 more wounded by Islamic jihadists. And a sharp-eyed reader might notice that the president's insistence on the need to "isolate" those "few extremists" contradict his administration's rote argument that the perpetrators of every new jihadist attack are already "isolated" individuals. Nevertheless, regardless of what India's Hindus— the prime victims of the Mumbai attack—thought of Obama's comments, his remarks seem to have fulfilled their purpose. As a *Times of India* headline stated, "Muslim leaders approve Obama's 'jihad' remarks."[21]

America's counter-terrorism policy, both at home and abroad, is being fatally undermined by the Obama administration's stubborn refusal to acknowledge the deep theological roots of violent jihad. In his NYU speech, Brennan declared to his audience that he "look[s] forward to an honest and candid discussion" about national security. But Brennan demonstrated in that very speech his fundamental inability to have such a discussion. In fact, throughout the speech he could not even bring himself to utter the phrase "Islamic terrorism," instead referring generically to "violent extremism"—a meaningless term that senators Lieberman and Collins, after investigating the Fort Hood massacre, specifically denounced as an indication of the flawed mindset that allowed the Fort Hood jihadist attack to occur.[22]

Brennan showed his true attitude toward an "honest and candid discussion" on terrorism when he met with *Washington Times* editors in June 2010. Questioning Brennan's characterization of jihad as peaceful and legitimate, an editor asked him to comment on the assertions of jihadists that Islamic scripture defines jihad as being inherently violent. Brennan responded by snapping, "I think we've finished. I have to get going." Then he stormed out of the room.[23] It was a stunning, physical depiction of the administration's petulant refusal to acknowledge the violent mandates of Islam.

Lieberman and Collins strongly admonished the administration to begin calling the threat we face by its proper name—"violent Islamic extremism." But that expression, of course, implies a connection between those three terms that Obama vehemently denies.

Until the U.S. government finds the courage to abandon its bromides about the glories of Islam and confront the cold, hard fact of violent jihadist ideology, we can expect to see a lot more Fort Hoods here at home, and a lot more Mumbais abroad.

★ ★ ★

Let's return for a moment to James Clapper's affirmation that the Muslim Brotherhood is a secular organization. How could the director of national intelligence be so wrong about such an influential jihadist group? That's a story in itself. By the time Clapper was soft-pedaling the Brotherhood threat, American Islamic groups associated with the organization had long positioned themselves as the go-to experts on Islam for the U.S. government. Since the 1993 World Trade Center bombing, whenever a terrorist attack has occurred or a terror plot has been thwarted—often involving individuals who were associated with and had been radicalized by Muslim Brotherhood ideologues—our government leaders time and again have turned to the Muslim Brotherhood's U.S. front groups for advice. These organizations are the government's "interfaith partners" who have been telling our homeland security, law enforcement, and intelligence agencies that the Brotherhood is a benign, peaceful organization that could be our greatest ally in the Middle East.

And every time our government gets burned by listening to and associating with these Brotherhood fronts, U.S. officials go right back to them for more advice. In late 2010, my friend, investigative reporter Patrick Poole, published a report reviewing some of the worst examples of the "blowback" from the government's outreach to the Muslim Brotherhood.[24] A few of the most glaring examples include:

- **Abdurahman Alamoudi.** The most frequent Muslim visitor to the Clinton White House and a consultant in establishing the Pentagon's Muslim chaplain program, Alamoudi was also al-Qaeda's top fundraiser in America and was eventually arrested and convicted in a Libyan intelligence plot to kill the Saudi crown prince. The government's former top Islamic adviser is currently serving a 23-year prison sentence.
- **Ali Mohamed.** Al-Qaeda's security chief, Mohamed infiltrated the U.S. Army Special Forces and was even used to

help train soldiers in Middle East affairs. While he was working with the FBI and CIA as an informant, he was secretly double-crossing these agencies and helped Osama bin Laden plan the 1998 attacks on the U.S. Embassies in Kenya and Tanzania.

- **Anwar al-Awlaki.** Before he fled the United States in 2002, al-Qaeda cleric al-Awlaki was mentor to at least three of the 9/11 terrorists, led Islamic prayers inside the U.S. Capitol for the Congressional Muslim Staffers Association, and was hosted at an "interfaith" lunch inside the still-smoldering Pentagon just after the 9/11 attacks.

- **Faisal Gill.** A former deputy of al-Qaeda fundraiser Abdurahman Alamoudi, Gill was appointed policy director for the Department of Homeland Security's Intelligence Division. Members of Congress later demanded an investigation into how Gill, with no previous intelligence experience, could have been hired to such a position with his terror-tied background. Gill resigned before the investigation could be completed.

The common thread among these incidents is the influence of the Muslim Brotherhood in America. And the U.S. government can't plead ignorance about the Brotherhood's goals. During the Holy Land Foundation terrorism financing trial in 2007 and 2008, federal prosecutors entered into evidence documents recovered in a raid of top Muslim Brotherhood leader Ismail Elbarasse's home in suburban Washington, D.C. One such document was a 1991 Muslim Brotherhood strategic memorandum that laid out the organization's ultimate goal in America:

The Ikhwan [Muslim Brotherhood] must understand that their work in America is a kind of grand jihad in eliminating and destroying the Western civilization from within and sabotaging its miserable house by their hands and the hands of the believers so that it is eliminated and God's religion is made victorious over all other religions.

How does the Brotherhood intend to do this? The memo directs the Brotherhood members to gain "mastery of the art of 'coalitions,' the art of 'absorption' and the principles of 'cooperation.'"[25] The document makes clear that the Brotherhood's chief tactic is to use our own democratic and pluralistic systems against us. One only needs to look at the laundry list of infiltrations and the government's failure to respond to those incidents to see that the Muslim Brotherhood's "grand jihad" on U.S. soil has been wildly successful.

That memo also lists what Brotherhood leaders call "our organizations." This list reads like a "Who's Who" of the U.S. government's Muslim outreach partners, including:

- The Islamic Society of North America (ISNA), the largest Islamic umbrella group in the country.
- The Islamic Circle of North America (ICNA), one of the ideological training arms of the Muslim Brotherhood.
- The North American Islamic Trust (NAIT), which holds the property titles to many American mosques.
- The Muslim Public Affairs Council (MPAC), which is a constant resource referred to by government agencies and the media.
- The Islamic Association for Palestine, which gave birth to another well-known Islamic organization, the Council on American-Islamic Relations (CAIR).

That the Muslim Brotherhood has the United States in its sights is hardly old news. As I described in chapter one, the supreme guide of the Muslim Brotherhood, Mohammed Badi, gave a sermon in October 2010 in which he openly declared war on America and Israel. The animosity of the Muslim Brotherhood toward the West and Israel goes back to the group's earliest days. In the 1930s and 1940s, the Muslim Brotherhood in Egypt maintained a special unit, called the "Secret Apparatus," which launched terror attacks against Western targets, hoping to purge Egypt of all Western influences. In 1948, a member of this "Secret Apparatus" gunned down the Egyptian prime minister. That was also the year that Israel was reborn as a Jewish nation, and Muslim Brotherhood founder and leader Hassan al-Banna sent troops to fight alongside Arab nations in an effort to crush Israel's nascent democracy. The animosity toward Israel and the West, and the burning desire for a Muslim conquest of both entities, has been a cornerstone of the Brotherhood's ideology ever since.

The Brotherhood's targeting of Israel took on a new level of intensity with the formation of Hamas in 1988. In fact, the Hamas Covenant specifically identifies the group as the Palestinian faction of the Muslim Brotherhood. That same covenant invokes *The Protocols of the Elders of Zion* and the notorious Islamic hadith that claims that Judgment Day will not come until Muslims rise up and murder all the Jews. As we'll see in the next chapter, this brand of eliminationist anti-Semitism is a bedrock of jihadist ideology, whether Sunni or Shia. That means, for U.S. government officials, it's just one more inconvenient truth that must be ignored at all costs.

CHAPTER NINE

FIRST THEY CAME FOR THE JEWS

I t's time for another round of "Who Said It? The Anti-Semitic Version."
Our first statement is a withering assault on the "Zionist entity"
that would make any Iranian ayatollah proud: "I am telling you that
what the Israelis are doing to the Palestinians is genocide. ... It is worse
than the Holocaust, of course."

So who said it? Was it Iranian "president" Mahmoud Ahmadinejad?
A leader of Hamas or Hezbollah? Or perhaps a spokesman for the Egyptian Muslim Brotherhood?

Try none of the above. The man behind this dose of anti-Semitic
bombast is actually a pillar of his Dearborn, Michigan community and
publisher of the largest Arab-American newspaper in the United States.

His name is Osama Siblani. And while he professed to be a non-
practicing Muslim when we spoke in the Dearborn offices of the *Arab-American News* in late 2005, his anti-Israel rhetoric would have fit quite
nicely at a Hamas rally in Gaza.

"Is Hezbollah a terrorist group?" I asked Siblani.

"No, they are not terrorists," he answered, deadpan. "Absolutely not. No. They are freedom fighters."

"What about Hamas?" I countered.

"Freedom fighters as well," Siblani responded emphatically.

Siblani, a native of Lebanon, began publishing the *Arab-American News* in 1984. He picked the perfect place to do it; Dearborn, located just outside Detroit, boasts one of the largest concentrations of Arab Muslims in the world outside the Middle East—comprising over 30 percent of the city's total population of roughly 100,000. A large chunk of those Arab residents hail from Lebanon, although there are significant numbers of Iraqis, Yemenis, and Palestinians as well. Accordingly, Dearborn is home to several sizeable mosques, including the nation's largest, the sprawling Islamic Center of America, which is located near the headquarters of the Ford Motor company.

I had journeyed to Dearborn with a CBN camera crew to investigate reports of widespread support among the city's residents for the Lebanon-based terrorist group, Hezbollah. I spent my first day in town walking the gritty streets of Dearborn's east and south sides—which were lined with row after row of businesses whose signs were written in Arabic, not English—to try to gauge the local pulse. Veiled women and men in Islamic garb were a common sight, and there was a distinctly Middle Eastern feel to the place.

Since my trip there a few years back, Dearborn's reputation as "Dearbornistan," an isolated Muslim enclave that is unfriendly to infidel outsiders, has only spread further. Several local residents have been arrested for aiding Hezbollah, and intelligence sources have confirmed to me that the city is, in fact, viewed as one of the epicenters for Hezbollah support in the United States. Unsurprisingly, aspects of sharia law, including the stifling of free expression and freedom of religion, have taken root. In June 2010, four Christian evangelists were arrested by Dearborn police for daring to engage a group of young Muslim attendees in a respectful religious discussion at the city's annual Arab International Festival.

The evangelists captured the incident on video. The clip, which they later posted on YouTube, showed that they never once raised their voices during their discussion with the Muslim youths, nor did they hand out Christian tracts or literature criticizing Islam that could incite an altercation.[1] Nevertheless, Dearborn police confiscated their cameras and led them from the festival in handcuffs. The four spent the night in jail for preaching the Gospel—in the United States of America. Dearborn Democratic mayor Jack O'Reilly, shamelessly seeking to curry favor with his restive Muslim constituency, later defended the arrests, characterizing the evangelists' peaceful activities as an "attack on the city of Dearborn."[2]

In the future, O'Reilly would be well advised to pay greater attention to potential attacks emanating *from* Dearborn against American targets, courtesy of the city's Hezbollah devotees.

As my interviews with Imam Mohammed Ali Elahi (the Iranian-born, Khomeinist cleric discussed in chapter eight) and Osama Siblani showed, support for Hezbollah is not just endemic among average Dearborners, it is also pervasive among acknowledged leaders of the city's Muslim community. Yet according to the *Arab-American News* website, Osama Siblani, the same guy who extolled Hamas and Hezbollah as "freedom fighters" during our interview and accused Israel of surpassing the worst genocide in human history, has been sought out by "successive American administrations" for his "counsel" on the Middle East. He has attended White House lawn picnics for the media and was even present for the White House signing ceremony of the Oslo Accords in 1993.[3] And despite his raw Jew-hatred and public praise for Islamic terrorist groups, Siblani has been honored by various educational institutions and media groups in the Detroit metropolitan area.

How deep does Siblani's support for Hezbollah and hatred of Israel run? As my cameraman and I were packing up our equipment and preparing to leave the offices of the *Arab-American News*, I asked Siblani his thoughts on Sheikh Hassan Nasrallah, the leader of Hezbollah and a man devoted to the destruction of both Israel and America. Siblani's response: "I know of no more honorable man in the world than Hassan Nasrallah."

Mind you, Siblani purports to be a secular Muslim. One can only imagine how the more devout of Dearborn feel about Nasrallah, who commonly refers to the United States as the "Great Satan" and has said of the Jews, "If they all gather in Israel, it will save us the trouble of going after them worldwide."[4]

My encounters in Dearborn helped shape one of my most tried-and-true principles in reporting on jihad and Islamism. To gauge whether a Muslim is moderate, I simply ask one question, usually near the beginning of the interview: "Do you recognize Israel's right to exist?" If I don't get an automatic, unequivocal "yes," I know I am dealing with someone who is not only hostile to Western, democratic values, but who is likely sympathetic to our jihadist enemies. It's simple: no Israel, no moderate. That is the ultimate litmus test, and it has never failed me. The question of Israel and its existence as a Jewish state cuts right to the heart of the matter—and straight through the disingenuous "we respect all religions" platitudes of smooth-talking Islamist mouthpieces in the United States.

Typically, these U.S.-based Muslim spokesmen will unreservedly condemn al-Qaeda and Osama bin Laden—but that's easy. Dig a little deeper and you'll find they inevitably blame terrorism on America itself—for its "imperialist" Mid-East policies and its support for Israel. Likewise, most American Islamists are shrewd enough to decry 9/11 when asked about it publicly, although one of their favorite lines—that the perpetrators were not "true Muslims"—is always good for a chuckle.

Bottom line: if someone tells you that Hamas and Hezbollah are in a different category than al-Qaeda, and that, unlike bin Laden's group, those two terrorist organizations are "resisting occupation" and their members are justified in blowing up themselves and Israeli women and children, you know immediately that you're not dealing with a moderate. In fact, you're dealing with a willing accessory to the Islamist plan to drive Israel into the sea and, ultimately, to erase the entire Jewish people from the face of the earth. Sheikh Yusuf al-Qaradawi, spiritual leader of the Muslim Brotherhood and one of the most influential Islamic clerics in the world, articulated that plan in his 2003 book, *Fatawa Min Ajl Falastin*, or "Fatwas on Palestine":

> [W]e believe that the battle between us and the Jews is coming....Such a battle is not driven by nationalistic causes or patriotic belonging; it is rather driven by religious incentives. This battle is not going to happen between Arabs and Zionists, or between Jews and Palestinians, or between Jews or anybody else. It is between Muslims and Jews as is clearly stated in the hadith. This battle will occur between the collective body of Muslims and the collective body of Jews i.e. all Muslims and all Jews.[5]

The hadith that Qaradawi invokes has been cited by jihadists throughout the ages—including by Hamas in their founding charter—to justify Muslim massacres of Jews. According to Islamic tradition, Mohammed told his companions:

> The last hour would not come unless the Muslims will fight against the Jews and the Muslims would kill them until the Jews would hide themselves behind a stone or a tree and a stone or a tree would say: Muslim, or servant of Allah, there is a Jew behind me; come and kill him. [41:6985]

That infamous hadith may be the most well known of the anti-Semitic references found in Islam's core texts, but it only scratches the surface. Consider the following sampling of Allah-sanctioned, Jew-hating venom from the Koran and hadiths:

- "Ignominy shall be [the Jews'] portion wheresoever they are found....They have incurred anger from their Lord, and wretchedness is laid upon them...because they disbelieve the revelations of Allah and slew the Prophets wrongfully...because they were rebellious and used to transgress." [Surah 111, v. 112]

- "And thou wilt find them [the Jews] the greediest of mankind." [Surah 11, v. 96]

- "[The Jews] are the heirs of Hell....They will spare no pains to corrupt you. They desire nothing but your ruin. Their hatred is clear from what they say....When evil befalls you they rejoice." [Surah 111, v. 117–120]

- "Because of the wrongdoing of the Jews....And of their taking usury....and of their devouring people's wealth by false pretenses. We have prepared for those of them who disbelieve a painful doom." [Surah IV, v. 160, 161]

- "Allah hath cursed [the Jews] for their disbelief." [Surah IV, v. 46]

- "[The Jews] will spare no pains to corrupt you. They desire nothing but your ruin. Their hatred is clear from what they say, but more violent is the hatred which their breasts conceal." [Surah III, v. 117–120]

- "And thou seest [Jews and Christians] vying one with another in sin and transgression and their devouring of illicit gain. Verily evil is what they do. Why do not the rabbis and the priests forbid their evil speaking and their devouring of illicit gain?...[E]vil is their handiwork." [Surah V, v. 62, 63]

- "O ye who believe! Take not the Jews and Christians for friends." [Surah V, v. 51]

- "The most vehement of mankind in hostility [are] the Jews and the idolators." [Surah V, v. 82]

- "Allah fighteth against [the Jews]. How perverse they are!" [Surah IX, v. 30]

- "[The Jews] spread evil in the land." [Surah V, v. 62–66]

- "[The Jews] knowingly perverted [the word of Allah], know of nothing except lies...commit evil and become engrossed in sin." [Surah II, v. 71–85]
- In addition, Jews are referred to as "apes and pigs" in no fewer than three Koranic verses. [2:62–65, 5:59–60, and 7:166]

In case you still don't get the picture, consider Mohammed's own personal example. Although Jews today are banned from entering Saudi Arabia, the Saudi city of Medina, Islam's second holiest city, was originally a Jewish settlement. Then along came Mohammed. Dr. Andrew Bostom, who's written two authoritative books on Islamic history, has recounted the behavior of Islam's prophet and founder following the Muslim victory over the Jewish Qurayzah tribe of Medina in 627 AD:

> [S]ome 600 to 900 men from the Qurayzah were led on Muhammad's order to the Market of Medina. Trenches were dug, and the men were beheaded; their decapitated corpses were buried in the trenches while Muhammad watched. Male youths who had not reached puberty were spared. Women and children were sold into slavery, a number of them being distributed as gifts among Muhammad's companions. According to Muhammad's biographer Ibn Ishaq, Muhammad chose one of the Qurayzah women (Rayhana) for himself. The Qurahzah's property and other possessions (including weapons) were also divided up as additional "booty" among the Muslims.[6]

And so the last remaining Jewish tribe of Medina was systematically exterminated, on Mohammed's orders, as he watched. Given this ugly precedent set by Islam's founder, not to mention the aforementioned verses from the Koran and hadiths, is it any wonder that a vast number of devout Muslims today wield a lethal hostility against the Jews?

I did not fabricate the anti-Jewish verses from Islam's core texts, nor did I create the story of the Medina massacre out of thin air. This is all part of the historical record, no matter how much our elected officials choose to ignore it. So are the various bloody pogroms waged against Jews living in Muslim countries throughout the centuries, not to mention the collaboration of Arab Muslims with the Nazis during World War II—which saw the leader of the Palestinians at the time, Grand Mufti Haj Amin al-Husseini, personally visit Nazi death camps and live as an honored guest in Berlin.

While in Germany, al-Husseini met with Adolf Hitler and the Nazi leadership and encouraged them to extend their genocidal plans for the Jews to the Arab world. Al-Husseini also helped recruit some 20,000 Bosnian Muslim volunteers for Hitler's Waffen SS. The Mufti's recruits went on to perpetrate some of the most vicious crimes of the Holocaust, wantonly slaughtering Jews throughout Croatia, Serbia, and Hungary.[7]

Yes, horrific pogroms and massacres against Jews occurred with shameful frequency for centuries in Christian Europe as well, with Nazi Germany, medieval Spain, and Tsarist Russia the most notorious culprits. Yet none of these so-called "Christian" regimes could point to any verse in the Bible, be it Old Testament or New, that would condone their brutal discrimination and violence against Jews—because such verses do not exist.

Indeed, the Bible is a book by and about the Jewish people. Moses, Abraham, Isaac, Jacob, Kings David and Solomon, and all of the prophets, from Daniel to Elijah to Ezekiel, were Jews. Likewise, Jesus was a Jew who deeply loved his people and the land of Israel. His mother Mary, his earthly father Joseph, and all twelve apostles were proud Jews as well.

The first Christians—comprising the first Church—were Jewish. And they all worshipped as Lord and Savior—as Christians do today—a Jewish carpenter from the Galilee region of Israel. So if you're a Christian with an ounce of anti-Semitism in your body, you'd be well advised to lose it. Needless to say, such feelings are antithetical to the Gospels. But as we've seen, sadly, they are not foreign to the Koran or the hadiths, and those Muslim SS units were, in their view, no doubt standing on solid theological ground.

So, too, were Muslims who chased out the nearly 1 million Jews who had been living in Islamic countries like Yemen, Egypt, and Libya before the re-establishment of the state of Israel in 1948.[8] For instance, that year, there were some 150,000 Jews living in Iraq. Today there are none. Most of these Jewish refugees, from Iraq and elsewhere, fled from persecution at the hands of their Muslim countrymen to the fledgling state of Israel. There, they would no longer be forced to live as tread-upon, second-class citizens, or dhimmis, as mandated by Islamic sharia law.

But even in Israel, Jews have not been able to enjoy a moment's rest from the murderous ire of their Islamic neighbors, who will not rest until the "sons of apes and pigs," as they quite commonly call the Jewish people, are driven into the sea once and for all. Incidentally, don't hold your breath waiting for the UN to begin a push for the hundreds of thousands of Jewish refugees from Muslim countries to reclaim the land and property that was stolen from them throughout the twentieth century. When it comes to these Jews run out of Muslim lands, the "international community" does not recognize any "right of return."

★ ★ ★

The typical response of my genuinely moderate Muslim colleagues—most of whom, tellingly, do not follow the Koran or hadiths literally—when challenged on Mohammed's behavior in Medina or the many anti-Jewish verses in Islam's holy texts is the same one they use to explain away the Verse of the Sword and Allah's other unsavory injunctions. They argue that Mohammed's revelations were confined to the milieu of seventh-century Arabia and were never meant to apply to the modern day. But as we've seen, that view is not shared by the vast majority of the world's Muslims and certainly not by the jihadists, who consider the commands of Mohammed open-ended and applicable to contemporary life—and that extends to their treatment of Jews.

Over the past ten years, I've covered several dozen cases of homegrown jihad plots on American soil. In every one of those cases, without fail, the jihadists in question held a burning hatred for Jews. Not just the state of Israel, but Jews in general. And Jewish targets were commonly among those being considered for attacks. Additionally, there have been countless instances of old-fashioned, anti-Jewish incitement and blood libels publicly spouted by radicalized American Muslims in recent years. Among them:

• On May 10, 2010, my friend, conservative activist and author David Horowitz, gave a speech at the University of California-Irvine. His appearance there was in response to an event called "Israeli Apartheid Week" that was being held at the same time by the school's Muslim Student Association. The MSA, as we discussed in chapter eight, is a Muslim Brotherhood-connected group that has seen several former leaders convicted on terrorism charges. During the Q-and-A session following Horowitz's address, a female MSA member named Jumanah Imad Albahri stood up and began to criticize him. So Horowitz cut to the chase and asked her if she supported the terrorist group Hamas, a question Albahri refused to answer. Their exchange then took an even more chilling turn:

> **Horowitz:** I am a Jew. The head of Hezbollah has said that he hopes that we will gather in Israel so he doesn't have to hunt us down globally. For it or against it?
>
> **Albahri:** For it.[9]

This unhesitant statement of support for genocide against the Jews was issued at a public forum on an American college campus. Yet Albahri was never reprimanded by UC-Irvine, and remained a member of the school's MSA chapter.

• In late December 2008, Israel finally responded to years of lethal rocket attacks launched from the Gaza Strip by conducting a three-week-long military operation against Hamas in Gaza. Operation Cast Lead, which ultimately resulted in a sharp decrease in rocket attacks and a weakening of Hamas's Gaza infrastructure, sparked worldwide Muslim protests against Israel, including throughout Europe and the United States. As I reported for CBN, shouts of "Allahu Akhbar," vicious anti-Jewish signs and rhetoric, and even physical violence were all commonplace at these marches, in which radical Muslims were joined by their fellow Israel-haters from the radical Left.

At one such event in Fort Lauderdale, Florida, a group of Jewish activists gathered to stage a peaceful counter-protest in support of Israel. It wasn't long before a Muslim woman in a hijab began to curse and shout anti-Semitic slurs at them. "Go back to the oven!" she shrieked, referencing one of the more notorious methods in which the Nazis murdered Jews during the Holocaust. "You need a big oven, that's what you need!" To drive the point home further, another Muslim protestor waved a sign that read, "Nuke Israel."[10]

• Over Labor Day weekend, 2010, the unholy alliance between the hard Left and Islamic supremacists reared its ugly head yet again at a venomous anti-Israel rally in Washington, D.C. The gathering, which featured Hezbollah flags waving side-by-side with banners bearing socialist slogans, was held to mark "Al-Quds Day"—an annual event where Muslims call for the "liberation" of Jerusalem from Israeli hands. And how would such a "liberation" occur if the Islamo-socialist alliance had its way? One speaker named Kaukab Siddique helpfully explained:

> We must stand united to defeat, to destroy, to dismantle Israel—if possible by peaceful means. Perhaps, like Saladin, we will give them enough food and water to travel back to the lands from where they came to occupy other people.[11]

Now, I personally don't know of any nation in human history that was destroyed "by peaceful means," but since Islamists always seem to find creative new ways to wreak havoc upon Jews, I suppose anything is possible. It's more likely, however, that Siddique's preferred method for destroying Israel is through armed jihad, as he made clear in further statements at the rally:

> For the Jews, I would say, see what could happen to you if the Muslims wake up. And I say to the Muslims, dear brothers and sisters, unite and rise up against this hydra-headed monster which calls itself Zionism. ... The Koran says drive them out from where they drove you out. There's no question of just dismantling the settlements. These settlements are only the tentacles of the devil that resides in Tel Aviv.[12]

This is rhetoric straight out of the Ahmadinejad playbook, delivered just minutes from the White House. And Kaukab Siddique isn't some young, radicalized Muslim who frequents al-Qaeda websites in his parents' basement. He is, in fact, an associate professor of English at Lincoln University, a small, historically African-American college outside of Philadelphia. Since 2003, the school has received almost $200 million in Pennsylvania state funds, despite employing a genocidal anti-Semite and unabashed Islamist—Siddique has also voiced support for the Taliban and for convicted al-Qaeda terrorists—as a member of its faculty.

When I contacted Lincoln University for comment about Siddique's remarks, the school's executive vice president told me that while Lincoln does not agree with Siddique's comments about Israel, the professor is tenured and has freedom of speech. He added that the school can't control what Siddique does or says on his own time as a private citizen. Something tells me Lincoln's brass would have been slightly more proactive had Siddique called for the extermination of Muslims, blacks, or homosexuals. But since Siddique—whose long track record of anti-Semitic statements includes Holocaust denial—was merely targeting those pesky Jews, Lincoln University continues to treat him as its very own "crazy uncle."

My story for CBN about Siddique's genocidal outburst in Washington was picked up by several national and international news outlets in October 2010 and was covered by both Bill O'Reilly and Glenn Beck on FOX News. In response to the ensuing uproar, the school issued a formal statement of condemnation of Siddique. Nevertheless, he remains on the school's faculty, comfortably tenured and free to call for Allah's wrath upon the Jews to his heart's content—on his own time, of course.

★ ★ ★

The Islamist onslaught against the Jews is just the beginning phase of a much larger plan. "First the Saturday people, then the Sunday people" has long been a rallying cry of jihadists, from Indonesia to Iran and beyond—meaning that once the Jews are wiped out, Christians will be next in the crosshairs. With Jews already forcibly evicted from Muslim countries, we now see the Christians of the Middle East being targeted for extermination by Islamic supremacists, to the point where the region may very well be nearing a day where it is practically bereft of any Christian presence at all, leaving Islam unchallenged.

Nevertheless, a narrative exists—particularly on the Left but also among the isolationist, Pat Buchanan/Ron Paul wing of the political Right—arguing that an end to America's support for Israel would mean an end to Islamic jihadists' war against America. Throw Israel under the bus, they say, and the likes of al-Qaeda and Iran will leave us alone; the jihadists are angry with us because we support their Israeli enemy, the great oppressor of Palestinians and the scourge of the Muslim world. Abandon Israel to its fate, they suggest, cut aid to those troublesome Jews, and eliminate their public support, and the Islamists will be content to remain in the deserts and mountains of the Middle East and South Asia, never to target America again.

This stance is not only immoral, it is inherently destructive to American interests. Above all, it flies in the face of Islamic history and ideology. Since its miraculous rebirth in 1948, the tiny state of Israel has borne the brunt of the fury of Islamic terrorism. And this outpost of democracy, freedom, and human rights has been the canary in the coalmine for the rest of Western civilization. Israel, surrounded by a sea of frothing Islamic radicals, is the first line of defense for the West in the struggle against global jihad. If this lone bastion of Western values in the world's most violent—and, due to oil, arguably its most strategic—region is overrun, the floodgates are open. Or as the former prime minister of Spain, José María Aznar, told me when I interviewed him for CBN in 2010, "If Israel goes down, we all go down."

Aznar was so dismayed by the Obama administration's abandonment of the Jewish State, which we'll examine shortly, that in 2010 he helped start an organization called "Friends of Israel" comprising several leading Western political figures and thinkers. Aznar and his colleagues fully grasp the ramifications of "First the Saturday people, then the Sunday people."

Islamist ideology demands that sharia law be established worldwide, and that any country not living under the banner of Islam is *Dar al-Harb*, or the land of war. In other words, Islam must be spread to the ends of the earth by any means necessary, as mandated by the Koran. That means, obviously, that the elimination of Israel is only the beginning. The throw-Israel-under-the-bus crowd, if it surveys Islamic history, has to know this. If Israel is indeed the root cause of Islamic rage against the West today, as they argue, then why did Muslims embark on two great waves of conquest against Europe—first in the eighth and ninth centuries and then again in the heyday of the Ottoman Empire—during a period when the state of Israel did not even exist?

From 70 A.D.—when the Romans destroyed the Second Temple in Jerusalem and the Jews were subsequently scattered around the globe—until 1948, there was no nation of Israel. Yet during that period, Muslims conquered Spain, Sicily, the Balkans, Bulgaria, Romania, Hungary, and Greece, drove to the gates of Vienna twice, and even reached as far as central France in the eighth century. They also frequently raided southern Italy, sacking Rome in 846 AD.

Since there was no Israel during this time, the unrelenting jihad against Europe clearly had to be motivated by something else. That something was Islamist ideology. Yet segments of the Left and isolationist Right would have us believe that the third great wave of jihad that began in the latter part of the twentieth century and persists today is due mainly to Israel's supposed occupation of "Palestinian land." As for the steady Islamic aggression against the West that transpired over much of the 1,378 years before the state of Israel was reestablished, why acknowledge the facts when you can blame that reliable scapegoat, the Jews?

Surveying the seething cauldron of terrorism and anti-Western animus that is the Middle East, the Obama administration, too, believes it's all Israel's fault. The central problem, we're led to believe, is Israel's construction of apartments in Jerusalem—for over 3,000 years, the capital of the Jewish people—and its building of additions, like a children's playroom for a growing family, onto existing homes. The Obamis argue that if only Israel would stop building so-called Jewish "settlements"—in places like East Jerusalem and the biblical heartland of Judea and Samaria, also referred to as the West Bank—then Israel and the Palestinians could finally come to a comprehensive peace agreement and all would be right with the world. They don't seem to notice that Israel's so-called "partner for peace," the Palestinian Authority, has little credibility on the West Bank street and only controls half the Palestinian territories (with the other half, Gaza, controlled by Hamas terrorists), or that Israel's withdrawal from both Gaza and southern Lebanon has resulted in both those areas becoming permanent jihadist bases used for attacking Israel.

Despite these glaring red flags and the steady diet of anti-Semitic blood libels and incitement broadcast daily by official Palestinian Authority television, the Obama White House believes now is the time for Israel to offer concessions to the Palestinians, cede Israeli territory—including half of Jerusalem—and strike a lasting peace deal. If Israel does so, three things will supposedly happen: 1) Other Arab regimes will be inspired to strike similar peace deals with Israel and will finally recognize the Jewish State's right to exist. 2) Other Arab regimes will join Israel and the West to form a united front that will successfully dissuade Iran from acquiring nuclear weapons. 3) Islamic terrorism against the West will decrease dramatically.

This theory is known inside the Washington beltway as "linkage," because it directly ties stopping Iran's nuclear weapons program to establishing a Palestinian state. Give the Palestinians a homeland of their own, the liberal political establishment intones, and Iran and its proxies will be significantly weakened, deprived of the "Palestinian card" they have used as a hammer against Israel for so long. Israeli leaders, quite rightly, would rather deal with Iran's nuclear weapons program first, and revisit the Palestinian issue down the road.

After all, the Iranian regime, which is devoted to Israel's destruction, may very well have a nuclear weapon by 2012. Such a development would pose an immediate threat to Israel's very existence and, in the Israelis' view, must be countered with the utmost urgency. On the other hand, the Palestinians are ruled by two opposing factions, Hamas and the Palestinian Authority—both of which refuse to recognize Israel's right to exist—and have shown no desire to renounce terrorism against Israeli interests. In other words, the Palestinians are a disjointed, radicalized mess with zero capability of forming any type of moderate, cohesive state in the near future. Therefore, let's deal with Iran first, the Israelis reason, and then we can talk about the Palestinian issue later. It makes perfect sense ... unless you are an Obama administration official.

In early February 2011, as Muslim nations like Tunisia, Egypt, Libya, Bahrain, and Yemen, among others, were being roiled by massive protests and civil unrest that had nothing whatsoever to do with Israel, recently retired Obama national security advisor James Jones delivered an address proclaiming—you guessed it—the importance of linkage. To make matters worse, Jones delivered his remarks before an Israeli audience:

> I'm of the belief that had God appeared in front of President Obama in 2009 and said if he could do one thing on the face of the planet, and one thing only, to make the world a better

place and give people more hope and opportunity for the future, I would venture that it would have something to do with finding the two-state solution to the Middle East.[13]

Something tells me God would not favor giving Palestinian Muslims half of Jerusalem—a city that is never even mentioned in the Koran but is mentioned in the Bible hundreds of times as Israel's eternal capital. Regardless, the ultimate problem with Jones's assessment is one of ideology, not theology. He and his former cohorts in the Obama administration have very publicly made "illegitimate" Israeli settlements, not Palestinian terrorism or Iranian belligerence, their core Middle East issue. From the cozy confines of Washington, D.C., they arrogantly dictate to the people of Israel, a sovereign nation, where Jews can and cannot live in the Jewish ancestral homeland.

Meanwhile, they refuse even to mention a fundamental problem with their plans—that Christian holy sites in East Jerusalem and elsewhere are far less likely to remain protected, as they have been for decades by the Israelis, if they are turned over to Palestinian control. Recall the desecration of Bethlehem's Church of the Nativity in 2002, when gunmen from the PLO, Hamas, and other Palestinian groups seized the building to avoid capture by Israeli troops. With the Israelis refusing to storm the church, a thirty-nine-day standoff ensued. During that time, in a house of worship revered as the birthplace of Jesus, the Palestinians held the clergy hostage, set fire to part of the church compound, looted golden icons, tore up Bibles, and most alarmingly, planted around forty bombs throughout the church that the Israelis had to dismantle after the attackers surrendered.[14]

The appalling violation of the church was by no means an isolated incident. Indeed, in recent years Middle Eastern Christians have been subject to a concerted attack by their Muslim neighbors. On March 8, 2011, thirteen people were killed in Cairo, Egypt, after a Muslim mob attacked thousands of Christians protesting the burning of a church by another Muslim mob.[15] This came just three months after twenty-one people were killed in a suicide bombing outside a Christian church in

Alexandria, Egypt. In light of similar, ongoing attacks on the dwindling Christian communities in Iraq, Indonesia, Pakistan, and beyond, the Obama administration's enthusiasm for securing Palestinian control of Christian holy sites seems incomprehensible. Yet, in light of Obama officials' unshakeable belief in the peacefulness and greatness and tolerance of Islam, and their dogged pursuit of Muslim outreach even at the expense of Americans' physical security, we see that their policy on this issue reflects a ruthless consistency in their agenda.

As part of this strategy, Obama administration officials have openly and repeatedly excoriated Israel over apartment units in Jerusalem, with UN ambassador Susan Rice, in an undiplomatic insult, labeling them as "folly" in February 2011.[16] Is it any wonder that concern is growing in Israel that the United States, under the Obama administration, can no longer be trusted to veto the Arabs' never-ending parade of anti-Israel measures at the UN?

The Obama administration's stunning disrespect for Israel reached a low point in March 2010, when Israeli prime minister Benjamin Netanyahu visited the White House. Netanyahu—the elected leader of a steadfast and pivotal U.S. ally—was ushered in the back door of the building and denied even the standard photo opportunity with Obama. The Israeli delegation was not invited to join the president for dinner, and Obama actually left them to dine on his own when they wouldn't agree to his demands to halt Jewish building in East Jerusalem.[17]

Rest assured that Israel's enemies were overjoyed when details of Obama's White House snub of Netanyahu emerged. In a vain attempt to appear "even-handed" and court America-hating jihadists, the Obama administration has made a great show of publicly slamming Israel—the only reliable and stable U.S. ally in the Middle East and a bulwark against Islamic terror. Their efforts have left Israelis feeling completely isolated at a dangerous time. Global anti-Semitism is on the rise, as is a movement advocating that nations divest from, boycott, and sanction Israel—the so-called "BDS movement." Furthermore, the European Union and the UN are applying relentless pressure on the Israelis to throw caution to the wind, surrender territory, and create a Palestinian state *right now*, current conditions on the ground and potential disastrous consequences be damned. And this solution, mind you, would largely consist of a peace treaty much like the one with Egypt for which Israel gave up the Sinai Peninsula—a treaty that leaders of the Egyptian Muslim Brotherhood, Egypt's possible future rulers, are already declaring "null and void."[18]

Israel surveys its immediate neighborhood and sees, aside from the looming threat of a nuclear-armed Iran, a Turkey that has gone from an ally to a heated Islamist adversary; an Egypt that has gone from friend (in relative terms) to possible Muslim Brotherhood-run foe; another relatively friendly country, Jordan, that is facing its own serious internal unrest, led largely by the Brotherhood; and nasty possible outcomes of revolutions in other Middle Eastern states where fanatical, anti-Israel Islamists could come to power. For Israel, circa 2011, the only thing that is 100 percent certain is that Iran, Syria, Hamas, and Hezbollah are licking their chops and waiting for the right moment to strike—we should take these entities' own word on that. Unwavering American support used to be a certainty as well, until President Obama decided to throw it out the window in favor of hopeless "engagement" with the sworn enemies of Israel and America.

One such example occurred in February 2010 when, just days after the Obama administration announced it was appointing an ambassador to Syria for the first time in five years—effectively rewarding a state sponsor of terrorism for continued bad behavior—Syrian president Bashar al-Assad held a public dinner meeting in Damascus with Iranian president Mahmoud Ahmadinejad and Hezbollah leader Hassan Nasrallah. In flaunting his relationship with Iran and Hezbollah, Assad delivered a message to Obama that was deliberate and clear: you can engage us all you want, but we will never respect you nor cease our quest to destroy the Jews. The next time the Obama administration accuses someone of "folly," it may want to look in the mirror.

★ ★ ★

As I write this, I'm sitting in a hotel room overlooking the Old City of Jerusalem. In my conversations with Israeli government officials, they keep their thoughts on the damaged relationship with America—damaged through no fault of Israel's—close to the vest, revealing precious little, and understandably so. Average Israelis that I talk to are a different story, however: practically everyone here expresses grave concern about the Obama administration, for the reasons outlined in this chapter and throughout this book. At the same time, they display an upbeat attitude of pride and perseverance. As a people who have survived countless centuries of murderous pogroms, persecution, and discrimination culminating in the horrors of the Holocaust, Jews have learned to deal with whatever is thrown their way. Through it all, Israel not only survives, it thrives.

Despite the wedge the Obama White House has attempted to drive between the United States and Israel, poll after poll shows that an overwhelming majority of Americans stands solidly behind the Jewish State, as does a majority of Congress on both sides of the political aisle. The reasons for that support are varied; for many Christians and Jews, it is a religious duty, as they take quite seriously the precept in the Book of Genesis that God will "bless those who bless [Israel] and curse those who curse [Israel]." Others see Israel as an emerging scientific, technological, and economic juggernaut that is in America's best interests to cultivate. Still others see Israel as an ocean of democratic stability and pro-American sentiment as well as a strategic asset in a region inherently hostile to the United States.

At the end of the day, however, it all boils down to common sense: Israel's enemies are America's enemies—period. Americans instinctively realize that fact, and that the true "underdog" in the Middle East is not the Palestinians—notorious purveyors of Islamic terrorism who danced in the streets when they learned of 9/11—but Israel, a tiny democratic nation of 7 million people (only 6 million of them Jews) surrounded by some 300 million hostile Muslims.

CONCLUSION

We Americans need to stare our enemies in the eyes and make an unflinching commitment to winning the war against global jihad and rooting out the terrorists next door. On a governmental level, a stronger campaign to crush al-Qaeda wherever it rears its head, particularly in the tribal regions of Pakistan—whether the Pakistanis like it or not—is paramount. So is the need not only to neutralize Iran's nuclear weapons program, but to cultivate regime change in Tehran. Other crucial steps include curtailing Muslim immigration to the United States, fixing or eliminating deeply flawed refugee resettlement programs, securing America's borders in a real and effective way, and continuously reducing the influence of Saudi Arabia in U.S. institutions and particularly in American Muslim communities.

Outlawing the Muslim Brotherhood on U.S. soil is another vital defensive measure. Instead of giving Brotherhood operatives an open door to the halls of power in Washington, D.C., we should use all possible legal means to marginalize and discredit them and their plans to build mega-mosques nationwide. The Muslim Brotherhood, whose own documents outline its plan to destroy America from within, is the enemy, and its American front groups should be treated as such.

That extends to the Middle East, where the Obama administration has apparently decided that it can work with the Brotherhood. How else to explain President Obama's infamous Cairo speech in 2009, for which he requested that members of the Egyptian Muslim Brotherhood be present?[1] And how else to explain his support for the ouster of Egyptian president Hosni Mubarak, when it was clear that Egypt's powerful and well-organized Brotherhood faction was most likely to benefit?

Former White House press secretary Robert Gibbs articulated the Obama administration's position in the waning days of Mubarak's regime, saying a reformed Egyptian government "has to include a whole host of important non-secular actors that give Egypt a strong chance to continue to be a stable and reliable partner."[2] The "non-secular actors" Gibbs spoke of were the Muslim Brothers. In essence, the Obama administration is pushing for the participation of an Islamic jihadist group in governing the largest and most influential Arab Muslim nation. This is pure madness, and unless Egypt suddenly blooms into an oasis of democracy after thousands of years of authoritarian rule, it may go down as one of the biggest foreign policy blunders in U.S. history.

When I travel the country to talk about the threats gathering against the United States, I'm constantly asked, "What can I do to help?" While there is no magic bullet to right this ship, there is plenty the average American can do to turn back the rising tide of jihad here at home. Above all, Americans must stay informed. Take at least twenty minutes each day to turn off your iPod, flip off the game, and get up to speed on current events, no matter how depressing you might find them. You owe it to yourself and your children to be aware of the rapidly advancing events in the Muslim world that will continue to affect every American, whether through a massive increase in oil prices or, God forbid, through Islamic terrorism.

Call me an alarmist, but given that we are locked in a civilizational struggle against folks who take the Koran and hadiths literally, it's probably a good idea that Americans be educated about them. Sadly, though, if you stop the average man on the street and ask if he's ever heard of jihad, sharia, or the Verse of the Sword, or if he's ever read Islam's core texts, you'll likely get a shrug of the shoulders and a blank stare before he buries his head back into his Blackberry to text about the results of *American Idol*.

Americans and all people of the West should know the names Charles Martel and Jan Sobieski. Nicknamed "The Hammer," Martel was the grandfather of the legendary Holy Roman Emperor Charlemagne. In the year 732 AD, in one of the pivotal battles of world history, known as the Battle of Tours, Martel led Frankish and Burgundian forces to victory over an advancing Muslim army near the villages of Tours and Poitiers, in north-central France. That's right: after conquering Spain, the armies of Islam advanced as far as central France, with designs on conquering all of Western Europe, until they were decisively defeated by The Hammer. Many historians believe Martel saved Europe and in the process, helped preserve Judeo-Christian, Western civilization. So why aren't Martel and the Battle of Tours taught in middle schools, high schools, and universities in every Western nation?

The same goes for Jan Sobieski, the Polish king who led a combined force of Poles, Austrians, and Germans to victory over the Turkish-led Ottoman Empire at the Battle of Vienna in 1683. It was the second time that the Ottoman Muslims had reached the gates of Vienna before being beaten back (the first being in 1571). In the battle's aftermath, the Ottoman Empire plunged into a long, downward spiral, while Sobieski was hailed by the Pope and others as the savior of Vienna and of Western European civilization. Again: the West is waging an existential struggle against Islamic aggression. Shouldn't Americans know that this is far from the first time that the West has been locked in such a struggle with the forces of Islamic supremacism, and draw inspiration from the courageous Western resisters to jihad that have come before us?

Recall that Ronald Reagan, years before he became president, would devour everything he could get his hands on about Communism, Marxism, and the Soviet system. By the time he was elected president he had a profound knowledge of the Soviet bloc, ultimately helping to lead the United States to victory in the Cold War.

For many people, 9/11 came out of nowhere. This time around, Americans have no excuse. Educate yourself. You don't need to become a news junkie or an Islamic expert, but at least get to know the basics about your enemy. Who is the Muslim Brotherhoood? What is jihad? What is sharia? What is the history of your local mosque, and have reporters uncovered jihadist sermons or jihadist literature there? What does the Koran say about non-Muslims? Learn it, commit it to memory, and tell your family, friends, and neighbors. No pressure or anything: we're only embroiled in a long, generational conflict in which the future of Western civilization is at stake.

Secondly, stay engaged. Join local and national organizations that not only oppose the Islamization of America, but that have real influence in state capitals and on Capitol Hill. The fierce grassroots opposition to the Ground Zero mosque is a perfect example of how average Americans can raise awareness about a topic and help influence the national discourse. Pressure your state and national representatives on issues that matter to America's security. Make your voice heard, especially at the ballot box. Today, with the rise of social media and YouTube, it has never been easier to organize with like-minded people and make a difference.

As I walk through the streets of Jerusalem, which have seen so many deadly "chip away" style attacks over the years, I can't help but wonder whether a day is fast approaching when America's schools, shopping malls, buses, and trains will fall victim to a similar jihadist onslaught. Islamists have made their intentions clear and provided us, through their actions, words, and writings, with their blueprint for destroying America. This information is readily available and time is short. It's long past due for Americans to get to know the enemy as well as the enemy knows us.

ACKNOWLEDGMENTS

I t isn't often that a guy from Fox Chase, Philadelphia gets the opportunity to write a book. That means I have a whole lot of people to thank for helping me get here.

Although the information in *The Terrorist Next Door* is often disturbing and frequently infuriating, the following acknowledgments are a celebration of all the people who showed me love, support, and guidance through the years and helped make this book possible.

The book was written over a period of seven months in planes, trains, hotels, subway cars, coffee shops, public libraries, and at home with an energetic 4-year-old nipping at my heels. For much of that time, sleep was only a rumor, but I lived to tell the tale. And I pray that the book impacts the national dialogue concerning America's struggle against Islamic jihadism—if nothing else, for our children's sake.

First, I want to thank my wife, Lori. Where do I even begin? When we met, we were just a couple of kids back in the neighborhood, without a care in the world. Since then, you have stood by me through good times and bad, tragedies and triumphs, setbacks and opportunities. We've gone through more in our fourteen years together than most people see in a lifetime, yet we're still standing, stronger than ever. I am eternally grateful for your boundless patience, understanding, and encouragement as I worked long hours to make this book a reality, with a newborn in the house, no less. It can never be repaid, and I know it would never even cross your mind to ask because that it is just who you are: a special, beautiful person. And pretty darn good-looking, too. You are a true blessing to me, and I thank God every day for bringing you into my life.

Speaking of blessings from above, my two daughters, Juliana and Leah, are the greatest gifts God could ever have given me. Special thanks go to the extraordinarily beautiful Juliana, for faithfully putting up with those weekends where Daddy would "disappear" to the library for a few hours to hammer out a chapter. It broke my heart every time I walked out the door to work rather than to stay home and play with you. But know that I wrote this book, ultimately, for you and your gorgeous little sister, Leah. I am determined to do everything in my power to ensure that you two little angels grow up in a free and prosperous America that is every bit as special and exceptional as the one I grew up in.

From the time I was just an outspoken little guy with big dreams, my mother Agnes and my late father Fred Sr. provided me with unending love, support, and encouragement in all my endeavors, no matter how improbable they may have seemed at first. Moreover, despite modest means, they did everything in their power to make those dreams a reality, sacrificing greatly to somehow send me to a prestigious high school that helped prepare me for college and my career beyond. Mom, you truly have a servant's heart: thank you a thousand times over for your patience with me, your forgiving nature, and for instilling a love of God in me at a young age. And Dad, you helped shape me into the man I am today. I know that you're reading a copy of this book in heaven and cheering me on the whole way. I love you and will see you again one day in a much better place.

My sister Judy and my brother Fred deserve special thanks for always picking up for their trouble-making, rowdy little brother in my pre-teen years, until I became a rowdy teenager who sprouted to 6 foot 4 and grew big enough to handle himself. Judy, you have been my greatest fan and supporter ever since I was a fifth grader shooting hoops with dreams of someday making it to the NBA. You are a blessing to me and to everyone who knows you and you have the kindest, most generous heart of anyone I have ever known. Thank you for your everlasting friendship and for taking the time to thoroughly read through each of these chapters. Fred, thank you for the thousands of hours of conversation over the years about life, politics, the Middle East, and everything in between. It helped shape the contents of this book. And thanks for letting me tag along with you and "the older guys" up the Rec. I have learned more from you—and from those legendary experiences—than you know.

The idea for this book began not with me, but with my fantastic literary agent, Maura Teitelbaum of Abrams Artists Agency. Maura, endless thanks for the confidence you've shown in my ability and your enthusiasm and persistence in making this project a reality. You have been a tireless advocate for my work and you would not rest until this book was a done deal. Thank you.

Special thanks go to Harry Crocker and the entire team at Regnery Publishing for giving me the opportunity to do this book and sound the alarm about the threats we're facing. It was an absolute pleasure working with the Regnery team from the beginning of the process to the end, and I am indebted to them for their confidence, honesty, and support.

My editor, Jack Langer, was the perfect fit for this book, and I believe that the final product reflects that. Jack's passion for and knowledge of issues relating to the Middle East and Islamic jihad, combined with his superb additions and editorial critiques, gave this project the polish and direction it needed. Jack was also unflappable when we got down to "crunch time," which was not surprising considering he, like me, hails from Philadelphia. Go Phils.

In addition to being one of America's finest investigative journalists and a foremost expert on the Muslim Brotherhood, Patrick Poole is a great friend. Pat, thanks for all of your guidance, suggestions, and insights pertaining to this book, particularly on chapter eight. You are a true watchman on the wall for our nation.

Thanks also to my friend, the great Michelle Malkin, who contributed an outstanding foreword that completely captured the tone and message of the book—no one could have done it better.

I would not be typing these words if it were not for my employer, the Christian Broadcasting Network, which took a flyer on me in 2005 and showed boundless patience as I grew and matured as an on-air presence. Thanks especially to Dr. Pat Robertson, Gordon Robertson, and Michael Little for their support and guidance through the years and for providing encouragement for this and every project I have embarked on during my time at CBN. The past six years working for CBN have brought one blessing after another, and I am very fortunate to call the network home.

I am also fortunate to have a news director at CBN, Rob Allman, who trusts my instincts and grants me the creative freedom to pursue the stories that I believe are important for our audience and our nation. Rob has stuck with me through growing pains and ups and downs, and has always been there to provide feedback and advice, not only professionally but on a personal level. I am extremely grateful.

What can I say about my colleagues at CBN's Washington, D.C. bureau? Simply put, you guys are family. Special thanks to bureau chief Robin Mazyck, for her daily support, guidance, and friendship, and her encouragement of this project; to David Brody, who has been a great and trusted friend and mentor since the day I began at CBN—they don't make 'em any better as a reporter or a human being; and to Matt Keedy and David Page, two dear friends and creative geniuses who have managed to make me look good for six years—you guys are true masters of your crafts. And hey, we've had a lot of fun doing it.

Many thanks also to my fearless cameramen Ian Rushing, Steve Jacobi, Jerome Young, and Royce Sallstrom, who have followed me into some very nasty places through the years and come face-to-face with evil men as a result. They've never flinched, no matter how hairy the situation may have become. They, and every D.C. crew member, are the unsung heroes of this book.

Big thanks to my fellow reporters John Jessup, Paul Strand, and Jennifer Wishon, for all the laughs, fellowship, and support; I'll stack our reporting corps up against anyone's. Thanks also to intrepid editor and good friend Jacob Moore; to Alegra Hassan, who was always there with a smile, a kind spirit, and great advice; to Crystal Woodall; and to the invaluable Pat Jenkins and Tamatha Papadeas, who make the whole thing run.

To everyone at CBN's Virginia Beach bureau: you guys are a joy to work with and there is no one I'd rather go to war alongside on a daily basis—period. Thanks most of all for your friendship. The same goes for the team at CBN's Jerusalem bureau, particularly my good buddy Chris Mitchell, who has helped me navigate the rough waters of the Middle East and more.

Thanks to my friends David Horowitz and Jamie Glazov, who gave me my first opportunity to write about the issues of Islamic jihad and the Middle East. I am eternally grateful. Thanks also to Steven Emerson of the Investigative Project on Terrorism, who gave me my first job in Washington, D.C. and greatly aided my development as a journalist.

Thanks to my good friend Nir Boms, a true freedom fighter who showed me the ropes of Washington, D.C., and to Daveed Gartenstein-Ross and Walid Phares, two indispensable allies in the fight to preserve our nation.

Thanks also to everyone at FOX News for their steady support and to the entire team at Christians United for Israel, especially my good friends David Brog and Ari Morgenstern.

To all my friends in Israel: stay strong, be blessed, and keep fighting the good fight. Know that I will stand with you always.

Closer to home, I'd like to thank everyone in Fox Chase. There are simply too many people to name. For anyone I ever shot hoops with, ate at Stoxy's with, dreamed with and shared a laugh with, thank you. I'll never forget. Fox Chase is a special place filled with special people who have impacted my life immeasurably. Know that I'm writing this book, ultimately, because I want to preserve the way we grew up for us and our kids. I love you all and remember fondly the days where all we had to worry about was running a full up the Rec on a hot summer night with good music playing in the background, hanging out, laughing and talking into the wee hours. You're friends for life.

To my late in-laws, Maz and Gigs, thank you for accepting me into your family, encouraging my career, and treating me as your own son. You are gone but not forgotten. The same goes for my late Uncle Jim, an Iwo Jima veteran and true American hero. And to my dearly departed friends Eddie Polec, who was taken from us much too soon, and Danny Kuhlmeier, who paid the ultimate sacrifice for our country, I'll see you when I get there.

Thanks to Jose and everyone on the block for all the good times.

Thanks to Steve Chadwin, Kristine Long, and Dr. Thomas Lombardi for seeing something in me, helping me to grow, and encouraging me to follow my dreams.

Thanks to all of the Stakelbecks and Kilkennys everywhere, and to the entire Berkery clan—especially Joe Marshall, for all the late night talks about the future of our nation.

Thanks to my friend Rudy Atallah for teaching me about the peace of the Lord, and to Tass Saada, for helping me to finally attain it.

Endless thanks go to the men and women of the U.S. military, the "shadow warriors," and all of the unsung heroes at home and in the trenches overseas who are battling to keep America safe and free.

At the end of the day, all credit for this book goes to my Lord and Savior, Jesus Christ. The Lord tugged on my heart for years and I resisted, trying to travel on my own path and on my own timetable rather than on His, which is always perfect. In 2009, I finally gave myself completely to Jesus, stopped fighting, and let Him take control of my life. Every day since then has been an adventure and a blessing. He truly changes lives— and I'll shout it from the mountaintops to anyone who will listen. Thank you, Lord, for everything.

NOTES

Foreword

1. "Malvo Case Defendant's Trial Exhibits," Fairfax County, VA, government website, http://web.archive.org/web/20041013003311/http://www.fairfax-county.gov/courts/cases/malvo_defendant_exhibits.htm (accessed February 24, 2011).
2. Joel Mowbray, "Open Door for Saudi Terrorists," National Review Online, July 2, 2002, http://old.nationalreview.com/mowbray/mowbray061402.asp (accessed February 22, 2011).
3. Domingo Ramirez, Jr., "College student in Texas arrested in terror case," *Fort Worth Star Telegram*, February 24, 2011, http://www.star-telegram.com/2011/02/24/2875816/college-student-in-texas-arrested.html (accessed February 24, 2011).

Introduction

1. Gordon Rayner and Duncan Gardham, "Cargo Plane Bomb Plot: Al-Qaeda Terrorists 'Threatened' Another Lockerbie," *Telegraph,* October 31, 2010, http://www.telegraph.co.uk/news/uknews/terrorism-in-the-uk/8100970/Cargo-plane-bomb-plot-al-Qaeda-terrorists-threatened-another-Lockerbie.html (accessed March 3, 2011).

2. "BA worker guilty of planning airline bomb plot," Reuters, March 1, 2011, http://www.reuters.com/article/2011/03/01/uk-britain-security-ba-idUSL-NE72002W20110301 (accessed March 3, 2011).

3. Raza Khan, "Al Qaeda extends to Somalia, Yemen," *Washington Times,* September 10, 2009, http://www.washingtontimes.com/news/2009/sep/10/al-qaeda-extends-reach/ (accessed March 3, 2011).

4. President Obama's remarks to students at St Xavier College in Mumbai, India, November 8, 2010. See video of his remarks here: http://www.youtube.com/watch?feature=player_embedded&v=vCllTEankoA (accessed March 3, 2011).

5. "The Future of the Global Muslim Population: Projections for 2010-2030," Pew Research Center, January 27, 2011, http://pewresearch.org/pubs/1872/muslim-population-projections-worldwide-fast-growth (accessed March 3, 2011).

6. "Far From Ground Zero, New Mosques Face Opposition," FOX News, August 8, 2010, http://www.foxnews.com/us/2010/08/08/away-raw-emotions-ground-zero-mosques-face-strong-opposition/ (accessed March 3, 2011).

7. WorldPublicOpinion.org Staff, "Public Opinion in the Islamic World on Terrorism, al Qaeda, and US Policies," WorldPublicOpinion.org, February 25, 2009, http://www.worldpublicopinion.org/pipa/pdf/feb09/STARTII_Feb09_rpt.pdf (accessed March 8, 2011).

8. "Muslim Americans: Middle Class and Mostly Mainstream," The Pew Forum on Religion & Public Life, May 22, 2007, http://pewforum.org/Muslim/Muslim-Americans-Middle-Class-and-Mostly-Mainstream%282%29.aspx (accessed March 3, 2011).

9. Edwin Black, *The Farhud: Roots of the Arab-Nazi Alliance in the Holocaust* (Washington, D.C.: Dialog Press, 2010).

10. Bill Warner, *Sharia Law for the Non-Muslim* (USA: CSPI , 2010), available online at http://www.cspipublishing.com/pdfs/WebSitePDF/Sharia_Law_for_Non_Muslim.pdf (accessed March 3, 2011).

11. "Darkening gloom," *The Economist,* February 4, 2011, http://www.economist.com/blogs/asiaview/2011/02/pakistans_blasphemy_law (accessed March 3, 2011).

Chapter One

1. Elisabeth Kaufmann, "In Murfreesboro, Tenn.: Church 'Yes,' Mosque 'No'," *Time,* August 19, 2010, http://www.time.com/time/nation/article/0,8599,2011847,00.html (accessed February 23, 2011).

2. Bob Smietnan, "Murfreesboro Mosque Spokeswoman Camie Ayash Has Felony Record," *The Tennessean,* September 20, 2010, http://www.tennessean.com/article/20100920/NEWS01/100920077/Murfreesboro-mosque-spokeswoman-Camie-Ayash-has-felony-record (accessed February 23, 2011).

3. Erick Stakelbeck, "Mega Mosque Plans Target America's Heartland," CBN. com, August 22, 2010, http://www.cbn.com/cbnnews/us/2010/August/ Mega-Mosque-Plans-Target-Americas-Heartland/ (accessed February 23, 2011).

4. Ibid.

5. Russell Goldman, "Islamic Center Backers Won't Rule Out Taking Funds from Saudi Arabia, Iran," ABCNews.com, August 18, 2010, http://abcnews. go.com/US/Politics/islamic-center-backers-rule-taking-funds-saudi-arabia/ story?id=11429998 (accessed February 23, 2011).

6. Michelle Theriault, "USA: Alaska's First Mosque," HalalFocus.com, August 12, 2010, http://halalfocus.net/2010/12/08/usa-alaskas-first-mosque/ (accessed February 23, 2011).

7. Jeff Jacoby, "The Boston Mosque's Saudi Connection," *The Boston Globe,* January 10, 2010, http://www.boston.com/news/globe/editorial_opinion/ oped/articles/2007/01/10/the_boston_mosques_saudi_connection/ (accessed February 23, 2011), and Senate Subcommittee on Terrorism, Technology and Homeland Security, *Wahhabism and Islam in The U.S.,* 108th Cong., 1st sess., 2003, available at the National Review Online, http://www.nationalreview.com/articles/207366/wahhabism-islam-u-s/stephen-schwartz (accessed February 23, 2011).

8. "Saudi Publications on Hate Ideology Invade American Mosques," Freedom House, http://www.freedomhouse.org/uploads/special_report/45.pdf (accessed February 23, 2011).

9. Holly Hayes, "Dome of the Rock, Jerusalem," SacredDestinations.com, last modified January 13, 2010, http://www.sacred-destinations.com/israel/ jerusalem-dome-of-the-rock (accessed February 23, 2011).

10. Javier C. Hernandez, "Planned Sign of Tolerance Bringing Division Instead," *New York Times,* July 13, 2010, http://www.nytimes.com/2010/07/14/ nyregion/14center.html (accessed February 23, 2011).

11. Andrew Malcolm, "At Ramadan Iftar Dinner, Obama Supports New Mosque On Private Property Near Ground Zero," *Los Angeles Times* Top of the Ticket, August 13, 2010, http://latimesblogs.latimes.com/washington/2010/08/obama-ramadan-iftar-remarks-text.html (accessed February 23, 2011).

12. Andrew Bostom, "Jihad, Dhimmitude, and Muslim Spain," *Andrew Bostom* blog, August 24, 2010, http://www.andrewbostom.org/blog/2010/08/24/ jihad-dhimmitude-and-muslim-spain/ (accessed February 23, 2011).

13. "Letters from the Imam," *The Wall Street Journal* Opinion Journal, September 1, 2010, http://online.wsj.com/article/SB10001424052748703632304 575451762406545760.html (accessed February 23, 2011); Michael Ledeen, "Imam Rauf's Love of 'Iranian Democracy,'" PajamasMedia.com, August 23, 2010, http://pajamasmedia.com/michaelledeen/2010/08/23/imam-raufs-love-of-iranian-democracy/?singlepage=true; and Tom Topousis, "Imam Terror Error: Ground Zero Mosque Leader Hedges on Hamas," *New York Post*, updated June 19, 2010, http://www.nypost.com/p/news/local/manhattan/imam_terror_error_efmizkHuBUaVnfuQcrcabL (accessed February 23, 2011).

14. "Iran Unveils Unmanned Bomber," *Morning Joe* video, Season 810: Episode 0823, aired August 23, 2010, available at clicker.com, http://www.clicker.com/tv/morning-joe/Iran-unveils-unmanned-bomber-1058862/ (accessed February 23, 2011).

15. Ron Radosh, "Imam Rauf and the State Department: The Truth About Our Man in the Middle East," PajamasMedia.com, August 23, 2010, http:// pajamasmedia.com/ronradosh/2010/08/23/rauf-and-the-state-department/ (accessed February 23, 2011).

16. Andrew C. McCarthy, "Rauf's Dawa from the World Trade Center Rubble," National Review Online, July 24, 2010, http://www.nationalreview.com/ articles/243536/raufs-dawa-world-trade-center-rubble-andrew-c-mccarthy (accessed February 23, 2011).

17. Ibid.

18. Abdul Rahman Al-Rashid, "A House of Worship or a Symbol of Destruction?" Asharq Alawsat, August 16, 2010, http://www.asharq-e.com/news. asp?section=2&id=21980 (accessed February 23, 2011).

19. Glynnis MacNicol, "Imam Rauf: Mosque Site is Not 'Hallowed Ground'," Mediaite.com, September 14, 2010, http://www.mediaite.com/online/imam-rauf-mosque-site-is-not-hallowed-ground/ (accessed February 23, 2011).

20. Jerry Gordon, "What is a Mosque? An Interview with Sam Soloman," *New English Review*, August 2010, http://www.newenglishreview.org/custpage. cfm/frm/68472/sec_id/68472 (accessed February 23, 2011).

21. Erick Stakelbeck and Reza Kahlili, "Inside Iran's Revolutionary Guards," *Stakelbeck on Terror* video, 28:36, CBN.com, December 27, 2010, http:// www.cbn.com/cbnnews/world/2010/December/Stakelbeck-on-Terror-Inside-Irans-Revolutionary-Guards/ (accessed February 23, 2011).

22. "9/11 Terror Mosque Shut: Hamburg Officials Raid Alleged Islamist Recruiting Site," Spiegel Online, August 9, 2010, http://www.spiegel.de/international/germany/0,1518,710845,00.html (accessed February 23, 2011).

23. Daniel Arrpospide "Swedish Politician Infiltrates Stockholm Mosque," YouTube video 1:03, from TV2Nydetene, posted by vladtepesblogdotcom on December 5, 2010, http://www.youtube.com/watch?v=_YfsNcqxpcw (accessed February 23, 2011).

24. "Turkey's Charismatic Pro-Islamic Leader," BBC News, November 4, 2002, http://news.bbc.co.uk/2/hi/europe/2270642.stm (accessed February 23, 2011).

25. Steven Emerson, "Another Islamist Rally for Hate in D.C.," The Investigative Project on Terrorism, September 4, 2010, http://www.investigativeproject. org/2162/another-islamist-rally-for-hate-in-dc (accessed February 23, 2011).

26. Patrick S. Poole, "Key Charlie Crist Ally Hosted Hamas Fundraiser in Florida Mosque," BigPeace.com, August 30, 2010, http://bigpeace.com/pspoole/2010/08/30/patrick-poole-key-charlie-crist-ally-hosted-hamas-fundraiser-in-florida-mosque/ (accessed February 23, 2011).

27. Olivier Carré and Michel Seurat, Les frères musulmans (1928–1982) (Paris: L'Harmattan, 1983), 221–22.

28. National Commission on Terrorist Attacks, The 9/11 Commission Report: Final Report of the National Commission on Terrorist Attacks upon the United States (New York: W.W. Norton, 2004).

29. Scott Shane and Souad Mekhennet, "Imam's Path From Condemning Terror to Preaching Jihad," New York Times, May 8, 2010, http://www. nytimes.com/2010/05/09/world/09awlaki.html?_r=1&hpw (accessed February 23, 2011).

30. Brian Fairchild, "The Muslim Brotherhood," Stakelbeck on Terror video, CBN.com, November 30, 2010, http://www.cbn.com/cbnnews/world/2010/September/Stakelbeck-on-Terror---The-Muslim-Brotherhood-in-America/ (accessed February 23, 2011).

31. "Muslim Brotherhood Supreme Guide: 'The U.S. Is Now Experiencing the Beginning of Its End'; Improvement and Change in the Muslim World 'Can Only Be Attained Through Jihad and Sacrifice,'" The Middle East Media Research Institute, October 6, 2010, http://www.memri.org/report/en/0/0/0/0/0/0/4650.htm (accessed February 23, 2011).

32. Ibid.

33. Patrick Poole, "The Muslim Brotherhood," Stakelbeck on Terror video, xx:xx CBN.com, November 30, 2010, http://www.cbn.com/cbnnews/world/2010/September/Stakelbeck-on-Terror---The-Muslim-Brotherhood-in-America/ (accessed February 23, 2011).

34. Laurie Goodstein, "A Nation Challenged: The Religious Opinion; Muslim Scholars Fight Back Against Terrorists," *New York Times,* October 12, 2001, http://www.nytimes.com/2001/10/12/us/nation-challenged-religious-opinion-muslim-scholars-back-fight-against.html?scp=6&sq=Imam%20feisal%20abdul%20rauf&st=cse (accessed February 23, 2011).

35. Steven Emerson, "Yusuf al-Qaradawi," The Investigative Project on Terrorism, July 9, 2008, http://www.investigativeproject.org/profile/167.

36. Department of Justice, "Justice Department Files Brief in Support of Continued Construction of Murfreesboro, Tenn., Mosque," United States Department of Justice, October 18, 2010, http://www.justice.gov/opa/pr/2010/October/10-crt-1162.html (accessed February 23, 2011).

Chapter Two

1. "N.J. suspects attended protests organized by radical Islamic group," CNN *This Just In,* June 11, 2010, http://news.blogs.cnn.com/2010/06/11/n-j-suspects-attended-protests-organized-by-radical-islamic-group/ (accessed February 23, 2011).

2. Ibid.

3. CNN Wire Staff, "Magazine details al Qaeda cargo plots," CNN.com, November 21, 2010, http://www.cnn.com/2010/WORLD/meast/11/21/al.qaeda.magazine/index.html?hpt=T2 (accessed February 23, 2011).

4. Ibid.

5. Greg Bruno, "Al-Qaeda's Financial Pressures," Council on Foreign Relations, February 1, 2010, http://www.cfr.org/publication/21347/alqaedas_financial_pressures.html (accessed February 23, 2011).

6. Jen Chung, "Al Qaeda Called Off a 2003 Cyanide Attack on NYC Subways," Gothamist.com, June 18, 2006, http://gothamist.com/2006/06/18/al_qaeda_called.php (accessed February 23, 2011).

7. A. G. Sulzberger and William K. Rashbaum, "Guilty Plea Made in Plot to Bomb New York Subway," *New York Times,* February 22, 2010, http://www.nytimes.com/2010/02/23/nyregion/23terror.html (accessed February 23, 2011).

8. Alastair Gee, "Mumbai terror attacks: And then they came for the Jews," *The Times,* November 1, 2009, http://www.timesonline.co.uk/tol/news/world/asia/article6896107.ece (accessed February 23, 2011).

9. "Pakistan Terror Commander Admits Aiding Mumbai Attacks," FoxNews.com, December 31, 2008, http://www.foxnews.com/story/0,2933,474384,00.html (accessed February 23, 2011).

10. Mark Mazzetti and Salman Masood, "Pakistani Role Is Suspected in Revealing U.S. Spy's Name," *New York Times,* December 17, 2010, http://www.

nytimes.com/2010/12/18/world/asia/18pstan.html?_r=1&hp (accessed February 23, 2011).

11. Carrie Johnson, "U.S. citizen David Coleman Headley admits role in Mumbai attacks," *Washington Post*, March 19, 2010, http://www.washingtonpost.com/wp-dyn/content/article/2010/03/18/AR2010031805407.html (accessed February 23, 2011).

12. Adam Gadahn, "Adam Gadahn March 7, 2010 Video with Transcript," Public Intelligence video from an As-Sahab video aired March 7, 2010, PublicIntelligence.com, posted March 17, 2010, http://publicintelligence.net/adam-gadahn-march-7-2010-video-with-transcript/ (accessed February 23, 2011).

13. "New issue of magazine offers jihadists terror tips," CNN.com, October 12, 2010, http://articles.cnn.com/2010-10-12/world/mideast.jihadi.magazine_1_yemen-terror-tips-al-qaeda?_s=PM:WORLD (accessed February 23, 2011).

14. Lucy Madison, "Attorney General Eric Holder: Threat of Homegrown Terrorism 'Keeps Me Up At Night,'" CBSNews.com, December 21, 2010, http://www.cbsnews.com/8301-503544_162-20026288-503544.html (accessed February 23, 2011).

15. Matthew Lysiak, Robert F. Moore, and Corky Siemaszko, "Gunman in Fort Hood shooting, Maj. Nidal Malik Hasan, shouted 'Allahu Akbar' before deadly attack," *New York Daily News*, November 6, 2009, http://www.nydailynews.com/news/national/2009/11/06/2009-11-06_susptected_gunman_in_fort_hood_shooting_maj_nidal_malik_hasan_shouted_allah_akba.html (accessed February 23, 2011).

16. "Fort Hood suspect Nidal Malik Hasan seemed 'cool, calm, religious,'" CNN.com, November 6, 2009, http://articles.cnn.com/2009-11-06/justice/fort.hood.suspect_1_nidal-malik-hasan-dr-hasan-fort-hood?_s=PM:CRIME (accessed February 23, 2011).

17. Mark Thompson, "Fort Hood: Were Hasan's Warning Signs Ignored?" *Time*, November 18, 2009, http://www.time.com/time/nation/article/0,8599,1940011,00.html (accessed February 23, 2011).

18. Ibid.

19. Peter Slevin, "Apartment Offers Glimpse At Suspect's Everyday Life," *Washington Post*, November 12, 2009, http://www.washingtonpost.com/wp-dyn/content/article/2009/11/11/AR2009111125063.html?hpid=topnews (accessed February 23, 2011).

20. Brian Ross and Rhonda Schwartz, "Major Hasan's E-Mail: 'I Can't Wait to Join You' in Afterlife," ABCNews.com, November 12, 2009, http://abcnews.go.com/Blotter/major-hasans-mail-wait-join-afterlife/story?id=9130339 (accessed February 23, 2011).

21. Anne Flaherty, "DoD finds officers made mistakes with Hasan," *Navy Times*, January 18, 2010, http://www.navytimes.com/news/2010/01/ap_ hood_risks_011510w/ (accessed February 23, 2011).

22. Richard Esposito, Rehab El-Buri and Brian Ross, "From Yemen, Anwar Awlaki Helped Inspire Fort Dix, Toronto Plots," ABCNews.com, November 11, 2009, http://abcnews.go.com/Blotter/anwar-awlakis-terrror-ties/ story?id=9055322&page=2 (accessed February 23, 2011).

23. Brian Ross and Rhonda Schwartz, "Major Hasan's E-Mail: 'I Can't Wait to Join You' in Afterlife," ABCNews.com.

24. Ibid.

25. "Napolitano Warns Against Anti-Muslim Backlash," FoxNews.com, November 8, 2010, http://www.foxnews.com/politics/2009/11/08/napoli-tano-warns-anti-muslim-backlash/ (accessed February 23, 2011).

26. Mark Thompson, "The Fort Hood Report: Why No Mention of Islam?" *Time*, January 20, 2010, http://www.time.com/time/nation/arti-cle/0,8599,1954960,00.html (accessed February 23, 2011).

27. Tabassum Zakaria, "General Casey: diversity shouldn't be casualty of Fort Hood," Rueters *Front Row Washington*, http://blogs.reuters.com/fron-trow/2009/11/08/general-casey-diversity-shouldnt-be-casualty-of-fort-hood/ (accessed February 23, 2011).

28. Ibid.

29. Joseph Lieberman and Susan Collins, "Lieberman, Collins: FBI and Pentagon could have stopped the Fort Hood shootings," *Washington Post*, February 4, 2011, http://www.washingtonpost.com/wp-dyn/content/arti-cle/2011/02/04/AR2011020403023.html (accessed February 23, 2011).

30. Dorothy Rabinowitz, "Major Hasan, 'Star Officer,'" *Wall Street Journal*, February 16, 2011, http://online.wsj.com/article/SB100014240527487044 09004576146001069880040.html?mod=googlenews_wsj (accessed February 23, 2011).

31. Chris Cuomo and Chris Vlasto, "A Life Thrown Away: Faisal Shahzad Went From MBA to Alleged Terrorist," ABCNews.com, May 4, 2010, http:// abcnews.go.com/WN/TheLaw/shahzad-leaves-traces-life-thrown/ story?id=10555970 (accessed February 23, 2011).

32. "Taliban's suicide-bomb trainer tutored NYK bombing suspect," *Hindustan Times*, May 6, 2010, http://www.hindustantimes.com/americas/Taliban-s-suicide-bomb-trainer-tutored-NYK-bombing-suspect/540098/H1-Arti-cle1-540060.aspx (accessed February 23, 2011).

33. "Faisal Shahzad's Pakistani Connections," TheWeek.com, May 24, 2010, http://theweek.com/article/index/203293/faisal-shahzads-pakistani-connections (accessed February 23, 2011).

34. "Shahzad on U.S. Travel Security List Since 1999," CBSNews.com, May 5, 2010, http://www.cbsnews.com/8301-31727_162-20004263-10391695.html (accessed February 23, 2011), and James Barron and Michael S. Schmidt, " From Suburban Father to a Terrorism Suspect," *New York Times*, May 4, 2010, http://www.nytimes.com/2010/05/05/nyregion/05profile.html?hp (accessed February 23, 2011).

35. Alison Gendar, James Gordon Meek, Rocco Parascandola, and Corky Siemaszko, "Pakistani-American Faisal Shahzad, suspect in foiled Times Square bomb plot, arrested at JFK," *New York Daily News*, updated May 4, 2010, http://www.nydailynews.com/ny_local/2010/05/03/2010-05-03_times_square_car_bomb_square_evidence_points_to_overseas_terrorist_involvement_w.html (accessed February 23, 2011).

36. David Montero, "US-born cleric inspired Times Square bomber Faisal Shahzad," *Christian Science Monitor*, May 7, 2010, http://www.csmonitor.com/World/terrorism-security/2010/0507/US-born-cleric-inspired-Times-Square-bomber-Faisal-Shahzad (accessed February 23, 2011).

37. Aaron Katersky and Richard Esposito, "Faisal Shahzad: 'War With Muslims Has Just Begun,'" ABCNews.com, October 4, 2010, http://abcnews.go.com/Blotter/times-square-bomber-faisal-shahzad-sentenced-life/story?id=11802740 (accessed February 23, 2011).

38. William K. Rashbaum, Mark Mazzetti, and Peter Baker, "Arrest Made in Times Square Bomb Case," *New York Times*, May 3, 2010, http://www.nytimes.com/2010/05/04/nyregion/04bomb.html (accessed February 23, 2011).

39. Stephen F. Hayes and Thomas Joscelyn, "Not A 'One-Off' Event," TheWeeklyStandard.com (blog), May 4, 2010, http://www.weeklystandard.com/blogs/not-one-event (accessed February 23, 2011).

40. "Eric Holder Refuses To Say 'Radical Islam,'" YouTube video from Testimony Before the House Judiciary Committee televised by C-SPAN 3 on May 13, 2010, posted by "keepamericasafecom," May 13, 2010, http://www.youtube.com/watch?v=HOQt_mP6Pgg (accessed February 23, 2011).

41. Katie Couric, "Bloomberg: 'No Evidence' Anyone Else Involved," CBSNews.com, May 3, 2010, http://www.cbsnews.com/stories/2010/05/03/eveningnews/main6457014.shtml (accessed February 23, 2011).

42. Steven Emerson, "Little Rock Shooter Eyed Bigger Targets," The Investigative Project on Terrorism *The Record*, June 4, 2009, http://www.investigativeproject.org/1286/little-rock-shooter-eyed-bigger-targets (accessed February 23, 2011).

43. James Dao, "A Muslim Son, a Murder Trial and Many Questions," *New York Times*, February 16, 2010, http://www.nytimes.com/2010/02/17/us/17convert.html (accessed February 23, 2011).

44. Richard Esposito, Pierre Thomas, and Jack Date, "Recruiter Shooting Suspect Under FBI Investigation," ABCNews.com, June 1, 2009, http://abcnews.go.com/Politics/story?id=7730637&page=1 (accessed February 24, 2011).

45. James Dao, "A Muslim Son, a Murder Trial and Many Questions," *New York Times*, February 16, 2010, http://www.nytimes.com/2010/02/17/us/17convert.html (accessed February 24, 2011).

46. Office of the Press Secretary, "Statement from the President on the Murder of Dr. George Tiller," The White House, May 31, 2009, http://www.whitehouse.gov/the-press-office/statement-president-murder-dr-george-tiller (accessed February 24, 2011).

47. "Attorney General on Murder of Doctor George Tiller," The United States Department of Justice, May 31, 2009, http://www.justice.gov/ag/speeches/2009/ag-speech-090531.html (accessed February 24, 2011).

48. La Shawn Barber, "Obama Finally Issues Statement on Pvt. William Long," La Shawn Barber's Corner (blog), June 4, 2009, http://lashawnbarber.com/archives/2009/06/04/obama-finally-issues-statement-on-private-william-long/ (accessed February 24, 2011).

49. Richard Sisk, James Gordon Meek, and Larry McShane, "U.S. officials investigating how Abdulmutallab boarded Flight 253 as more red flags surface," *New York Daily News*, January 3, 2010, http://www.nydailynews.com/news/national/2010/01/03/2010-01-03_plane_questions_dont_fly_right_warning_signs_were_evident_yet_bomb_suspect_still.html?page=1 (accessed February 24, 2011).

50. Mark Hosenball, "The Radicalization of Umar Farouk Abdulmutallab," *Newsweek*, January 2, 2010, http://www.newsweek.com/2010/01/01/the-radicalization-of-umar-farouk-abdulmutallab.html (accessed February 24, 2011).

51. Claudia Rosett, "Not So Isolated, And More Than Extremist," *Forbes*, January 1, 2010, http://www.forbes.com/2009/12/31/airline-terrorism-al-qaida-opinions-columnists-claudia-rosett.html (accessed February 24, 2011).

52. "Abdulmutallab: Cleric Told Me to Bomb Jet," CBSNews.com, February 5, 2010, http://www.cbsnews.com/stories/2010/02/04/national/main6174780.shtml (accessed February 24, 2011).

53. "CQ Transcript: Homeland Security Secretary Napolitano on CNN's 'State of the Union,'" RollCall.com, December 27, 2010, http://www.rollcall.com/news/75036-1.html?cqp=1 (accessed February 24, 2011).

54. Julia Davis, "Convicted Terrorists Living Next Door, Deadly Terror Plot Devised Inside California Prison," Examiner.com, January 28, 2010, http://www.examiner.com/homeland-security-in-los-angeles/convicted-terrorists-living-next-door-deadly-terror-plot-devised-inside-california-prison?render=print (accessed February 24, 2011).

55. Gary Stoller, "Can trains, subways be protected from terrorists?" *USA Today*, December 27, 2010, http://www.usatoday.com/money/industries/travel/2010-12-27-railsecurity27_CV_N.htm (accessed February 24, 2011).

56. Erick Stakelbeck, "Intel Source: 12 'Terrorist Teams' Spread Out Across U.S. and Europe," *Stakelbeck on Terror*, CBN.com (blog), October 1, 2010, http://blogs.cbn.com/stakelbeckonterror/archive/2010/10/01/intel-source-12--terrorist-teams--spread-out-across.aspx (accessed February 24, 2011).

Chapter Three

1. "Welcome to Holy Islamville: Jamaat ul-Furqra Gilani Followers Conducting Paramilitary Training in U.S.," Regional Organized Crime Information Center, Special Research Report, 2006, available online at http://media.charleston.net/2010/pdf/rocicreport_042510.pdf (accessed February 24, 2011), and John J. Miller, "A Junior al Qaeda…Right Here at Home: Meet al Fuqra," *National Review*, January 31, 2001, http://old.nationalreview.com/flashback/flashback-miller013102.shtml (accessed February 24, 2011).

2. "Welcome to holy Islamville: Jamaat ul-Furqra Gilani Followers Conducting Paramilitary Training in U.S.," Regional Organized Crime Information Center, Special Report, 2006.

3. "Patterns of Global Terrorism 1999," Department of State Publications, April 2000, http://www.state.gov/www/global/terrorism/1999report/1999index.html (accessed February 24, 2011).

4. Mark Steyn, "Linkage Logarithms," *Washington Times*, October 19, 2003, http://www.washingtontimes.com/news/2003/oct/19/20031019-112022-5881r/ (accessed February 24, 2011).

5. John J. Miller, "A Junior al Qaeda…Right Here at Home: Meet al Fuqra," *National Review*, January 31, 2001.

6. Mira L. Boland, "Sheikh Gilani's American Disciples," *Weekly Standard*, March 18, 2002, http://www.weeklystandard.com/Content/Public/Articles/000/000/000/996lxfmd.asp?page=1 (accessed February 24, 2011).

7. Ibid.

8. "Frightening Film on U.S. Terrorism Training Camps," FoxNews.com, February 17, 2009, http://www.foxnews.com/story/0,2933,494424,00.html (accessed February 24, 2011).

9. "Terrorist Training in Rural America?" video transcript, CBN.com, http://www.cbn.com/media/browse_videos_info.aspx?s=/vod/EST30v1 (accessed February 24, 2011).

10. TMO, "Atlanta gets its largest mosque," Community News (V10-I35), *The Muslim Observer*, August 21, 2008, http://muslimmedianetwork.com/mmn/?p=2745 (accessed February 24, 2011).

11. Diane Macedo, "Plans to Build Massive Islamic Center Raise Concerns in Tennessee," FoxNews.com, August 9, 2010, http://www.foxnews.com/us/2010/08/09/plans-build-tennessee-islamic-centers/ (accessed February 24, 2011).

12. Ibid.

13. Ibid.

14. "Profile: Abu Hamza," BBC News UK, November 5, 2010, http://www.bbc.co.uk/news/uk-11701269 (accessed February 24, 2011).

15. "From community activist to alleged terror conspirator," CNN.com, August 29, 2002, http://articles.cnn.com/2002-08-29/justice/ujaama.background_1_james-ujaama-day-james-earnest-thompson-qaeda?_s=PM:LAW (accessed February 24, 2011).

16. Declan Walsh and Daniel Nasaw, "Background: 'North Carolina Taliban,'" *Guardian*, September 3, 2009, http://www.guardian.co.uk/world/2009/sep/03/background-daniel-boyd-fbi-case (accessed February 24, 2011).

17. "FY 2009 Performance and Accountability Report," Department of Justice, http://www.justice.gov/ag/annualreports/pr2009/sect2/sg1.pdf (accessed February 24, 2011).

18. David E. Kaplan, "Homegrown Terrorists: How a Hezbollah cell made millions in sleepy Charlotte, N.C.," *U.S. News & World Report*, March 2, 2003, http://www.usnews.com/usnews/news/articles/030310/10hez.htm (accessed February 24, 2011).

19. John S. Pistole, Testimony Before the House Committee on Financial Service Subcommittee on Oversight and Investigations, Washington, D.C., Federal Bureau of Investigation, September 24, 2003, http://www.fbi.gov/news/testimony/the-terrorist-financing-operations-section, and "Federal Judge Hands Downs Sentences in Holy Land Foundation Case," The United States Department of Justice, May 27, 2009, http://www.justice.gov/opa/pr/2009/May/09-nsd-519.html (accessed February 24, 2011).

Chapter Four

1. "Secretaries of Defense," Historical Office, Office of the Secretary of Defense, http://osdhistory.defense.gov/SODs/aspin.html (accessed February 24, 2011).

2. Mohamed Sheikh Nor, "Somali Militants Announce Merger, Threaten Attacks," *Washington Examiner*, December 23, 2010.

3. Jeremy Sare, "Adrift in the UK," *Guardian*, June 5, 2008, http://www.guardian.co.uk/commentisfree/2008/jun/05/immigration.immigrationpolicy (accessed February 24, 2011).

4. Urmila Ramakrishnan, "Swedish delegates study Mpls Somali population," MNDaily.com, October 25, 2010, http://www.mndaily.com/2010/10/25/swedish-delegates-study-mpls-somali-population?quicktabs_6=1 (accessed March 1, 2011).

5. "Population 1st January 2006 and 2007 and changes in 2006, by immigrant category and country background," Statistics Norway, 2007, http://www.ssb.no/english/subjects/02/01/10/innvbef_en/arkiv/tab-2007-05-24-01-en.html (accessed February 24, 2011).

6. "Population; sex, age, origin and generation, 1 January," *Statline*, September 28, 2010, http://statline.cbs.nl/StatWeb/publication/?DM=SLEN&PA=37325eng&D1=a&D2=187&D3=0&D4=0&D5=0&D6=6-12&LA=EN&HDR=T&STB=G1,G2,G3,G4,G5&VW=T (accessed February 24, 2011).

7. See Statistics Denmark, http://www.statbank.dk/statbank5a/default.asp?w=1280 (accessed February 24, 2011).

8. "Ethnic Origins, 2006 counts, for Canada, provinces and territories – 20% sample data," Statistics Canada, October 6, 2010, http://www12.statcan.ca/census-recensement/2006/dp-pd/hlt/97-562/pages/page.cfm?Lang=E&Geo=PR&Code=01&Table=2&Data=Count&StartRec=1&Sort=3&Display=All&CSDFilter=5000 (accessed February 24, 2011).

9. Cameron Stewart, "Somalis in Australia quizzed over pirate links," *The Australian*, November 22, 2008, http://www.theaustralian.com.au/news/somalis-quizzed-over-pirate-links/story-e6frg6uf-1111118108007 (accessed February 24, 2011).

10. Andrew Liepman, "Violent Islamist Extremism: Al-Shabaab Recruitment in America," Hearing before the Senate Homeland Security and Governmental Affairs Committee, March 11, 2009, http://hsgac.senate.gov/public/_files/031109Liepman.pdf (accessed March 8, 2011).

11. Kevin Diaz, "FBI Tracks Somali Terror Links in Minneapolis, Elsewhere," *Star Tribune*, March 12, 2009, http://www.startribune.com/local/41082717. html?page=1&c=y (accessed March 8, 2011)

12. "Violent Islamist Extremism: Al-Shabaab Recruitment in America," Hearing before the Senate Homeland Security and Governmental Affairs Committee, March 11, 2009, hsgac.senate.gov/public/_files/031109Liepman.pdf (accessed February 24, 2011).

13. Ibid.

14. Erick Stakelbeck, "Somali Muslims Changing Small Town," CBN.com, May 19, 2009, http://www.cbn.com/cbnnews/566637.aspx (accessed February 24, 2011).

15. "How Did We Get So Many Somali Refugees – The Numbers Are Telling," Refugee Settlement Watch (blog) posted by acorcoran, updated November 13, 2010, http://refugeeresettlementwatch.wordpress.com/2008/09/10/how-did-we-get-so-many-somali-refugees-the-numbers-are-telling/ (accessed February 24, 2011).

16. Office of the Press Secretary, "Presidential Memorandum--Refugee Admissions," Presidential Determination No. 2011-2, The White House, October 8, 2010, http://www.whitehouse.gov/the-press-office/2010/10/08/presidential-memorandum-refugee-admissions (accessed February 24, 2011).

17. Catherine Herridge, "FBI Director: Al-Qaeda-Linked Somali Group Could Attack U.S.," FoxNews.com, October 2, 2009, http://www.foxnews.com/politics/2009/10/02/fbi-director-al-qaeda-linked-somali-group-attack/ (accessed February 24, 2011).

18. David Johnston, "Militants Drew Recruit in U.S., FBI Says," *New York Times*, February 23, 2009, http://www.nytimes.com/2009/02/24/washington/24fbi.html?_r=2 (accessed February 24, 2011).

Chapter Five

1. Andrea Eger, "Blast victim was a loner," *Tulsa World*, last modified May 24, 2008, http://www.tulsaworld.com/news/article.aspx?articleID=051003_To_A1_Blast (accessed February 24, 2011).

2. Carol Cole, "Police bomb expert shares details of OU bombing," *The Norman Transcript*, March 1, 2006, http://normantranscript.com/local/x518944679/Police-bomb-expert-shares-details-of-OU-bombing (accessed February 24, 2011).

3. Ibid.

4. The United States Department of Justice, Office of Public Affairs, "Federal Judge Hands Down Sentences in Holy Land Foundation Case," May 27, 2009, National Security Division, 09-519, http://www.justice.gov/opa/pr/2009/May/09-nsd-519.html (accessed February 24, 2011).

5. Annie Jacobsen, "How Normal Is Norman?" osint@yahoogroups.com, posted January 4, 2006, http://www.mail-archive.com/osint@yahoogroups.com/msg18108.html (accessed January 23, 2011).

6. *The United States of America v. Zacarias Moussaoui*, In the United States District Court for the Eastern District of Virginia, Alexandria Division, December 2001 Term, http://www.justice.gov/ag/moussaouiindictment.htm (accessed February 24, 2011).

7. Islamic Society of Norman, "New Masjid Annur," http://www.masjid-annur.org/main/page_new_masjid.html (accessed January 23, 2011).

8. Koco.com, "Student Leader: Hinrichs Not Muslim," October 5, 2005, http://www.koco.com/news/5063479/detail.html (accessed February 24, 2011).

9. AP Wire Service, "Bombing at OU was not terrorism, FBI agent declares," *Tulsa World*, July 17, 2006, http://www.tulsaworld.com/news/article.aspx?articleID=060717_Ne_A10_Bombi2626 (accessed February 24, 2011).

10. Andrea Eger, "Blast victim was a loner," *Tulsa World*.

11. Dina Temple-Raston, "Jihadi Cool: Terrorist Recruiters' Latest Weapon," NPR, March 26, 2010, http://www.npr.org/templates/story/story.php?storyId=125186382 (accessed February 24, 2011).

12. Adam Gadahn, "Legitimate Demands," YouTube video, 6:31, posted by fullosseousflap, May 29, 2007, http://www.youtube.com/watch?v=nE2sh2VISTI (accessed February 24, 2011).

13. Haaretz Service, "American Al-Qaida member acknowledges his Jewish roots," Haaretz.com, June 14, 2009, http://www.haaretz.com/jewish-world/news/american-al-qaida-member-acknowledges-his-jewish-roots-1.277913 (accessed February 24, 2011), and Jon Konrath, Xenocide 5, 1993, http://www.rumored.com/xenocide/xenocide5.txt.

14. Adam Yahiye Gadahn, "Becoming Muslim," Muslim Student Association of USC, November 1995, available at: http://www.freerepublic.com/focus/f-news/1482394/posts (accessed March 1, 2011).

15. Raffi Khatchadourian, "Azzam The American," *The New Yorker*, January 22, 2007, 50, http://www.newyorker.com/reporting/2007/01/22/070122fa_fact_khatchadourian?currentPage=all (accessed February 24, 2011).

16. Ibid.
17. Adam Yahiye Gadahn, "Becoming Muslim."
18. Ibid.
19. Raffi Khatchadourian, "Azzam The American," *The New Yorker.*
20. Ibid.
21. Dirk Johnson, "Suspect in Illinois Bomb Plot 'Didn't Like America Very Much,'" *New York Times*, September 27, 2009, http://www.nytimes. com/2009/09/28/us/28springfield.html (accessed February 24, 2011).
22. Ibid.
23. Ibid.
24. Bruce Rushton, "Man accused in bombing plot known for strong stance on Islam," PJStar.com, September 24, 2009, http://www.pjstar.com/archive/ x1800826354/Man-accused-in-bombing-plot-known-for-strong-stance-on-Islam (accessed February 24, 2011).
25. Ibid.
26. Dirk Johnson, "Suspect in Illinois Bomb Plot 'Didn't Like America Very Much,'" *New York Times.*
27. Bruce Rushton, "Man accused in bombing plot known for strong stance on Islam," PJStar.com.
28. Madeleine Gruen, "Attempt to Attack the Paul Findley Federal Building n Springfield, Illinois," Target America, NEFA Foundation, Report 23, 8, http://www.nefafoundation.org/newsite/file/nefa_fintontargetamerica.pdf (accessed February 24, 2011).
29. Bruce Rushton, "Man accused in bombing plot known for strong stance on Islam," PJStar.com.
30. Chris Megerian, "N.J. Men Accused in Somalia Terror Plot Downloaded Videos, Writings of al Qaeda Leaders," nj.com, June 7, 2010, http://www. nj.com/news/index.ssf/2010/06/nj_men_accused_in_somalia_terr.html (accessed February 25, 2011).
31. Bruce Rushton, "Alleged bomber knew of authorities' interest," SJ-R.com, September 24, 2009, http://www.sj-r.com/archive/x576522186/Alleged-bomber-knew-of-authorities-interest (accessed March 1, 2011).
32. Kareem Fahim, Richard Perez-Pena, and Karen Zraick, "From Wayward Teenagers to Terror Suspects," *New York Times*, June 11, 2010, http://www. nytimes.com/2010/06/12/nyregion/12suspects.html?pagewanted=all (accessed February 24, 2011).
33. Chris Megerian, "N.J. Men Accused in Somalia Terror Plot Downloaded Videos, Writings of al Qaeda Leaders," NJ.com.

34. Perry Chiaramonte and others, "Bloodlust of NJ 'jihadists,'" *New York Post*, June 7, 2010, http://www.nypost.com/p/news/local/bloodlust_of_tjU-WgKCSnGMpRDcz9eUBXJ (accessed February 24, 2011).

35. Kareem Fahim, Richard Perez-Pena, and Karen Zraick, "From Wayward Teenagers to Terror Suspects," *New York Times*.

36. Ibid.

37. Griff Witte, Jerry Markon, and Shaiq Hussain, "Pakistani Authorities Hunt for Alleged Mastermind in Plot to Send N. Virginia Men to Afghanistan to fight U.S. Troops," *Washington Post*, December 13, 2009, http://www.washingtonpost.com/wp-dyn/content/article/2009/12/12/AR2009121201598.html?sid=ST2009121002234 (accessed February 24, 2011).

38. Peter Bergen and Dr. Bruce Hoffman, "Assessing the Terrorist Threat," Bipartisan Policy Center, September 10, 2010, http://www.bipartisanpolicy.org/library/report/assessing-terrorist-threat (accessed February 24, 2011).

39. Griff Witte, Jerry Markon, and Shaiq Hussain, "Pakistani Authorities Hunt for Alleged Mastermind in Plot to Send N. Virginia Men to Afghanistan to fight U.S. Troops," *Washington Post*.

40. "Americans Sentenced in Pakistan for Attempting to Join Terrorist Groups and Fight U.S. Forces," Anti-Defamation League, updated June 24, 2010, http://www.adl.org/main_Terrorism/americans_detained_in_pakistan.htm (accessed February 24, 2011).

41. Ibid., and The Investigative Project on Terrorism, "Hand Book Shows ICNA's True Goals," *IPT News*, December 6, 2010, http://www.investigativeproject.org/2373/hand-book-shows-icna-true-goals (accessed February 24, 2011).

42. Aamer Madhani, "Cleric al-Awlaki dubbed 'bin Laden of the Internet'," *USA Today*, updated August 25, 2010, http://www.usatoday.com/news/nation/2010-08-25-1A_Awlaki25_CV_N.htm (accessed February 24, 2011).

43. Greg Miller, "Muslim cleric Aulaqi is 1st U.S. citizen on list of those CIA is allowed to kill," *Washington Post*, April 7, 2010, http://www.washingtonpost.com/wp-dyn/content/article/2010/04/06/AR2010040604121.html (accessed February 24, 2011).

44. Jana Winter, "Some Muslims Attending Capitol Hill Prayer Group Have Terror Ties, Probe Reveals," FoxNews.com, November 11, 2010, http://www.foxnews.com/politics/2010/11/11/congressional-muslim-prayer-group-terror-ties/ (accessed February 24, 2011).

45. Catherine Herridge, "Exclusive: Al Qaeda Leader Dined at the Pentagon Just Months After 9/11," FoxNews.com, October 20, 2010, http://www.

foxnews.com/us/2010/10/20/al-qaeda-terror-leader-dined-pentagon-months/ (accessed February 24, 2011).

46. Scott Shane and Souad Mekhennet, "Imam's Path from Condemning Terror to Preaching Jihad," *New York Times*, May 8, 2010, http://www.nytimes.com/2010/05/09/world/09awlaki.html?_r=1 (accessed February 24, 2011).

47. The Investigative Project on Terrorism, "Dar Al-Hijrah Official's Deception on Awlaki," *IPT News*, November 18, 2009, http://www.investigativeproject.org/1521/dar-al-hijrah-officials-deception-on-awlaki (accessed February 24, 2011).

48. Scott Shane and Souad Mekhennet, "Imam's Path from Condemning Terror to Preaching Jihad," *New York Times*.

49. Joseph Rhee and Mark Schone, "How Anwar Awlaki Got Away," ABC News, November 30, 2009, http://abcnews.go.com/Blotter/FtHoodInvestigation/anwar-awlaki/story?id=9200720&page=1 (accessed February 24, 2011).

50. Imam Johari Abdul-Malik, interview by Michel Martin, "Devout Muslims Sometimes Split On Beliefs," NPR News *Tell Me More*, November 12, 2009, http://www.npr.org/templates/story/story.php?storyId=120344756 (accessed February 24, 2011).

51. Patrick Poole, "Hatred in the Heartland," FrontPageMag.com, May 20, 2008, http://archive.frontpagemag.com/readArticle.aspx?ARTID=30943 (accessed February 24, 2011).

52. James Gordon Meek, "Yemeni Cleric Anwar al-Awlaki Wants U.S. Citizens Dead, Is Targeted By CIA for Assassination," *New York Daily News*, updated May 23, 2010, http://www.nydailynews.com/news/world/2010/05/23/2010-05-23_yemeni_cleric_anwar_alawlaki_wants_us_citizens_dead_is_targeted_by_cia_for_assas.html (accessed February 24, 2011).

53. Erick Stakelbeck, "Al Qaeda Cleric's Recordings Sold at Va. Store," CBN.com, June 2, 2010, http://www.cbn.com/cbnnews/us/2010/June/Al-Qaeda-Clerics-Recordings-Sold-at-Va-Store-/ (accessed February 24, 2011).

54. Scott Shane and Souad Mekhennet, "Imam's Path from Condemning Terror to Preaching Jihad," *New York Times*.

55. Carrie Johnson, "JihadJane, An American Woman, Faces Terrorism Charges," *Washington Post*, March 10, 2010, http://www.washingtonpost.com/wp-dyn/content/article/2010/03/09/AR2010030902670_2.html (accessed February 24, 2011).

56. J. J. Green, "What is Anwar al-Awlaki's appeal.?" WTOP.com, March 24, 2010, http://www.wtop.com/?nid=778&sid=1918625 (accessed February 24, 2011).

57. Carrie Johnson and Alice Crites, "'JihadJane' Suspect Dropped Out Before High School, Married at 16," *Washington Post*, March 11, 2010,

http://www.washingtonpost.com/wp-dyn/content/article/2010/03/10/
AR2010031003722.html?hpid=moreheadlines (accessed February 24, 2011).

58. Ibid.

59. "Police say suspect in terror plot attempted suicide in 2005," CNN.com,
March 10, 2010, http://articles.cnn.com/2010-03-10/justice/jihad.jane_1_
plot-boyfriend-arrested?_s=PM:CRIME (accessed February 24, 2011).

60. Corky Siemaszko, "Paulin-Ramirez's Family Feels 'Pity' For 'Jihad Jamie';
say she was likely egged on to join plot," *New York Daily News*, March
15, 2010, http://www.nydailynews.com/news/national/2010/03/15/
2010-03-15_paulinramirezs_family_feels_pity_for_jihad_jamie_say_she_
was_likely_egged_on_to_.html (accessed February 24, 2011).

61. Ibid.

Chapter Six

1. Erick Stakelbeck, "U.S. Designated Global Terrorist Sits Down with Stakelbeck on Terror," *Stakelbeck on Terror*, CBN.com (blog), February 18,
2010, http://blogs.cbn.com/stakelbeckonterror/archive/2010/02/18/
u.s.-designated-global-terrorist-sits-down-with-stakelbeck-on-terror.aspx
(accessed February 25, 2011).

2. "Treasury Department blocks assets of men accused of supporting al-
Qaeda," *USA Today*, December 21, 2004, http://www.usatoday.com/news/
washington/2004-12-21-terror-assets_x.htm (accessed February 25, 2011).

3. Ibid.

4. Martin Smith, "'Zubaydah Is Dead,'" PBS.org, August 13, 2010, http://
www.pbs.org/wgbh/pages/frontline/shows/search/journey/2.html (accessed
February 25, 2011).

5. Stephen Gray, *Ghost Plane: The True Story of the CIA Rendition and Torture Program* (New York: St. Martin's Press, 2007), 33.

6. "Attorney General Alberto R. Gonzales Highlights Success in the War on
Terror at the Council on Foreign Relations," United States Department of
Justice, December 1, 2005, http://www.justice.gov/opa/pr/2005/Decem-
ber/05_opa_641.html (accessed February 25, 2011).

7. Michael Seamark, "Does this photograph prove Abu Qatada is flouting his
bail?" *Daily Mail*, August 30, 2008, http://www.dailymail.co.uk/news/
article-1050754/Does-photograph-prove-Abu-Qatada-flouting-bail.html
(accessed February 25, 2011).

8. "Interview: Yasser El-Sirri," Frontline, PBS.org, September 2001, http://
www.pbs.org/wgbh/pages/frontline/shows/terrorism/interviews/el-sirri.html
(accessed February 25, 2011).

9. Erick Stakelbeck, "London's Islamic Radicals Speak Out," CBN.com, February 16, 2010, http://www.cbn.com/cbnnews/world/2010/February/How-London-Became-a-Terrorist-Hotbed/ (accessed February 25, 2011).

10. "Britain Monitoring 30 Terror Plots," *The Australian*, April 13, 2008, http://www.theaustralian.news.com.au/story/0,25197,23531768-2703,00.html (accessed February 25, 2011).

11. Jack Doyle, "Mohammed is now the most popular name for baby boys ahead of Jack and Harry," *Daily Mail*, October 28, 2010, http://www.dailymail.co.uk/news/article-1324194/Mohammed-popular-baby-boys-ahead-Jack-Harry.html (accessed February 25, 2011).

12. Melanie Phillips, "British police running from Muslim demonstrators, a Christian nurse facing the sack for offering to pray for a patient – this is the way society dies," *Daily Mail*, February 4, 2009, http://www.dailymail.co.uk/debate/article-1134042/MELANIE-PHILLIPS-British-police-running-Muslim-demonstrators-Christian-nurse-facing-sack-offering-pray-patient--way-society-dies.html (accessed February 25, 2011).

13. "Sharia law in UK is 'unavoidable,'" BBC News, February 7, 2008, http://news.bbc.co.uk/2/hi/7232661.stm

14. David Harrison, "Christian Preachers Face Arrest in Birmingham," *The Telegraph*, May 31, 2008, http://www.telegraph.co.uk/news/uknews/2058935/Police-advise-Christian-preachers-to-leave-Muslim-area-of-Birmingham.html (accessed February 25, 2011).

15. "PM's speech in Turkey," Number10.gov.uk, July 27, 2010, http://www.number10.gov.uk/news/speeches-and-transcripts/2010/07/pms-speech-in-turkey-53869 (accessed February 25, 2011).

16. Hear the exchange here: http://www.youtube.com/watch?v=pxY7Q7CvQPQ (accessed February 25, 2011).

17. Watch the attack here: http://www.youtube.com/watch?v=gYjkLUcbJWo& feature=relmfu (accessed February 25, 2011).

18. Morrigan Emmaleth and Cassandra Victoria, "EDL forms Jewish Division," JihadWatch.org (blog), posted by Robert Spencer, Dir., July 18, 2010, http://www.jihadwatch.org/2010/07/edl-forms-jewish-division.html (accessed February 25, 2011).

19. Sue Reid, "Special investigation: How predatory gangs force middle-class girls into the sex trade," *Daily Mail*, August 7, 2010, http://www.dailymail.co.uk/news/article-1301003/Special-investigation-How-predatory-gangs-force-middle-class-girls-sex-trade.html# (accessed February 25, 2011).

20. Chris Brook, "Top detective blasts 'culture of silence' that allows Asian sex gangs to groom white girls ... because police and social services fear being branded racist," *Daily Mail*, January 5, 2011, http://www.dailymail.co.uk/news/article-1344218/Asian-sex-gangs-Culture-silence-allows-grooming-white-girls-fear-racist.html#ixzz1ELa1XOST (accessed February 25, 2011).

21. Neil Sears, "Swilling beer, smoking dope and leering at porn, the other side of hate preacher 'Andy' Choudary," *Daily Mail*, January 5, 2010, http://www.dailymail.co.uk/news/article-1161909/Swilling-beer-smoking-dope-leering-porn-hate-preacher-Andy-Choudary.html (accessed February 25, 2011).

22. "4 men sentenced to prison for Muhammad cartoon protest in London," ReligionNewsBlog.com, July 18, 2007, http://www.religionnewsblog.com/18771/islamic-terrorists (accessed February 25, 2011).

23. Abul Taher, "A third of Muslim students back killings," *The Times*, July 27, 2008, http://www.timesonline.co.uk/tol/news/uk/article4407115.ece (accessed February 25, 2011).

24. Sean O'Neill, "Analysis: Tanweer video gives credence to al-Qaeda link," *The Times*, July 6, 2006 http://www.timesonline.co.uk/tol/news/uk/article683841.ece (accessed February 25, 2011).

25. Jason Burke, "Channel tunnel is terror target," *The Guardian*, December 24, 2006, http://www.guardian.co.uk/world/2006/dec/24/politics.terrorism (accessed February 25, 2011).

26. Daniel Pipes, "Britain's new export: Islamist carnage," *The Jerusalem Post*, August 3, 2010, http://www.jpost.com/Opinion/Columnists/Article.aspx?id=183551 (accessed February 25, 2011).

Chapter Seven

1. Phil Stewart and Adam Entous, "Iranian missile may be able to hit U.S. by 2015," *The Economist*, April 19, 2010, http://www.reuters.com/article/2010/04/20/us-iran-usa-missile-idUSTRE63J04H20100420 (accessed February 25, 2011).

2. Glenn Kessler, "Obama Shakes Hands with Gaddafi," *Washington Post*, July 9, 2009, http://voices.washingtonpost.com/44/2009/07/09/obama_shakes_hands_with_gaddaf.html (accessed February 25, 2011).

3. "Handshake With Obama Belies Chavez's Contempt for America," FOX News, April 20, 2009, http://www.foxnews.com/politics/2009/04/20/handshake-obama-belies-chavezs-contempt-america#ixzz1CB3OlZub (accessed February 25, 2011).

4. "Chavez to Obama: 'I want to be your friend,'" MSNBC, April 18, 2009, http://www.msnbc.msn.com/id/30271562/ns/world_news-americas/ (accessed February 25, 2011).

5. Peter Nicholas, "Obama defends greeting Hugo Chavez," *Los Angeles Times*, April 20, 2009, http://www.latimes.com/la-fg-obama-americas20-2009apr20,0,1717554.story (accessed February 25, 2011).

6. David Jackson, "Another Obama 'bow' flap," *USA Today*, April 13, 2010, http://content.usatoday.com/communities/theoval/post/2010/04/another-obama-bow-flap/1 (accessed February 25, 2011).

7. "Obama's bow in Japan sparks some criticism," MSNBC, November 16, 2009, http://www.msnbc.msn.com/id/33978533/ns/politics-white_house/ (accessed February 25, 2011).

8. Beth Fouhy, "Obama: Would meet Iranian as president," *USA Today*, September 24, 2007, http://www.usatoday.com/news/politics/2007-09-24-1364154241_x.htm (accessed February 25, 2011).

9. Jason Djang, "A New Year, A New Beginning," The White House, March 19, 2009, http://www.whitehouse.gov/Nowruz/ (accessed February 25, 2011).

10. Ali Akbar Dareini, "Iran's Supreme Leader Dismisses Obama Overtures," *Huffington Post*, March 21, 2009, http://www.huffingtonpost.com/2009/03/21/irans-supreme-leader-dism_n_177617.html (accessed February 25, 2011).

11. "Obama Offer Is Denounced by Ayatollah," *New York Times*, March 21, 2010 http://www.nytimes.com/2010/03/22/world/middleeast/22iran.html (accessed February 25, 2011).

12. Alexander Burns, "President Obama expresses 'deep concerns' about Iran election," *Politico*, June 16, 2009, http://www.politico.com/news/stories/0609/23804.html (accessed February 25, 2011).

13. "Protesters Stage Somber Rally In Iran," CBS News, June 18, 2009, http://www.cbsnews.com/stories/2009/06/18/world/main5095264.shtml (accessed February 25, 2011).

14. "Gibbs: Ahmadinejad 'elected leader' of Iran," Breitbart, August 4, 2009 http://www.breitbart.com/article.php?id=D99S89DO0&show_article=1 (accessed February 25, 2011).

15. Josh Rogin, "Cat and mouse: Iranian foreign minister shakes hands with senior U.S. official…but dodges Hillary Clinton," *Foreign Policy*, December 4, 2010, http://thecable.foreignpolicy.com/posts/2010/12/04/iranian_foreign_minister_shakes_hands_with_senior_us_official_but_dodges_hillary_cl (accessed February 25, 2011).

16. David Ignatius, "Obama offers Iran an opening on engagement," *Washington Post*, August 5, 2010, http://www.washingtonpost.com/wp-dyn/content/article/2010/08/04/AR2010080406238.html (accessed February 25, 2011).

17. Stephen F. Hayes and Thomas Joscelyn, "Obama's Iran Fantasy," *Weekly Standard* Vol. 15, No. 45, August 16, 2010 http://www.weeklystandard.com/articles/obama-iran-fantasy (accessed February 25, 2011).

18. Ibid.

19. Jennifer Griffin, "Iranian Weapon Shipment to Afghan Taliban Raises Alarm," FOX News, October 19, 2010, http://www.foxnews.com/politics/2010/10/19/iranian-weapon-shipment-afghan-taliban-raises-alarm/ (accessed February 25, 2011).

20. Hamid Shalizi, "Karzai says his office gets 'bags of money' from Iran," Reuters, October 25, 2010, http://www.reuters.com/article/2010/10/25/us-afghanistan-karzai-idUSTRE69O27Z20101025 (accessed March 9, 2011).

21. Colonel Timothy J. Geraghty, "15 Years Later: We Came in Peace," *USNI Proceedings Magazine*, October 2008 Vol. 134/10/1,268, http://www.usni.org/magazines/proceedings/2008-10/25-years-later-we-came-peace (accessed February 25, 2011).

22. "Hostages taken at the U.S. Embassy in Tehran," November 4, 1979, PBS.org, *Terrorist Attacks on Americans*, 1979–1988, http://www.pbs.org/wgbh/pages/frontline/shows/target/etc/cron.html (accessed February 25, 2011).

23. Dan Darling, "Mind of Mugniyeh," *Weekly Standard* (blog), July 25, 2006 http://www.weeklystandard.com/Content/Public/Articles/000/000/012/466aubsk.asp

24. Jeffrey Goldberg, "In the Party of God," *The New Yorker*, October 28, 2002 http://www.newyorker.com/archive/2002/10/28/021028fa_fact2?currentPage=all (accessed March 8, 2011).

25. Adam Zagorin and Joe Klein, "9/11 Commission Finds Ties Between al-Qaeda and Iran," *Time*, July 16, 2004, http://www.time.com/time/nation/article/0,8599,664967,00.html (accessed February 25, 2011).

26. Anna Mahjar-Barducci, "Iran Placing Medium-Range Missiles in Venezuela; Can Reach the U.S.," *Hudson New York*, December 8, 2010, http://www.hudson-ny.org/1714/iran-missiles-in-venezuela (accessed February 25, 2011).

27. "Rafsanjani Says Muslims Should Use Nuclear Weapon against Israel," Iran Press Service, http://www.iran-press-service.com/articles_2001/dec_2001/rafsanjani_nuke_threats_141201.htm (accessed February 25, 2011).

28. Richard Lloyd Parry, "Clinton says US would arm its allies against a nuclear Iran," *Sunday Times*, July 23, 2009, http://www.timesonline.co.uk/tol/news/world/asia/article6723037.ece (accessed March 1, 2011).

Chapter Eight

1. "Exploding Misconceptions," *The Economist*, December 16, 2010, http://www.economist.com/node/17730424 (accessed March 1, 2011).

2. Barry Rubin, "The Region: Revolutions, Walk-Outs and Fatwas," *Jerusalem Post*, January 16, 2011, http://www.jpost.com/Opinion/Columnists/Article. aspx?id=203876 (accessed March 1, 2011).

3. Translation by MEMRI, "Leading Sunni Scholar Sheik Yousuf Al-Qaradhawi Calls for the Egyptian Army to Replace the Government and Prays to Allah for the Conquest of the Al-Aqsa Mosque," http://www.memritv.org/clip_transcript/en/2815.htm (accessed March 1, 2011).

4. Watch the chant here: http://www.youtube.com/watch?feature=player_embedded&v=du5emnvGgvg (accessed March 1, 2011).

5. See the IHW website here: http://www.islamichouseofwisdom.com/. See the clip of Elahi's pro-Khomeini sermon here: "Imam Elahi: Imam Khomeini More Than a Political Leader," http://www.youtube.com/watch?v=5P3HRc7GLlw&feature=player_embedded (accessed March 1, 2011).

6. Tawfiq Hamid, "The Development of a Jihadi's Mind," *Current Trends in Islamist Ideology* 5 (2007), pp. 18–19.

7. Mitchell D. Silber and Arvin Bhatt, *Radicalization in the West: The Homegrown Threat*, New York City Police Department, August 2007.

8. Ibid., 15.

9. Ibid., 20.

10. Milton J. Valencia, "Muslim community rallies behind Sudbury man charged by the FBI," *Boston Globe*, March 8, 2009, http://www.boston.com/news/education/higher/articles/2009/03/08/muslim_community_rallies_behind_sudbury_man_charged_by_the_fbi/ (accessed March 1, 2011).

11. Joseph Lieberman and Susan Collins, "Lieberman, Collins: FBI and Pentagon could have stopped the Fort Hood shootings," *Washington Post*, February 6, 2011, http://www.washingtonpost.com/wp-dyn/content/article/2011/02/04/AR2011020407034.html (accessed March 1, 2011).

12. Bridget Johnson, "Mullen: Broadly tackling extremism will undermine 'uneducated' mullahs," *The Hill*, November 12, 2010, http://thehill.com/blogs/blog-briefing-room/news/129029-mullen-tackling-extremism-through-development-will-undermine-uneducated-mullahs- (accessed March 1, 2011).

13. Thomas Jocelyn, "The Pope of Terrorism, Part I," *Weekly Standard,* July 25, 2005, http://www.weeklystandard.com/Content/Public/Articles/000/000/005/880qqeoh.asp (accessed March 1, 2011).

14. Jonathan Karl, "Director of National Intelligence James Clapper: Muslim Brotherhood 'Largely Secular'," ABC News *The Note,* February 10, 2011, http://blogs.abcnews.com/thenote/2011/02/director-of-national-intelligence-james-clapper-muslim-brotherhood-largely-secular.html (accessed March 1, 2011).

15. See the video of Brennan's remarks here: http://www.whitehouse.gov/photos-and-video/video/john-brennan-speaks-national-security-nyu (accessed March 1, 2011).

16. "NASA Chief: Next Frontier Better Relations With Muslim World," FOX News, July 5, 2010, http://www.foxnews.com/politics/2010/07/05/nasa-chief-frontier-better-relations-muslims/ (accessed March 1, 2011).

17. "U.S. wants to build up Hezbollah moderates: adviser," Reuters, May 18, 2010, http://www.reuters.com/article/2010/05/19/us-lebanon-usa-hezbollah-idUSTRE64I0UM20100519 (accessed March 1, 2011).

18. "Counterterror Adviser Defends Jihad as 'Legitimate Tenet of Islam'," FOX News, May 27, 2010, http://www.foxnews.com/politics/2010/05/27/counterterror-adviser-defends-jihad-legitimate-tenet-islam/ (accessed March 1, 2011).

19. Andrew Bostom, "John Brennan: Witless for the defense," *Washington Times,* July 12, 2010.

20. See Obama's remarks here: "Obama regrets distortion of Islam to justify violence," YouTube.com, http://www.youtube.com/watch?feature=player_embedded&v=vCllTEankoA (accessed March 1, 2011).

21. Bhaskar Roy, "Muslim leaders approve Obama's 'jihad' remarks," *Times of India,* November 8, 2010, http://timesofindia.indiatimes.com/india/Muslim-leaders-approve-Obamas-jihad-remarks-/articleshow/6885197.cms (accessed March 1, 2011).

22. Joseph Lieberman and Susan Collins, "Lieberman, Collins: FBI and Pentagon could have stopped the Fort Hood shootings," *Washington Post,* February 6, 2011, http://www.washingtonpost.com/wp-dyn/content/article/2011/02/04/AR2011020407034.html (accessed March 1, 2011).

23. "WH counter-terrorism adviser Brennan storms out of TWT offices," *Washington Times,* August 23, 2010, http://www.washingtontimes.com/blog/watercooler/2010/aug/23/wh-counter-terrorism-adviser-brennan-storms-out-tw/.

24.   Patrick Poole, 10 Failures of the U.S. Government On the Domestic Islamist Threat, Center for Security Policy, November 2010.

25.   Jason Trahan, "Muslim Brotherhood's papers detailed plan to seize U.S.," *Dallas Morning News*, September 17, 2007.

Chapter Nine

1.   Video and transcript of *Stakelbeck on Terror Show*, August 24, 2010, http://www.cbn.com/cbnnews/world/2010/August/Stakelbeck-on-Terror-Show1/ (accessed March 2, 2011).

2.   "Background on Arab Fest Arrests," City of Dearborn, Michigan press release, http://www.cityofdearborn.org/government/city-services/public-information/press-releases/441-arab-fest-response (accessed March 2, 2011).

3.   About Publisher Osama Siblani, *Arab American News* website, http://www.arabamericannews.com/news/footer/osama-siblani.html (accessed March 2, 2011).

4.   Deborah Passner, "Hassan Nasrallah: In His Own Words," Camera.org, July 26, 2006, http://www.camera.org/index.asp?x_context=7&x_issue=11&x_article=1158 (accessed March 2, 2011).

5.   Jeffrey Goldberg, "Sheikh Qaradawi Seeks Total War," *The Atlantic*, February 23, 2011, http://www.theatlantic.com/international/archive/2011/02/sheikh-qaradawi-seeks-total-war/71626/ (accessed March 2, 2011).

6.   Andrew Bostom, *The Legacy of Jihad*, Note on Cover, AndrewBostom.org, http://www.andrewbostom.org/loj//content/blogcategory/21/33/ (accessed March 2, 2011).

7.   Video and transcript of *Stakelbeck on Terror Show*, "The Arab-Nazi Alliance in the Holocaust," January 27, 2011, http://www.cbn.com/cbnnews/world/2011/January/Stakelbeck-on-Terror-The-Arab-Nazi-Alliance-in-the-Holocaust/ (accessed March 2, 2011).

8.   "The Forced Migration of Jews from Arab Countries and Peace," Prof. Ada Aharoni, August 2002, http://www.hsje.org/forcedmigration.htm (accessed March 2, 2011).

9.   David Swindle, "'For It': MSA Student Confesses She Wants a Second Holocaust," News Real Blog, May 11, 2010, http://www.newsrealblog.com/2010/05/11/for-it-msa-student-confesses-she-wants-a-second-holocaust/ (accessed March 2, 2011).

10.   Joseph Abrams, "Protestor Calls for Jews to 'Go Back to the Oven' at Anti-Israel Demonstration," FOX News, January 8, 2009, http://www.foxnews.com/story/0,2933,477450,00.html (accessed March 2, 2011).

11. Erick Stakelbeck, "College Professor Calls for Israel's Destruction," CBN News, October 19, 2010, http://www.cbn.com/cbnnews/us/2010/October/College-Professor-Calls-for-Israels-Destruction/ (accessed March 2, 2011).

12. Ibid.

13. Herb Keinon, "Jones: Israeli-Palestinian strife still core of ME ills," *Jerusalem Post*, February 8, 2011, http://www.jpost.com/MiddleEast/Article.aspx?ID=207259&R=R1 (accessed March 2, 2011).

14. Dore Gold, *The Fight for Jerusalem* (Washington, D.C.: Regnery, 2007), 19-20.

15. "Chaos deepens as clashes in Egypt kill 13," Associated Press, March 9, 2011, http://news.yahoo.com/s/ap/20110309/ap_on_re_mi_ea/ml_egypt.

16. Susan E. Rice, "Explanation of Vote by Ambassador Susan E. Rice, U.S. Permanent Representative to the United Nations, on the Resolution on the Situation in the Middle East, including the question of Palestine, in the Security Council Chamber," United States Mission to the United Nations, February 18, 2011, http://usun.state.gov/briefing/statements/2011/156816.htm (accessed March 2, 2011).

17. Adrian Blomfield in Jerusalem, "Obama snubbed Netanyahu for dinner with Michelle and the girls, Israelis claim," *Telegraph*, March 25, 2010, http://www.telegraph.co.uk/news/worldnews/barackobama/7521220/Obama-snubbed-Netanyahu-for-dinner-with-Michelle-and-the-girls-Israelis-claim.html (accessed March 2, 2011).

18. "Israel peace treaties, null and void - Muslim Brotherhood member," Ahlul Bayt News Agency, February 24, 2011, http://www.abna.ir/data.asp?lang=3&id=228023 (accessed March 2, 2011).

Conclusion

1. "Muslim Brotherhood Members to Attend Obama's Cairo Speech," FOX News, June 3, 2009, http://www.foxnews.com/politics/2009/06/03/muslim-brotherhood-members-attend-obamas-cairo-speech/ (accessed March 2, 2011).

2. Paul Richter and Peter Nicholas, "U.S. backs 'non-secular' groups as part of Egypt's government," AZCentral.com, February 1, 2011, http://www.azcentral.com/news/articles/2011/02/01/20110201us-brotherhood0201.html (accessed March 2, 2011).

INDEX